PRINCIPLES OF FLIGHT

PRINCIPLES OF FLIGHT

**Flying Bush Planes
Through a World of War,
Sexism, and Meat**

BILL HATCHER

Lantern Books | New York | A Division of Booklight Inc.

2018
Lantern Books
128 Second Place
Brooklyn, NY 11231
www.lanternbooks.com

Some names have been changed.
All dollars are US currency, unless indicated otherwise.

Printed in the United States of America

Library of Congress Cataloging-in-Publication Data

Names: Hatcher, Bill, author.
Title: Principles of flight : flying bush planes through a world of war, sexism, and meat / Bill Hatcher.
Description: New York : Lantern Books, 2017. | Includes bibliographical references.
Identifiers: LCCN 2017054036 (print) | LCCN 2017052911 (ebook) | ISBN 9781590565759 (ebook) | ISBN 9781590565742 (pbk. : alk. paper)
Subjects: LCSH: Hatcher, Bill. | Bush pilots—Africa, East—Biography. | Geography teachers—United States—Biography. | Africa, East—Description and travel. | Social justice.
Classification: LCC TL540.H2588 (print) | LCC TL540.H2588 A3 2017 (ebook) | DDC 629.13092 [B] —dc23
LC record available at https://lccn.loc.gov/2017054036

Also by Bill Hatcher

The Marble Room
How I Lost God and Found Myself in Africa

For my parents, whose love prepared me.
For Kim, whose love inspires me.
For the exploited, whose love can heal us all.

Supporters

I wish to thank the following, whose generous support
helped fund this book's publication.

Keith C. Bartels

Christine A. Borner

Pat Bousliman

Dee Brake

Carol Chapman

Aaron Conrad

Phillipa Conrad

Kathy Dunham

Atif Faridi

Shazia Faridi

Jeffrey Goveia

James Livaccari

Michael Maher

Liza Marron

Lucy Probert

Brooke Romano

Dan Romano

Jim Schneider

Carolyn G. Smoyer

Kim Smoyer

Under the Rainbow Tree, LLC

Debbie Westra

Steve Westra

East Africa

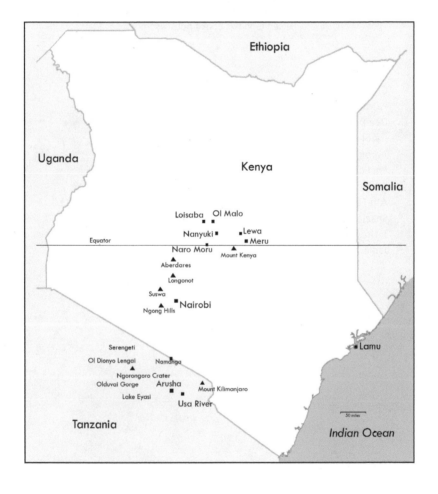

Ethiopia

Uganda

Kenya

Somalia

Loisaba ■ Ol Malo

Nanyuki ■ ■Lewa
Equator ■ Meru

Naro Moru ▲
Mount Kenya ▲

Aberdares ▲

Longonot ▲

Suswa ▲

Ngong Hills ▲ ■Nairobi

Serengeti

Ol Dionyo Lengai ▲ Namanga

Ngorongoro Crater ▲

Olduvai Gorge ■ Arusha ▲

Lake Eyasi Mount Kilimanjaro ▲

Usa River ▲

Tanzania

■Lamu

Indian Ocean

50 miles

Alaska

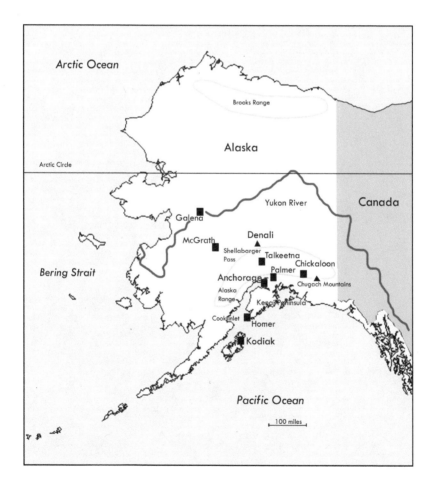

Arctic Ocean

Brooks Range

Alaska

Arctic Circle

Galena

Yukon River

Canada

McGrath

Denali

Shellabarger Pass

Talkeetna

Chickaloon

Palmer

Anchorage

Chugach Mountains

Bering Strait

Alaska Range

Kenai Peninsula

Cook Inlet

Homer

Kodiak

Pacific Ocean

100 miles

Contents

contents continued

BOOK ONE

Old Empires

CHAPTER 1

The Red Planet

I HELD ON with all my strength, though it would not save me. Far below, the plane's shadow dashed over a stand of cottonwood trees, whose yellow leaves fluttered in the setting sun as if waving hello or goodbye. They reminded me of when I was a boy, and the seasons I had spent hunting with my father. Today was his birthday.

My copilot had set the emergency transponder code to 7700 and radioed mayday, while I searched for a landing site and tried not to fixate on the altimeter. It read nine thousand feet above sea level, which was four thousand feet AGL (above ground level). At sixty-five knots—the plane's best glide speed—we could fly for five minutes, or seven miles, over the Utah desert. The nearest airport was twelve miles away and surrounded by subdivisions.

My SoftComm headset blocked all sound except a high-pitched whir of blood that sang in my ears. Like a tombstone, the propeller stood motionless in front of the engine cowling. I could not remember how long it had been that way.

At three thousand feet over the Green River, I spotted a short, dirt airstrip intended for ultra-light aircraft. It ran to the edge of a low mesa. At two thousand feet, I made shallow turns to align our plane with the runway, a maneuver that stole altitude faster than I expected, and we lost another thousand feet. On final approach, we came in short. Our Cessna 172 sank below the level of the runway and sailed toward the side of the mesa as our shadow raced up to meet us. A light on the instrument panel blinked red, and I recalled the pilot's memory aid: *White, you're light. Red, you're dead.*

Before my next thought, which was after the end but before the beginning, the yoke column sheared, bones shattered, and my head smashed into the instrument panel.

Still, I could not let go, even if it killed me.

Red earth blurred past the Jeep's window. Ten months had passed since the crash, and all I remembered of it was a flash of sagebrush gilded in sunset on the slope ahead. We had expected to die. I later learned what happened and why I lived, but the crash continued to haunt me in ways more sinister than mortality alone. It compelled me to reassess the profound shift in worldview I had experienced during my service in Peace Corps Tanzania in the mid-1990s. By the end of my time there, I had flown free of the religious jingoism and racism of my youth, yet I continued to float in the rapture of those insights, afraid of what they foreshadowed. I refused to come down, and so the completion of that shift remained unrealized. Perhaps my shadow self—my inner conflict—caught up with me the day I crashed in 2000. It called me to return to Africa, and by August 2001, I had made it back.

"Will!" shouted Vijay from the driver's seat. His Jeep had no muffler. "You wanna stop? It's two more hours!" He held up two fingers.

I shook my head. "I'm good!"

"*Kitu*, something!" he yelled, and laughed, which exposed his overbite. I knew the Swahili word for "something" was *kitu*, though I did not see the connection. I laughed anyway, relieved to forget about the crash, relieved to be back in East Africa.

The sun shone hard on the blacktop highway and the crops that ran to the horizon on either side. To the east, long rows of leafy green tea flickered by like pages in a book, and to the west bloomed thousands of hectares of red and white chrysanthemums. Big agribusiness grew the flowers for a natural insecticide called pyrethrum, and the fruity, almost minty bouquet filled the air in the Jeep.

We had left the city, but people clustered along the highway. Women carried baskets of mangoes or oranges piled high on their head, and men pedaled or pushed one-speed bicycles, all black and chrome, laden with burlap bags of beans or millet or maize. A short distance off the road, a zebra stood in the shade of an African tulip tree, or flame tree. The zebra took no interest in the bright red flowers and instead only flicked its tail and scratched its rump against the bark. It seemed content but had strayed too close to town, and I feared poachers might take advantage of its carelessness. I was glad when we passed by and could no longer see the zebra.

Vijay had picked me up at the airport in his old green Jeep, and now we drove northeast on Kenya Highway A2 to the East Africa branch of the National Outdoor Leadership School, or NOLS. The branch was situated on the lower western slopes of Mount Kenya.

His Jeep may have lacked a muffler, but it did have a tape player.

"You like Spice Girls?" he shouted, waving a cassette.

I gave a thumbs-up.

The crash had compromised my short-term memory. I had difficultly remembering what someone had just asked me or if I had already responded. But though I had heard of the Spice Girls, I honestly knew none of their songs.

"*Spice up your life!*" he sang, yelling the lyrics over the roar of the engine. His window was rolled down to help ventilate the cab, and every moment or two he smoothed his wavy black hair back out of his eyes, which did little good in the turbulence.

"*What?*"

"The song! 'Spice Up Your Life!'" He glanced at me, then at my neck, at the highway again, then back to me. "What is it?" he said, pointing at the tattoo partly visible above my shirt collar.

I pulled down the collar to expose the image of a phoenix.

"Mexico!"

"What?"

"I got it in Mexico!" I shrugged. To me, the tattoo represented how I had overcome the bigoted thinking of my childhood—Christianity, white privilege, male superiority. Brought up in an evangelical household in the Bible Belt, I had lost direction when my parents' marriage crumbled. I responded by marrying young in an attempt to repair my concept of a Christian family. But after only two and a half years, I too divorced. My key to salvation came from an unlikely source: a flyer calling for Peace Corps Volunteers. Peace Corps stationed me in Tanzania, where I taught geography at an all-girls' boarding school. I had expected to broaden students' horizons. Instead, my views were challenged—by encounters with local shamans, dangerous ascents on Mount Kenya, Kilimanjaro, and Mount Meru, and a special friendship that developed between a Muslim girl and me.

Vijay pulled up his shirtsleeve to expose a floral tattoo on his upper left arm. "Me, too!" he shouted.

Vijay was an Indian Kenyan who observed certain Hindu practices, but said he was not religious, *per se*. His more immediate concerns involved a girl he had met in Nairobi, an Irish woman named Moira. He beamed a phosphoric smile when he talked about her, but because the engine was so loud, he said he would tell me more when we arrived at the branch.

We were both field instructors for NOLS and had met at the school's headquarters in Lander, Wyoming. Founded in 1965, NOLS specializes in wilderness leadership and was originally established to train instructors for its sister school, Outward Bound. Over time, its focus evolved to include a wide range of student populations and outdoor skills. I first learned about NOLS from a Peace Corps friend, and now I had returned to Africa on a yearlong contract to lead mountaineering, backpacking, and sailing courses in Kenya and Tanzania.

After the town of Thika, we passed the Del Monte Pineapple Farm. The fields soon gave way to forests of candelabra, wild fig, umbrella trees, and sausage trees, so-called for the elongated seedpods that dangle from their branches. In their shade, vendors sold papayas, avocados, and many other fruits. I smiled with a thousand memories at the sounds of Swahili and bicycle bells, and at the organic smells of wood smoke, manure, and humanity. Surely, I thought, Africa would help me become whole again.

By late afternoon, the road turned north into a broad valley, where cumulus clouds gathered over the Aberdare Range to the west and Mount Kenya to the east.

We slowed down as we approached a police checkpoint, and Vijay grumbled.

"What's wrong?"

"Cops," he said. "They are such assholes, especially these Kikuyus."

"Why?"

"They stop me all the time and demand money if my lights are dirty or my door squeaks."

"A squeaky door?"

"Anything. They're so corrupt and array."

I knew he probably meant to say *awry*, as in deviant, but I did not correct him. Nor did I ask why he thought Kikuyus were bad people. I was tired and wanted to fit in. I needed a friend.

Peugeot taxis and Isuzu transport trucks had pulled onto the shoulder of the road. The police wore blue berets and clean blue uniforms. A braided cord passed through the epaulette on the left shoulder of each officer's shirt. With glib superiority, they inspected the vehicles. However, they seldom inspected Land Rovers and Land Cruisers, and when they saw me in the passenger's seat of Vijay's Jeep, they waved us through. In the Peace Corps, I had learned that police did not stop vehicles carrying white people, because East Africa received foreign aid from wealthy nations in the global North. I suspected racial prejudices were also at work. From experience, I knew that Africans extolled all things European and American. Many considered the United States the most inventive and powerful nation on Earth, and as an American—and a white male, to boot—I received preferential treatment. As such, I was ushered to the front of customer lines, given the best seats on buses, and paid special attention to whenever I spoke—though times were changing. Still, the association made me uneasy, because while I opposed discrimination, it was a built-in cultural boon that worked in my favor, and I enjoyed it, tacitly.

As we sped past, Vijay rolled down his window and stuck his hand out and waggled his middle finger. "Asshole!" he shouted in English.

The police narrowed their eyes but made no attempt to stop us.

"Are you nuts?"

"They won't do anything as long as you're here," he said. "Anyway, they're too dumb to know what I said."

I knew that black Africans and Indian Africans, or *Wahindi*, harbored old grievances against each other. A current of mistrust had permeated their affairs since the latter sailed from the British Indian Empire to British East Africa around the turn of the twentieth century. They came as indentured laborers to build roads, railroads, and bridges, and also to work as traders and shopkeepers. British colonials highly regarded their familiarity with English, as well as their lighter skin, and awarded them greater esteem and opportunities.

Once past the checkpoint, we turned onto a dirt road toward Mount Kenya. Dark clouds gathered over the peaks. Mud-wattle huts stood every hundred yards or so along the road. Some had grass roofs, others corrugated tin, though each hut had a garden of cabbage or sweet potatoes or corn staked out with string. Chickens and goats ran loose.

Then I saw it. To the side of the road sat a small, unassuming kiosk fashioned of sticks and grass like so many I remembered in Tanzania. The familiar red, white, and blue "wave" logo of a sun-bleached Pepsi sign hung over the counter. The slogan on its banner declared, *chaguo ni lako* ("The Choice Is Yours"). But I had not yet made my choice. I was still too afraid to return to Earth.

Vijay shifted to a lower gear that growled like an airplane engine and reminded me of flying. "Do you know of any little airports around?"

He pointed back to the turnoff. "There's one like twenty minutes north. You wanna go?"

With occasional exceptions, Vijay was fluent in English. Part of his panache in demonstrating his command of the language was to employ informal contractions like *wanna* and *gonna* and American slang. His parents spoke Hindi and English, his first and second languages, respectively. Swahili came in third, followed by a smattering of some Kenyan tribal languages.

"Not today. But I'm a pilot, so I'd like to see—"

"No shit!"

I was happy it impressed him. "Yeah, for the last eight years."

"Hey, you should talk to Kabiru. He's an instructor. You know him?"

I shook my head, but the name sounded familiar.

"He's a pilot, or he used to be. He'll tell you."

Ten minutes later, we turned onto a rutted lane that had clumps of grass growing down the middle. A wooden NOLS sign hung from an iron rod to the side. We approached a grove of tall trees and a fence with a metal gate. An *askari*, or watchman, dressed in the traditional Maasai manner, stood next to the gate. He was tall and thin and very dark and wore a long *shuka* with a red tartan pattern knotted over his left shoulder. According to custom, each of his earlobes was incised and stretched to leave an opening of perhaps three inches. I had seen younger men insert film canisters in the openings to maintain their shape and keep them from shrinking. But this man was older, and the holes were too large for film canisters. For convenience, he had wrapped the lobes over the tops of his ears. He also carried a wooden spear, though he used it as a walking staff as we drove up.

Vijay waved. The *askari* smiled and waved back, and smiled and nodded at me, too. Two of the man's lower front teeth were missing, another Maasai custom. He opened the gate, and we drove through.

"Is he an *askari*?"

"For nighttime," said Vijay. "His shift starts about now, I guess."

"He looks pretty old for that, don't you think?"

"Yeah, but Peter likes to give work to the locals." Peter managed the branch.

Eucalyptus trees and green lawns grew around a ranch-style home, cabins, and other buildings. In the back, the yard sloped down to a wooden gazebo. A stream flowed through a grove of trees behind the gazebo. At eight thousand feet above sea level, this British colonial homestead was built in the 1920s and exuded a secure, albeit privileged tranquility.

We parked next to three 1980s vintage Land Rovers, each of them green with a white roof. Vijay jumped out and unloaded my backpack from the rear seat. I grabbed my guitar case.

"Your cabin's this way," he said.

As we walked across the lawn, a droning noise grew louder. We ducked when a small plane skimmed the treetops.

"*Jesus!*"

Vijay laughed and pointed. "That's Bongo! You should meet him."

"Bongo?"

"You know, like the striped antelope. That's what he's named after."

Flight had long fascinated me. As a boy, I launched model rockets and wrote stories of travel to distant worlds, especially Mars, the red planet named after the Roman god of war. One summer, I nailed a short strip of steel ribbon and a length of baling wire to a block of wood. Then I climbed on top of our chicken coop and reached as high as I could to wind the wire around a nail in an adjacent telephone pole to serve as an antenna. Whenever I heard a plane, I ran outside and climbed up. Crouching on the metal roof—too hot to sit on—I tapped the metal ribbon against the nail in the block of wood, generating what I imagined to be Morse code. I was certain the pilot would receive it and wave the plane's wings. In my head, he did so every time.

I also read about Charles Lindbergh, who had undertaken the first nonstop solo transatlantic flight in his monoplane,

Spirit of St. Louis, in 1927. Lindbergh visited Kenya in 1964 and wrote an essay about his trip called "Is Civilization Progress?" In it, he remarked, "If I had to choose, I would rather have birds than airplanes." I admired Lindbergh, but his comment puzzled me. The words of World War I flying ace, Captain Jacques De Sieyes inspired me more: "Aviation is a game—an amazing game, a game of adventure, of countless thrills, of soul-stirring excitement."

Bongo's plane flew east toward the craggy, glaciated peaks of Mount Kenya. I was keen to be back in Africa, but a crisis loomed. Did I hope to close the circle, let go, and finally grow up? Or did I work to prolong the bliss of transformation and float in noncommittal youth forever? Either way, a deep sense of unfinished business demanded to be resolved.

I was not alone. My story merged with that of millions of other Americans. Together, we unwittingly approached a cultural wind shear that could no longer support our avarice, gluttony, and chauvinism. Impact was certain.

On the grandest scale, the world itself indulged in patterns of fear and violence so pervasive and so ingrained that few recognized they participated in its carnage every day, because it was normal. It was business as usual. The consequences ranged from perpetual warfare, sexism, racism, and environmental ruin to the very food on our plate. We had turned our planet red, though we managed to remain detached, floating above it all.

But no one can stay aloft forever.

CHAPTER 2

Principles of Flight

MY CABIN WAS the second to the right from the branch manager's house. It bordered the west side of the property. Each cabin was named after a different animal, such as *Simba*, for lion, and *Tembo*, for elephant, which was the most spacious cabin. A tag on my door read *Swara*: gazelle in Swahili.

Swara occupied one hundred square feet and had no plumbing. Temperatures dropped into the fifties most nights, especially during the two rainy seasons, and the cabin had no heat, so I covered myself with a woolen blanket to sleep. A mosquito net was unnecessary, since malaria was not a problem at this elevation.

Daylight filtered through red, safari-print muslin on the room's only window. For evening light, an incandescent bulb hung from a wire in the center of the tin ceiling, but since the power often went out, a hurricane lamp and a box of matches rested on a desk in the corner. Woven grass mats covered the dirt floor, and sheets of blue polyurethane blanketed the interior walls. The people who had built the cabin had nailed the polyurethane to the smooth sides of horizontal wooden planks to provide the room with a modest degree of insulation, privacy, and protection from insects and snakes. Outside, the planks retained their bark, giving the cabin a pioneer look.

I shoved my Dana Design backpack and gear under the bed and arranged my "town clothes" on a set of bookshelves opposite the door. When finished, I put my journal, compass, and floppy safari hat on the desk. I treasured these three items. They were tokens of my identity, and they comforted me. However, I did not display my most prized item.

Reaching into my pocket, I pulled out a small flake of aluminum, nearly flat and about the size of a fifty-cent piece. One side was faded green, the other shiny metallic. I had sanded the edges smooth. Slender and thin, it felt warm from my pocket, and I rolled it between my thumb and index finger.

For the past year, since before the crash, I had carried it everywhere, though I was not superstitious and did not believe it held magical powers. To me, it was merely a token that symbolized flight and my ambitions to become a good pilot, certainly better than I had so far demonstrated. If I could just meditate on it long enough, I was certain my wishes would come true. I was less confident in my ability to ignore how it also symbolized violence and death.

In June 1943, a B-17 Flying Fortress left Pendleton, Oregon, to join the war in Europe. It flew east across the nation with a crew of nine men. At midnight on June 28, the pilot radioed the airport in Gillette, Wyoming. He estimated their position to be near the town of Powder River. They were never heard from again.

The Army scoured the Bighorn and adjacent mountain ranges, but no wreckage was found. Two summers later, cowboys noticed the sun reflecting off of a shiny object in the mountains near Cloud Peak. When they investigated, they found the debris and the remains of the crew. One had survived the impact, but both his legs were broken. He wrote in a journal that the plane had been slightly off-course before it raked the top of the mountain. He died a few days later.

In August 2000, I led a NOLS course in the Bighorn Mountains. Halfway through the thirty-day course, we climbed Bomber Mountain, named after the incident. The summit is a field of shattered granite that covers one square mile at nearly thirteen thousand feet above sea level. Wreckage from the plane is strewn over several hundred yards, and I imagined how it must have nearly cleared the top. The radio-shack portion of the fuselage was mostly intact, with two wheels and their ancient rubber tires turned brittle in the high-altitude sun. I saw sections of wing here, a radial engine cylinder there, but the rest was mostly scraps of mangled aluminum wedged between slabs of rock.

Our group rested nearby, and the rock I sat on seesawed beneath my boots. I glanced down, and in a cleft of red granite was a flake of aluminum, a fragment of the plane's skin. It did not shine in the sun because it lay in shadow, and its drab paint concealed it. In that moment, the thought of having it possessed me. I desired it, that it might remind me why I flew airplanes and justify my hesitation to grow up.

While no one looked, I reached down and took it.

The piece of metal glinted like a talisman, and I turned it over in my fingers. The green side evoked fantasies of heroism and courage, while the shiny side looked ordinary and reflected my guilt in having taken it. In a deeper sense, the painted side signified my persona, aloof from the sexism, violence, and environmental ruin of the world. The other side revealed willing ignorance.

I rubbed it until the friction made it hot and then slipped it back into my pocket.

Vijay dropped by later that afternoon. On the way to the cookhouse for dinner, he told me he had talked to Moira. His cell battery had run down, but not before they made plans to meet in Nairobi and spend time together before our wilderness course started in a few weeks. If I was in town, he said, we should all have dinner together. He was excited to introduce her to me and show her off to me, but I asked him to let me think about it. I had just arrived and wanted to learn the lay of the land.

People sat at picnic tables under a pavilion outside the cookhouse as we walked up. On weekdays, the cooks served dinner free of charge for branch staff; many people ate from plates with their fingers in the traditional manner. A white-and-brown chicken loitered at the corner of the cookhouse.

Vijay plugged his flip phone into a wall outlet before turning to introduce me. "Will, this is Peter and his wife, Charlotte."

A white middle-aged couple stood and wiped their hands. The man reached out, and I shook his hand.

"Welcome!" said Peter. His forehead wrinkled under salt-and-pepper hair. "Except, I was expecting Bill."

"I thought I'd try something new." Subconsciously, I had taken the alternate name as a way to exert control over my volatile life.

Charlotte smiled and nodded, as if she understood. "So, Will, Peter tells me you lived in Africa before?" She was about forty and spoke with a light accent I could not identify.

We sat down, and I told them my story. I then learned that Charlotte was Dutch, and Peter, American. Schooled in wildlife biology, he had worked as a NOLS field instructor for many years before his current position as branch manager. He was about fifty with short hair and an earring stud in his left ear. He and Charlotte had a son about four years old named Miles and an adopted Kikuyu girl, Mary, who was still in diapers.

I enjoyed their company and the free meal—chicken masala with rice and *sukuma wiki*, a Swahili term that means "push the week." *Sukuma wiki* is prepared from minced kale, boiled for hours, and is eaten as a last resort before payday and before one can buy fresh food at the market. Because of his ethics, Vijay abstained from the chicken but ate the kale, the rice, and a local staple made of flour and water called *ugali*. It had no flavor, and I picked at it. But the chicken was fresh, and I stripped every bone, leaving only the gristly parts at the joints.

I had grown up in the rural Midwest, hunting and keeping livestock, some of which were chickens. But over the past five years, my taste for meat had waxed and waned. The reasons were vague—or rather, I kept them vague for fear they might make cooking inconvenient and eating less pleasurable. Leaving meat on the menu eased the pressure so I could focus on more important matters.

Vijay's phone rang. He jumped up and ran to the electrical outlet to disconnect it from the charging cord. It was Moira, and with a great smile he excused himself and walked behind the cookhouse with the phone pressed to his ear. Charlotte excused herself from the table, too. As she walked to her and Peter's home across the yard, the chicken I had noticed earlier zigzagged past her feet as if petitioning for help. Charlotte said something to the chicken I could not hear, something kind, which seemed contradictory, given we had just eaten one of her kin and would likely see this one in the pot soon.

Peter and I bussed our table and walked over to a building where students were outfitted and field rations prepared. The door to the gear room stood open. Inside, a black man inspected ropes, webbing, harnesses, and metal hardware used for rock climbing. He wore a red Chicago Bulls baseball cap and turned to peer at us over his large-framed glasses.

"Will, this is Kabiru," said Peter, "one of our most senior instructors."

"Oh! You mean to say, one of your oldest instructors," Kabiru said, and chuckled.

He stood three inches shorter than me and sported a round tummy unusual for a NOLS instructor—or a Kenyan, for that matter—but it suited him and only added to his jolly, avuncular manner. His smile revealed teeth stained yellow from decades of black tea, and when he pushed up his glasses onto the bridge of his nose, I saw that the iris in one of his eyes was glazed gray-white.

He reached out, and we shook hands. "Yes, Mister Will. Or is it Bill?"

"You two know each other?" asked Peter.

"We met once in Lander," said Kabiru. "I was leading a course in Wyoming, and if I'm not mistaken," he dipped his chin and peered over his glasses, "you were with a certain woman, yes?"

My pulse quickened. Amy was an instructor I had met before the crash. To me, she resembled a curvier, bohemian version of actress Amanda Peet, who played opposite Bruce Willis in *The Whole Nine Yards*. Amy made it clear she was attracted to me one evening when she asked if I would come to her room and give her a massage.

We spent the next three months behind locked doors. I felt like a teenager again, though with greater understanding and endurance. We rendezvoused in her room, in my room, in bathtubs, in hot tubs, and in every room of three different homes we housesat during our winter of love.

I had been celibate since my divorce seven years earlier, so perhaps my explosion of desire was due to an accumulation of lust, though it more likely represented a lack of directional control in my life. By attaching myself to *her* needs and *her* life, I avoided confronting my own.

Growing up in America's heartland, I learned about sexual puritanism from an early age. I had always reserved sex for true love—until Amy. The discrepancy troubled me. I resolved it by writing a love song for her on my guitar. I went ice climbing and rock climbing and skiing with her to showcase our common interests outside the bedroom. I prepared halibut with chard—her favorite—and even turned down an offer from the NOLS staffing office to guide courses in the Chilean Andes because I could not fathom spending time apart from my beloved. After three months of sex, attended with flashes of romance, I bared my soul and pledged my love to her.

She left the next day.

I was crushed. No one could break up with me, I thought. I was too good-looking, earnest, and sweet. In a rush of self-preservation, I convinced myself that I'd had my way with her and was now stronger. The fantasy boosted my little-boy ego, enough to fly more often, move to the NOLS base in Vernal, Utah, and learn to fly bush planes.

I shook my head. "No. We're not—"

Kabiru nodded. "I see. But Vijay, he tells me you are a pilot, yes?"

"Yes. And you, too?"

He scratched his forehead under his Bulls cap. "Well, I used to fly, too much, mostly these twin-engine turboprops. But you, you have your PPL, is it?" (A PPL is a Private Pilot's License.)

"Single-engine, land. American."

"Very good. But you will also need a Kenyan PPL, which you can get at Wilson Airport in Nairobi."

"Wilson."

"Yes. I trained there."

"Vijay mentioned an airport between here and Nanyuki. Did you fly there, too?"

He laughed. "No. That's Tropic Air. But Jamie, he's the owner. He's one of those, you know, Kenya Cowboys," he said, chuckling as he turned to Peter. The term was borderline pejorative and referred to the older, British-Kenyan families who continued to nurse fantasies of colonialism and white privilege.

"Like Bongo?"

"No, Bongo, he's not so bad. In any case, use my old textbooks. I'll bring them for you tomorrow. And when you go to Wilson, look for the last hangar on the left. The flight school is there."

Kabiru came to my cabin the next day. He handed me four volumes of the Trevor Thom series called *The Air Pilot's Manual*. Each covered technical aspects of the flight environment, aviation weather, and the airplane—or aeroplane, its British spelling.

I was ecstatic. On my first day back in Africa, my wish for adventure had been granted. Romantic visions of flying over the savanna wearing a baseball cap and chewing on a cigar possessed me. Perhaps my talisman held powers after all.

Kabiru had not elaborated on his career as a pilot, so when he dropped off his books, I asked.

"Oh," he said, and chuckled lightly as he took off his thick-lensed glasses. A gray film covered the iris in his left eye.

"I was a fresh NOLS instructor, trying to light our little stove, and I sat too close, no glasses, and it exploded. My vision was ruined. I never flew again."

"I'm sorry."

He clicked his tongue. "Oh! Don't be. I hated flying."

I almost jumped back.

"You see, it was just *so boring*! All you do is fly up to this altitude, set the controls, and sit. Then you come down, you land, park the plane. You see? Very boring."

But I heard none of it.

"Anyway, pay special attention to that one, the first one," he said, tapping *Volume One* at the top of the stack I held. "It stresses the four principles of flight: gravity, lift, power, and drag. Learn them, and never forget them."

"I will. And thank you for the books. I'll study hard."

"Yes, you had better."

CHAPTER 3

The Principle of Gravity

THE HILLS AND bends in the road looked almost familiar when Vijay drove me to Nairobi. I hoped to enroll in flight school at Wilson Airport, but I also wanted to find a tutor so I could improve my Swahili, or Kiswahili, as the language is technically called. I had not spoken it in over five years, and if I wanted to live and work long-term in East Africa, I needed to brush up on the language spoken by nearly everyone in Kenya, Tanzania, Uganda, and the bordering areas.

NOLS kept two apartments at the Kivi Milimani Hotel in downtown Nairobi—one for itinerant instructors, and another for Peter and his family. Along with Kabiru's flight manuals, I took with me my Jeppesen-Sanderson PJ-1 plotter, a manual flight computer, and a pilot's clipboard with Velcro that strapped to the thigh so you could write notes and make calculations during the flight. I thought of nothing else but flying bush planes, and for once, Vijay might have been relieved his Jeep made too much noise to allow for conversation.

Vijay dropped me at the apartment. Down the street, I found an Internet café and a restaurant, and since it was getting dark, I ducked into the restaurant. The interior lighting was low and the decor cowboy-themed, with posters of John Wayne and Clint Eastwood. A steer's horns were mounted over the bar. The music of a modern African group called *Simba Wanyika*, or Plains Lions, played over the sound system, but the rest of the bar's motif was imported from the United States. Around the bar, Kenyan prostitutes pawed at affluent men of every racial category, although I noticed the white men were getting more attention than any other group.

A waitress brought a menu and winked. I blushed and acted like I had not noticed. I was flattered, and she was certainly pretty, but I knew better. The risk of catching STIs, including HIV/AIDS, was not inconsiderable. Furthermore, in spite of my newly discovered lust, I retained a commitment to genuine relationships and not just sex for hire, or even for simple companionship.

The restaurant's menu was committed to meat: ribs, tenderloins, racks and rumps of lamb, fish (filleted and whole), and chickens' legs and breasts. I ordered a cheeseburger with fries, or chips, as they called them in this former British colony. I also ordered a Tusker Lager, Kenya's premium beer. The woman took the order, and I could not help but notice the motion of her hips in her black leather skirt as she walked away. She was undeniably attractive and pleasing to watch, yet it felt cheap to ogle her. I looked away, uncomfortable at what it said about me.

As I waited for my order, I noticed most men at the bar had taken off their suit coats but left their ties on and loosened while they puffed cigarettes. The women wore very little. It could have been a scene from almost any place on the planet: clothed men who fancied themselves power brokers fraternizing over meat while virtually naked women competed to serve them to earn money.

The inequities were obvious. Yet I did not perceive a deeper level, one explored by Carol J. Adams in her book *The Sexual Politics of Meat: A Feminist-Vegetarian Critical Theory*. In this now classic text, Adams investigates how meat and women's bodies are cognate symbols of male power and domination. Animals are consumed literally, and women are consumed visually and sexually. Advertisements that substitute cuts of meat for parts of a woman's body seem playful and innocuous—to the conditioned mind. Adams suggests that eating meat (and eggs and milk, which she calls "feminized protein") is a manifestation of the fragmentation and consumption of women themselves. A manly man eats meat and controls women. This worldview is nearly universal and nearly invisible. For instance, no one objects when fathers "give away" their daughters but not their sons in wedding ceremonies. This custom is a toned-down version of a time not long past when women were considered property to be bought, sold, abandoned, mutilated, or murdered as their male masters—and male-authored holy books—saw fit. In some parts of the world, such practices persist.

Sitting in the cowboy bar, I did not see the connection between meat, women, and violence. I flew far above this reality, even though its atmosphere kept me aloft. When my waitress brought me my cheeseburger, I ate it and never gave either of them a further thought.

Flight school at Wilson Airport was my objective the next morning. I walked to a bus stand down the street, and in five minutes, two dangerously packed commuter vans, called *matatus* in Kenya, pulled up. Young men stood on the running boards of the *matatus*, taking fares and shouting destinations. All *matatus* and buses have mottos painted on the front or back, many of which are religiously themed. PARTY FOR JESUS was painted above the rear window of the first *matatu*. The second van was named THE SWORD OF GOD, a phrase derived from the scriptures of the three Abrahamic religions: Judaism, Christianity, and Islam. PARTY looked more fun, but SWORD was closer, so I jumped on the latter when both vans gunned their engines to leave. In ten minutes, its driver dropped me, although a heathen, safely at the airport.

Following Kabiru's directions, I found the flight school, deposited one thousand US dollars, and began lessons immediately. My instructor's name was Major Kabuthu, chief of the flight school. Unfortunately, the Major, as he liked to be called, was rather full of himself and often smelled of liquor. As we continued to fly together, he would either bark orders or become so exasperated with my ineptitude that he would take control of the plane lest he die of a stroke or heart attack or, conceivably, boredom.

We flew a Piper Cherokee. The Cherokee is a single-engine, low-wing plane of a design I had no experience flying, so I spent several lessons becoming acquainted with its idiosyncrasies. In the process, I learned Wilson Airport shared airspace with Jomo Kenyatta International. This made for a very busy sky, plus the air traffic controllers spoke in a mixture of British, Kenyan, and Indian accents and used terminology foreign to me. And the program was expensive. My first thousand dollars soon evaporated, so I deposited another thousand. A few lessons later, the toll topped three thousand. No matter: each time I sailed into the air, exhilaration straight out of a boyhood adventure story once again filled me.

On some days, we flew only touch-and-goes. This maneuver involves landing on a runway and taking off again without coming to a full stop, repeating the circuit over and over again. The Major pointed out landmarks to help me know when to turn the plane. The white monastery was for crosswind, the lake for downwind, the racetrack for base, and the water tower for the final approach. But there were so many lakes and water towers that I often missed a turn. The horizon also distracted me. The volcanic mountains of Suswa and Longonot rose to the west, and the savanna of Nairobi National Park lay just south of the city, where acacia and baobab trees dotted the open grasslands. The park merged with the vast Athi plains farther south, and I imagined giraffe and wildebeest at watering holes and prides of lions lazing in the shade of rocky outcrops, keeping an eye on migrating ungulates. Maasai people roamed that country, too. And farther southwest, in Tanzania, the Rift Valley opened into Olduvai Gorge, where humanity itself was born.

"*What are you doing?*" shouted the Major.

We had gained two hundred feet during my daydream. I strained to identify a landmark, but the plane's low-wing configuration obscured the ground, and we dipped and climbed as I tried to spot one.

"Give it to me!" he shouted, and grabbed the controls. He mumbled something in Kikuyu and pointed the plane straight at the ground with full right rudder and full left aileron to enter a steep descent called a sideslip. My head grew hot, and my stomach leaped into my throat. My ears popped. Beads of sweat coalesced and trickled into my eyes. The salt stung, so I squeezed them shut, which only intensified the queasiness.

I swallowed hard, and my stomach twitched, when a lost memory appeared.

Cool liquid spills over my forehead and scalp. My eyes flutter, and I wake up. I lie on my back in a small room filled with a droning sound. The glare from two fluorescent bulbs obscures the ceiling. The surface vibrates under me.

I hear a voice, and a woman stares into my face. Her mouth moves, but her voice is muffled, and I do not understand. Someone else holds the sides of my head. The smell of vomit is strong.

Sounds sharpen, and the room bounces and jostles. I hear a siren. More cool liquid pours over my scalp, but I cannot move my hands or legs. Rather, I cannot feel them, as though I am a disembodied head, and I do not know what has happened or where I am.

"What's your parents' phone number?" shouts the woman.

I remember my sister's number. The woman scribbles it down. I cough and taste blood and vomit. The person holding my head looks down at me. It is a man's face. He is upside down to me and looks alien. The sight startles me.

"You're gonna make it," he says. "Your friends weren't so lucky."

He continues to talk, but I pass out.

"*Open your eyes!*" yelled the Major as he leveled out the plane.

The imposed gravity of the maneuver made it difficult for me to lift my eyelids. During the dive, a memory of the minutes or hours after the crash had broken into my consciousness, and although I was glad the pieces were beginning to fall into place, I feared what they might reveal.

As for the Major, he gaped as if I were a pathological idiot. "*Do not forget gravity!*" he shouted. "It is the first principle of flight! It acts in *one* direction—*straight down!*"

He shook his head and then motioned me to take the yoke, or control wheel. I took the controls, set the flaps, pulled the power back, and managed to land the plane, though it was not pretty. I pulled the plane onto the apron in front of the flight school and parked. The Major got out without speaking a word and shook his head as he marched to his office for a cognac.

That evening, I was alone at the apartment, which was on the third floor of the hotel. I tried to concentrate on my studies, although the clamor on the streets made it difficult to focus. From the living room, I watched a plastic shopping bag blow around outside. The thin bag was one of millions of "flowers" that "bloom" all over Africa, a curse that ends up in all sorts of flora and fauna. This one was printed with an image of the Marlboro Man, and it looped around the parking lot as if gravity held no power over it and it was free to go and do as it pleased. At one point, I was sure it would reach the ground and snag on a bush and be unable to free itself, and I leaned out over my table to see, but a breeze kept it aloft. It soared again and sailed out of sight over the roof of the next building. Perversely, I was relieved it got away.

The black-corded phone on the coffee table startled me when it rang. I picked up the receiver.

"Will," said Vijay. "Peter called. He said two more American instructors arrive Tuesday, and he needs me to collect them at the airport. We brief next Friday at the branch. Are you ready to go back?" The next round of wilderness courses was set to kick off, and all instructors were expected to attend the meeting.

"I'll be ready. But what about Moira?"

"It's okay. We'll meet you for dinner another time."

Time was short, so the next morning I called the Kenya Civil Aviation Authority to schedule my written test. Days later, I caught a bus across town, sat in a classroom with a dozen other student pilots, and took the exam. I was the last to finish. The test proctor—or invigilator, as the British call it—said results would be mailed in four weeks. My field contract started in one. The practical portion of my flight training would have to wait, but I needed a break from the Major anyway.

Most field courses lasted thirty days or less. The one about to begin was sixty-five days long and included three weeks of backpacking on Mount Kenya, three more in the Serengeti, and the remainder on the Indian Ocean sailing Arabian dhows (lateen sailboats). I was headed into the African bush and would not climb into a cockpit again until December.

Matt and Kirsten arrived, tired but excited. As a couple, they would share the larger Tembo cabin. Staffing scheduled them to work together on one of the two courses that ran at any given time from the East Africa branch. I helped lead the concurrent course. The idea was to keep at least one American instructor on each course so that students, who were mostly Americans, would have an instructor to whom they might better relate. It also meant I never worked with Matt or Kirsten.

When we arrived at the branch Tuesday evening, the air was noticeably cooler, and I slept well my first night back in Swara cabin. I rose early to go for a run in the forest at the boundary of Mount Kenya National Park. Before starting, I went to the instructors' kitchen for a glass of orange juice. The kitchen had a refrigerator, a gas stove, a sink with running water, and a linoleum floor. The flooring in the rest of building was solid teak, and most walls were plastered and painted white or blue. The ranch house also contained administrative offices, a bathroom with a flush toilet and a hot shower, and an instructors' lounge with a television and an old fireplace. An adjacent room had been retrofitted to house a library. In addition to books, it contained a telephone and a desktop computer—a Power Macintosh 7600. This was not the African bush I experienced in the Peace Corps, but I wasn't about to complain about the luxuries.

I carried my glass of orange juice to the instructors' lounge and flipped on the television. The news broadcast at that hour was in Swahili. I tried to watch the news each day to sharpen my language skills, so it surprised me when I heard American English being spoken. A reporter stood in a street and interviewed a woman, who looked frightened. Around her, people had stopped their cars and gotten out to talk and point up at the buildings. They were in New York City, huddling in patches of morning sun, so I knew it had to be at least one day old, given the time-difference between here and there.

Then came the screams, and cacophony overpowered the interview. A shadow leaped up the windows of a skyscraper as a passenger jet slammed into the tower. Fire and smoke erupted and debris rained down. Another plane had crashed into an adjacent tower, and now that building imploded under the inexorable force of gravity.

Everything was about to change.

CHAPTER 4

Boys Will Be Boys

WE SAT IN a circle on wooden desk chairs. Twenty of us had planned our week around this meeting on the sunny lawn behind the instructors' lounge, and now we had nothing to say. Many sipped black tea with whole milk and sugar and stared at the ground. Matt and Kirsten sat close together, holding hands, and Peter wore his reading glasses, absorbed in an email he had printed out that morning. Across the yard, a young Kenyan man washed clothes in an outdoor sink. The slap of wet clothes and the strong smell of OMO detergent helped me imagine the day was normal, like any other, and the horror of previous day had been only a bad dream, one we all shared.

A small bird startled me when it landed on the ground near my bare feet, but I remained still, as I had learned to do as a boy when hunting with my father. My legs extended straight out, down to the ground, with my feet crossed in the grass, and the little bird hopped onto the big toe of my lower foot. I caught my breath but did not move. Someone giggled, and everyone forgot the concerns of a moment earlier. Peter sat several places to my left and bent forward to see.

The bird had a white belly and black shoulders. Black plumage marked its face like a mask, and it made a *chat-chat* sound and jerked its head as if scolding me to get up and go somewhere new if I felt so sad.

"What is it?" I whispered, not moving a muscle.

"Flycatcher," said Vijay, seated immediately to my left. "Or maybe—"

"No, that's right," said Peter. "Flycatcher family. A species of northern wheatear."

The bird hopped to my upper foot and scaled the toes, skipping some in a single bound. Its tiny claws did not hurt, but they did tickle, and I struggled not to flinch.

"They migrate to Alaska every spring," Peter continued, "and return here in the fall. Longest migration in the world." He directed his next comment to the bird. "But you're back early this year, aren't you?"

In two seconds, it jumped and glided to a tomato stake in the garden, thirty yards away. Everyone watched. Some pointed and spoke in low voices.

Vijay tapped me on the arm. "I think he's your friend," he said.

I secretly agreed, or at least hoped so, perhaps because he could fly so far and stay aloft so long.

But the spell was broken. Peter took off his glasses and rubbed his eyes. He was in no hurry to speak and waited for everyone to quiet down.

"So, as you might have heard," he said, "all flights from the United States are canceled, and several students have dropped out."

People murmured to their neighbors, but Peter had more to say, so Kabiru spoke up. "Please!" he said. "Quiet, so he can talk."

Anxious faces returned to Peter. "Right now," he said, "about half our students have canceled, but the Admissions Office got commitments from the other half, who still want to come. So, we intend to honor those commitments and go ahead with both courses."

Chatter resumed. A Kenyan woman sat to my right. She held a cup of black chai and a cookie called a glucose digestive biscuit. She had dunked the cookie into her tea and taken a bite, when she addressed the group in English. "But hey, you guys." No one paid attention, so she spoke louder, causing bits of cookie to fly from her mouth. "You guys!" The clamor died. "What about their flights? Our permits may expire before they get here. So, when can we start?" Her questions were really for Peter, and she continued to chew her cookie while she waited for an answer.

She and Kirsten were the only two women present. The number of women who worked as instructors for NOLS had increased from near zero in the 1960s to nearly a third. This was more than any other outdoor school, except for women-focused programs, such as Women's Wilderness Institute.

"We're not sure yet," said Peter. "At least a week, maybe two. Logistics and rations are set, and we'll work with the parks to extend our permits. But it's important we remember how much these students want to be here in spite of everything, and we should strive to run these courses like normal."

The Kenyan woman turned to me. "Not exactly normal," she whispered, and took another bite of the cookie she had dunked.

Her name was Mukina. I had met her in Lander a year earlier. One of her upper front teeth was missing and caused her to pronounce sibilants such as "*th*" and "*s*" with a lisp, which I found endearing. She was smart and bubbly, and she laughed at the silliest things in such a wheezing, belly-cramping manner I could not help but laugh, too. Today, however, was not a day for laughter.

"I am praying for those families and for our students," she said, pulling the cross at the end of her necklace toward me like an exorcist holds a crucifix.

Mukina's reminded me of the cross necklace my former wife had given me after we married. Mine was made of little nodules of gold, and the facets seemed to sparkle even in the dark, a symbol of our faith. After we divorced and I moved to Tanzania, I discovered the veneer concealed junk metal, a more accurate symbol of religious myopia, and I threw it away. The piece of metal from the crashed plane was my talisman now.

"President Bush, I hope he kills every last Taliban," said Mukina, who literally spat into the grass. I nodded and tacitly agreed that the perpetrators must surely pay. Several others in the group grunted approval, though Kabiru sat quietly, thoughtfully, wearing his Bulls cap and holding his chin. He glanced sideways at me through his large-framed glasses as if to gauge my reaction to her comment. "These people, they are snakes!" she went on. "Hyenas! I am certain they cannot even read their so-called holy book."

Kenyans and Americans shared a tragic bond. In 1998, Al-Qaeda had bombed the American embassy in Nairobi, killing 213 people, including 12 Americans. A simultaneous explosion destroyed the American embassy in Dar es Salaam, Tanzania, killing 11.

We were relieved that both semester courses would run, though a cloud of uncertainty descended, and I was unsure how to interpret my emotions. Africans were not alone in fantasizing about the United States as a utopia, free from disease, poverty, and worry. Americans had invented telephones, automobiles, and airplanes and had sent men to the moon. American farmers grew crops in such abundance that they fed most of it to their cows and pigs (75 percent of all grains) and converted it to ethanol to run their cars (20 percent). Still, enough remained for Americans to have their fill and donate the remainder to people in Africa. America was clearly invincible and beyond quotidian concerns.

The word *utopia* derives from the Greek and translates as "not a place" or "nowhere." It exists only in the imagination. This reality sank in for everyone on 9/11, and with it, new questions emerged: Who could commit such an act of terror? Who was capable of such violence? And the question on everyone's mind, *why?* What grievance had America committed that warranted this level of retribution? We searched our collective memory and came up empty.

Personally, I sensed a shift in energy. I still wanted to fly bush planes, but I was less certain about Kenya. An impulse beckoned me home to show solidarity with my people, whose self-identity as a beneficent actor on the global stage—an assumption rooted in the belief in our inherent superiority—had been violated. It demanded revenge.

As a young boy, I had been given toy guns and knives and swords and encouraged to "play war." In elementary school, my favorite book was *Johnny Reb and Billy Yank*, which I read cover to cover. I imagined fighting in the American Civil War as a Confederate soldier, a true rebel. I intuitively knew slavery was unjust and that it had been a major factor behind the war, yet I dismissed it as a footnote and wrote a revised version in my journal of why the war had started.

Confederate flags adorned my bedroom, and saloon doors blocked its entry (a feature that would expose several embarrassing moments as I entered my teens). Rabbits' feet (for luck), rubber tomahawks, and live ammunition (rifle cartridges and shotgun shells) decorated my Old West roll-top desk. Toy six-shooters bedecked the lamp on my night table under a squirrel skin I had tanned, and leather-bound cow

horns were mounted on the wall over my bed. The shag carpet was blood red. Clearly, I belonged in that cowboy-themed
bar in Nairobi!

I also pretended to be an officer in Nazi Germany, but
switched to G.I. Joe after learning my grandfather had fought
against Germany in that war. Whichever war I reenacted, I
gave myself regular promotions, lost enough battles to make
my inevitable triumph more hard-fought and interesting, and
wrapped up any given campaign in time for dinner. At the
table, when my mother expressed her concern that I was con-
ducting my military campaigns with too much zeal, my father
dismissed it with that age-old defense, "Boys will be boys."

My interest in the elements of war was not entirely imagi-
nary. In our house, shotguns and rifles were kept unloaded
and on display in a gun rack next to the fireplace, and I was a
proud junior member of the National Rifle Association. My
favorite TV shows were reruns of *Gunsmoke*, *Bonanza*, and
Hopalong Cassidy because my father had watched them as a
boy. As with most young men, I modeled my ideal of strength
and courage after my father and wanted him to be proud of
me. He was my hero. (Around this time, American troops in
Vietnam booed John Wayne off the stage at a USO performance when he swaggered up to the mike in a cowboy costume. To these soldiers, he represented a Hollywood version
of warfare that mocked the nightmares they had witnessed.)

Socially, I was trained to be a soldier. My grandfathers had
served in the Navy, and I inherited military relics from both.
My father's mother sewed a Revolutionary War costume for
me to wear on Halloween when I was eight. I liked it so
much I squeezed into it the next year, too.

However, I never actually fought in a war, and neither did
my father. Before graduating from high school, he enrolled
in trade school to become a pipefitter-welder, and at eighteen

he married my mother and I was born. This helped ensure his number would not come up early in the draft. Meanwhile, as I engaged in my mock battles, the United States was roiled by the civil rights, feminist, and environmental movements, as well as by protests against the Vietnam War, worries about human overpopulation, and the ever-present threat of nuclear holocaust.

Two weeks after 9/11, Vijay, Peter, and I drove the Land Rovers to Nairobi. I had not been allowed to drive as a Peace Corps volunteer, so this was my first day behind the wheel in Africa. The driving lane in Kenya is (as a former British colony) on the left, speed limits and distances are marked in kilometers, and road signs have unfamiliar shapes and colors. The Land Rover's steering wheel was on the right, and I had to operate the stick shift, mounted on the floor, using my left hand. Thankfully, the shifting pattern, as well as the clutch, brake pedal, and gas pedal followed the same arrangement as in the United States.

Nairobi traffic at rush hour was a mass of black exhaust, clogged roundabouts, street vendors, bicycles, children hawking trinkets, and the occasional goat wandering into traffic. I drove to the apartment at the Milimani Hotel and collapsed on the couch. Peter had business at the immigration office. Vijay said he was "making a bee-line" to see Moira.

In the morning, I walked downtown to the Sarit Centre, a three-level indoor mall complete with gift shops, boutiques, music stores, and a food court. At the mall's theater, I bought a ticket to see *The Ghosts of Mars*, starring Ice Cube and Natasha Henstridge. The movie's premise sounded interesting, if pulpy: humans had colonized Mars in the late twenty-second century and established a matriarchal society. Women were in charge. However, while working at a remote mine, several men unwittingly release a gang of subterranean "ghosts," which possess the men and turn them into zombies.

Unfortunately, the dialogue was stilted, the effects mediocre, and the background music a constant pulse of heavy metal power chords. I was embarrassed such rot could be produced in the United States and was certain every Kenyan in the theater was eyeing me with contempt. I snuck out after twenty minutes.

Outside, I wandered through a maze of kiosks and shops. I needed nothing, but felt guilty, as I was wearing New Balance tennis shoes, Levi's jeans, and a North Face jacket tied around my waist. An elderly woman in one of the kiosks sold necklaces strung with flakes of metal and seeds. The metal resembled scraps of copper cut from a pipe, and the seeds were black like those from the fruit of a baobab tree. I pulled out my money clip. It was not made of gold, but it looked like gold and had my initials engraved on the flat side. The garish status symbol enhanced my discomfort, yet made me feel important and superior. Deep down, I knew I was neither of those things, and how much I needed that validation disturbed me.

I bought two necklaces and put them on, and the woman smiled and nodded. "*Mzuri sana*" (Very good), she said. "*Wanaofanana pete yako*" (They match your ring). She meant the copper ring on my right ring finger that my mother had given me.

While we talked, the stalls cleared out, and the old woman glanced around. It was getting dark.

"*Ni mwisho sasa. Nenda nyumbani*" (It's late now. Go home), she said, with a flash of concern in her eyes. I thanked her again and walked away.

Vijay said he and Moira would be having dinner at the InterContinental Hotel, and that I should join them. I could finally meet his girlfriend. Furthermore, he said, the hotel had live music and dancing and great food.

I crossed Kenyatta Avenue to the hotel and heard the band playing "Route 66" before I reached the double doors. The floors were made of marble, and the mirrors that lined the walls reflected light from a great chandelier.

I saw Vijay in the lounge and waved. Moira sat next to him. She was pretty and 100 percent Irish, with red hair, freckles, and skin the color of skimmed milk. We introduced ourselves and made small talk, but the topic soon turned to 9/11. It was on everyone's mind, and we had to address it. We agreed that Osama bin Laden would surely pay. A wave of needing revenge rippled through me that felt both reckless and righteous, as if being an American endowed me with a certain authority, a sanctioned grievance that trumped all others. It made me feel powerful and gave me a cause.

Nonetheless, it was hard to nurse the righteous intensity of revenge for very long when we were there to have fun and enjoy ourselves. With little effort, the conversation turned to the upcoming course and the students we would greet at the airport in a couple of days.

We danced when the band played Marvin Gaye's "I Heard It Through the Grapevine," and Vijay and Moira continued to dance when the song changed to Percy Sledge's "When a Man Loves a Woman" and the music was slow. From my chair, I watched them whisper in each other's ears and laugh. They were about to spend nearly three months apart, and I was happy to give them space. I felt a twinge of envy. I hoped that I, too, might find love in Kenya.

Around ten o'clock, I left the InterContinental. A fleet of taxis had lined up outside, but the apartment was less than a mile away. I had only ten dollars in my money clip, probably not enough for a cab, so I decided to walk, just as I had a hundred times before as a Peace Corps volunteer in Tanzania.

Nairobi is situated at over five thousand feet above sea level, so it was chilly, and I put on my North Face jacket. I thought it strange how the streets, earlier filled with chaos, were now empty. The clap of my shoes on the sidewalk echoed off the buildings, as the music from the hotel faded behind me.

Kenyatta Avenue was deserted when I crossed over. Shrubbery lined the sidewalk next to Uhuru Park, and streetlamps cast pools of light that turned gray in between. I almost wished the lamps were dark so I could see the constellations stretched out across the African sky, though I would have that delight soon enough. The thought made me smile, and I felt strong, confident, and carefree.

I never heard them coming.

CHAPTER 5

Crusaders

TWO MEN GRABBED my arms and lifted me off the ground, while a third man clubbed me over the head from behind again and again. A fourth man appeared in front of me. Barefoot and dressed in rags, he was shorter than the others and pummeled my face with a police baton.

I struggled, but they were strong. A flood of adrenaline numbed me to the pain but did little to squelch the terror of knowing I had lost control of my situation. The man behind me continued to beat my neck, shoulders, and head, and I heard a roaring sound when he smashed my right ear.

Suddenly, I could not hear anything from either ear. The man in front pointed his baton in my face. He shouted, but I heard only a high-pitched whir, as if we were underwater, similar to the sound in my headphones when my plane had been about to crash. He jabbed his baton toward the bushes bordering the park, and the men hauled me into the darkness. A wave of panic gripped me, as I was certain that if they carried me off the street, behind the bushes, they would slip a knife between my ribs, and no one would know till morning. This was my last chance. With all my strength, I fought and let out a primal scream I could hear only inside my head, but they were too strong. My struggle brought only more blows from the man I could not see behind me, and they hauled me into the shadows.

"*Bwana, chukua vitu vyangu tu*" (Mister, just take my things). I did not know if they spoke Swahili, but I said it in the most disarming tone I could muster, though it was strange to speak without hearing my voice. "*Sitakupa shida*" (I won't give you any trouble).

They wrenched the North Face jacket off me and forced me to the ground on my back. The same two men held my arms, and the one who had beaten my face with the police baton glared at me. The look in his eyes was wild and menacing. Anything could happen. He bent down and shook the baton in my face and said something I could not hear. I tried a gentle smile and tasted blood. Again, I told him to take whatever he wanted and assured him I would make no trouble.

Meanwhile, the man who had beaten me from behind hopped down next to my legs. He pulled the shoes and socks off my feet and dug into my pockets. He took my gilded money clip with my ID and MasterCard and a Kenyan one-thousand-shilling note, worth about ten dollars. He tried my other pockets, but the talisman was all that remained. He held it up to examine. In spite of my injuries and utter helplessness, I felt an urge to shout and demand he return it to me at once. Fortunately, I said nothing.

He handed everything over to the man with the police baton, who appeared to be their leader, and then jammed his hand down my pants, rooting around my genitals and crotch, searching for a money belt or hidden stash. My assailants were experienced. I was relieved when he withdrew his hand, though he saw my necklaces and yanked them off. He then went to my outstretched hands and took my wristwatch and the copper ring my mother had given me.

In a moment, the high-pitched whir faded—first in my left ear, then in my right—and I could hear again. The two men holding my arms to the ground released me and walked several paces away to join their leader and the man who had groped me. The four of them huddled and appraised their booty. The leader kept the cash but tossed my driver's license, work permit, and MasterCard on the ground. The men were probably illiterate, so they could not use those things. The leader also took my North Face jacket, and the man who had groped me already wore my socks and shoes. But everything else—the shiny money clip, my ring, watch, necklaces, and the talisman—went to the henchmen, who were complaining about how little cash I carried.

They skulked off, deeper into the park, and as I got up, the adrenaline began to wear off. A sharp pain pierced my head and radiated into my neck. My face throbbed, and I wondered if bones were broken.

I picked up my ID cards and credit card and walked to the gap in the bushes that led onto the sidewalk. I was disoriented and feared they might yet pursue me, so I turned once to look, but they had withdrawn beyond the threshold of light—all except one. With his back to me, he had stopped to inspect something in his hands. "*Hakuna kitu*" (This is nothing), he said, and tossed the talisman aside before disappearing into the park.

I hurried over. It had landed shiny side up and reflected the streetlight, so it was easy to find, and I grabbed it. None of the other things mattered now, and it cheered me to know I still possessed this one thing, this fragment of identity that represented my crusade to freedom. I slipped it into my empty pocket and staggered out of the park.

Under the streetlight, drips of blood spattered onto the sidewalk. Red specks dotted my white T-shirt and the name of my college alma mater printed on the front—Southern Illinois University. I touched my face and head. A nasty cut crossed both lips, now swollen, and I tasted blood, but I felt around in my mouth with my tongue—I still had all of my teeth. I found another cut and a hematoma on my left cheek, and the bridge of my nose was tender. Blood had caked around my lips and under my chin. Lumps throbbed on my scalp, but my hands were covered in blood, so I could not tell if the lumps bled.

Most of the blood came from my right ear. The man behind me had hit me so hard that the earlobe and outer helix of the ear dangled from a strand of flesh.

Carefully, I pulled my bloody T-shirt over my head, balled it up, and pressed it against my injured ear. I was exhausted. Yet as I walked, an older anxiety crept in, one I had not felt since the crash. A sense of mortality expanded into feelings of emptiness, self-doubt, and loss of control. Into and out of spots of light, I continued toward the apartment, barefoot, when a memory of the crash bled into my consciousness. And now I could not stop thinking of it.

The smell of antiseptics is strong. Ceiling lights make me squint, and people move around me. They wear blue masks and blue latex gloves. I try to move, but straps restrain me. My right forearm is bent at a severe angle, and a bone juts out near the wrist. Blood drips from my fingertips.

"Diprivan!" shouts a man in a white coat.

I writhe and groan.

A woman stoops near my face. "Focus. Breathe," she says, coaching me as if I were giving birth.

I squirm. "I gotta pee!"

The man in the white coat motions to the woman.

Holding a thin tube, she reaches under the sheet that covers my lower body and grabs my penis. I feel a sharp pinch, then relief.

I pass out.

It was almost midnight when I knocked on the door. No one stirred, so I knocked again. This time, two people mumbled, and a light blinked on through the door's peephole

"Who is it?" Peter asked.

"It's me, Will." I licked my lips. They tasted metallic like the iron in blood.

Keys jingled, the tumblers and latches of three locks clicked and rattled, and Peter opened the door. He wore a white robe and squinted into the light of the open, concrete corridor.

"*Jesus!* What happened?" he asked.

He brought ice wrapped in a towel and forgave me for waking him up. I got a spare shirt from my room in the instructors' flat next door and told him everything as he drove me to the emergency room at Nairobi Hospital.

We sat in the waiting room for an hour, listening to people cough and groan. Two young men sat in a row of molded plastic chairs behind me, facing away. They must have been waiting for someone being seen by a doctor, because they sounded perfectly healthy, and I overheard them talking in English about 9/11.

"You know," said one to the other, "the Americans will make them pay too much," as in *so* much.

My pride swelled, and I forgot about my ear and contusions. No one could attack the United States without suffering severe consequences, I thought.

"Did you hear George Bush's speech?" he went on. "He said they will wage a crusade, a holy war, on all Muslims."

I had not heard this news, and it popped my bubble. I knew Bush was a right-wing Christian conservative who believed in a literal reading of the Bible. Many Bible stories concerned battles and massacres—from Sodom and Gomorrah to genocides committed by the Israelites to prophecies of Armageddon—and Christians saw these stories as life lessons. I knew this personally. As a boy in church, I sang praises to the Lord with such hymns as "Onward, Christian Soldiers! (Marching as to War)," "A Mighty Fortress Is Our God," "Am I a Soldier of the Cross?", and many more. Our religion of love betrayed itself with horrendous acts of violence.

But surely, I thought, the president would never make such an incendiary remark. It recalled, even if unintentionally, the Christian Crusades—holy wars instigated by Pope Urban II in the eleventh century that continued until the fifteenth. The Pope had contrived an urgent need to establish safe passage to Jerusalem for Christian pilgrims. Yet Christians and Jews already lived in the holy city, as Muslims considered both groups "people of the Book." Scholars now believe the Pope's true motive was to unite the Eastern and Western branches of Christianity (Catholicism and Orthodoxy) and appoint himself supreme head of the Church.

The young man's friend in the waiting room had another opinion. "No, I am telling you, the American Imperialism, it is self-destructing," he said. "They have controlled the twentieth century, just as British controlled the nineteenth century. The twenty-first century will belong to China, and we must curry their favor if we hope . . ."

I stopped listening. My face flushed hot, and my ear stung. I would have turned in my chair and set them straight, but I was bleeding and disoriented. At the same time, I could not help but ask myself if America was not as all-powerful as I had imagined—as everyone had imagined—and if omnipotence was, in any event, the ultimate measure of success. We Americans liked to run our flags up the pole in our yards and march and sing and launch fireworks displays (the cost of which matched the GDP of some nations), all the while congratulating ourselves on our inventiveness, resourcefulness, and power. Could so much chest-pounding, I wondered, be a symptom of self-doubt, loss of control, and a creeping sense of mortality? At that moment, the question was eerily self-descriptive.

Around two in the morning, a black man—a male nurse—called my name. The image of a white woman, usually blonde and curvaceous (such as Nurse Goodbody on *Hee Haw*), still informed my imagination when I heard the word *nurse*. When I thought of a doctor, I pictured a white man with graying hair and bushy eyebrows, like my childhood pediatrician. But I was in Kenya and (so I liked to think) had evolved in my attitudes toward gender and race. Thus, I remained unconcerned, even cheerful, when a black woman doctor sewed up the dangling portion of my ear and treated the contusions on my head, neck, and face. I had no broken bones. She applied Neosporin, gauze, and tape and told me that cartilage heals remarkably well and the damage should be negligible. She also said I was lucky: victims of Nairobi muggings often lost more than a little blood and their dignity.

Peter paid my emergency room tab—eight hundred shillings, or about eight dollars—and we were back at the apartments within the hour. I could not sleep. I thought about the attack, the flashback of an operating room, and what the two young men in the hospital waiting room had said about Bush's crusade. Try as I might to deny it, what the president had said spoke to me—and not just about 9/11. My American identity had been violated, and I wanted revenge.

Early the next morning, I took a taxi to the Central Police Station on Moi Avenue. Flame trees and eucalyptus trees shaded the lawn and might have given the place a relaxed, breezy feel were it not for a platoon of officers standing guard with AK-47s. A lorry pulled up, and the police unloaded a gang of handcuffed men and shoved them into the station, while prostitutes strolled around like they owned the place. The interior of the station evoked a sense of hopelessness, but I stood in line, and after an hour I reported to an officer at a desk. He embodied indifference. With great effort, he opened a thick black ledger and added my name and story to the saga of Nairobi, better known as "Nairobbery" by casualties like me.

Nonetheless, like a crusader for good, I felt vindicated. I had done my part to see that justice was served and my ego massaged. I also knew nothing would happen. The police force, which struck me as just a more organized band of brigands, would probably raid the slums and harass people who had nothing to do with any crimes. I fantasized about how swiftly the US Armed Forces would exact their particular form of justice if the job were left to them. Civilian casualties, I assumed, would be negligible.

Yet the possibility that the United States might become embroiled in a holy war—one launched to massage our own bruised ego—tempered my zeal for righteous revenge. I retreated to lick my wounds and comfort myself with the facts that I was white, American, and male . . . and I still had my talisman.

CHAPTER 6

Animal Husbandry

I FELT WELL enough to drive to the airport, but kept the doors locked and the windows rolled up, even though it was hot and the Land Rover had no air conditioning. On Kenyatta Avenue, I glanced at the bushes along Uhuru Park. The memory caused me to take a sharp breath, which surprised me. I was most surprised by how my emotions surrounding the attack mixed with those of my crash, 9/11, and a growing sense of violence. They forced me to glimpse a world I normally ignored. Perhaps I could ignore it again, but I could not forget.

Peter and Vijay also drove Land Rovers to the airport. Our students arrived in approximately equal numbers of men and women. They ranged in age from nineteen to twenty-one, and all were taking their semester in Africa for college credit.

That evening, we drove the students to the Milimani Hotel, and then to the branch the next day. My face was black and blue with bruises and cuts, and my ear was taped up, so some students asked about my injuries. The attack was fresh in my mind, and I hesitated to tell the story, but Peter encouraged me. He hoped it might motivate them to be vigilant, especially in Nairobi. Vijay could not believe my stupidity.

After pitching their tents in the yard near the gazebo, we outfitted the students with gear and rations for the next sixty-five days—about four thousand pounds of food. We also selected books and photocopied articles to carry as reference materials in the field. The transportation crew checked vehicles, and everyone pitched in to help load provisions. Everything was set.

The attack had left me feeling more vulnerable, as I was after the crash. I needed to reclaim control, so after locking my cabin, I went to the toolshed and borrowed a hammer and nail. Crouched over my talisman, I punched a hole near the edge of it, threaded it with a spare shoestring, and slipped it over my head. At first, it felt cold on my sternum. I turned it so the green side faced out, but it flipped over to the shiny side, as if it had a secret to tell or a warning to give—Stanford's warning. I flipped it back again, but it would not stay hidden.

Stanford Addison was a Northern Arapaho spiritual healer who lived on the Wind River Indian Reservation in Wyoming. Two months after my plane crash, I met a woman in Lander named Lisa Jones who was writing a book about him called *Broken: A Love Story*. She invited me to accompany her to the reservation and do a "sweat" with her and her Native friends. At the last minute, she had to cancel, but said I should go anyway and called ahead to tell Stanford to expect me.

At the age of twenty, Stanford had lost the use of his legs in an automobile accident and slipped into depression. However, he soon discovered that he had a gift: to mend tribal depression and tame wild horses with trust and love instead of force. He was a real-life horse whisperer.

The sweat lodge stood between Stanford's doublewide mobile home and a corral, where several Arabian horses huddled for warmth. The walls and ceiling of the lodge were made of old rugs, tarps, and quilts strung together with nylon cords over a framework of red willow branches. About six feet high in the center and twenty feet in diameter, the lodge's profile resembled a turtle, which symbolizes the womb of creation in Plains Indian mythology.

The heat inside the lodge contrasted with the December air, and the wood smoke and chanting Indians evoked for me scenes from Kevin Costner's *Dances with Wolves*. After the sweat, Stanford held a midnight feast in his home. But it was his warning I remembered most: "There's something you've been avoiding, something you oughta give back," he told me from his electric wheelchair. "You gotta let it go."

I was certain he meant the talisman, and part of me wondered if my guilt for having taken it was somehow responsible for the crash. At the time, I had planned to return it—as soon as my pilot's license was reinstated and I saved enough money to rent a plane and fly it over, and I was not too busy.

Wearing it now as a necklace reminded me that I had neglected Stanford's advice. But the gesture also made it easier for me to accept the talisman as my personal possession. I owned it. It was mine, and that made it easier to forget I had promised to let it go.

Peter assigned Vijay, Mukina, and me to proctor one of the two courses. A proctor stays with a course throughout each of its sections, while other instructors rotate in and out. For the next ten weeks, we would spend nearly every hour of every day with one another and our students.

The first section of the course was on Mount Kenya. Kabiru led this section, and we approached the mountain from the west via the obscure Gathiuru Route, one that is little known and less used. The trail soon converged with elephant paths that meandered through forests of bamboo and aromatic jasmine. Higher up, the bracken became nearly impenetrable, which forced us to use a *panga*, or machete, to make progress. Once above tree line on the open moors, however, my hiking pole became useful for balance and traction. Mukina said it looked like a cane and giggled about it. I insisted on calling it my staff.

Each morning, we reshuffled students into three groups of four. One or two instructors went with each group, hoping to rendezvous by day's end. We backpacked off-trail using maps with eighty-foot contour intervals; so, at this scale, we could never be sure if the route was passable or if a seventy-nine-foot cliff barred the way. Despite tricky spots that required vertical pack-passes (passing our backpacks down to one another over short crags, no more than ten feet high, to make descent safer and more manageable), we circumnavigated the mountain at roughly fourteen thousand feet above sea level. The strange-looking plants at this altitude included furry lobelias, heathers that resembled giant cabbages, and the senecios that stood ten feet tall and reminded me of the Joshua trees in southern California. U-shaped valleys, waterfalls, and house-sized boulders suggested the mountain's glacial history, most of which is never perceived by park visitors. Poachers and poaching patrols, however, traveled this country all the time. We were lucky and did not encounter any poachers, although the park warden flew over nearly every day in his white Piper Cub, confirming that they were around.

Mukina had studied biology, so she taught this subject on the course. She said she loved animals but also loved to eat them and could not imagine doing without meat.

"I will be working so hard," she said to us, "carrying such a heavy pack in these mountains, so I need my protein."

To satisfy her appetite, she had a cooked goat's leg in her pack. Every evening, she hunkered down in our Mountain Hardware tent and gnawed on the leg. She was not concerned when it began to turn green.

Since, for reasons of hygiene, students had no meat in their rations, Mukina kept the leg out of sight. Everyone else carried bulk foods, such as beans, rice, lentils, flour, pasta, cheese, dried fruits and vegetables, powdered sauces, and various spices and cooking oils. Homemade pizza, fried pasta, and homemade cinnamon rolls were favorites. We also carried Ketepa black tea and Africafe instant coffee and added sugar and powdered milk to each.

Vijay avoided eating the meat of mammals and birds, though he sometimes ate fish. He also practiced an aspect of Vedantic Hinduism called Swara Yoga. (Here, *swara* is Hindi for breath, not to be confused with the Swahili word *swara*, or *swala*, for gazelle.) Every morning, he sat in his sleeping bag with the hood pulled over his head and meditated. At intervals, he covered his nose with his right hand in a fashion that resembled Spider-Man activating his web. With the right nostril closed, he inhaled through his left nostril. Then he closed his left nostril and exhaled through the right. (I later learned this practice is called *Nadi Shodhana* in yoga.)

He noticed me watching him. Mukina was still asleep in her sleeping bag. Kabiru slept in his own tent.

"You wanna try?" he whispered.

"What does it do?"

"Each nostril is connected to the opposite hemisphere of the brain, so your right brain controls the left nostril, which is feminine. The left brain is masculine and controls the right nostril. By breathing in through the feminine left, I invite friendship, peace, and life into my body from the cosmos, and when I exhale through the masculine right, I eliminate violence and destruction and death. Like this," he said, and demonstrated.

To me, it sounded like New Age mumbo-jumbo. I needed coffee.

"Try it," he said. "Do like this."

Reluctantly, I copied the Spider-Man hand configuration and inhaled through the left and out through the right, but my breaths and nostril closures were uncoordinated, and I felt silly.

Mukina moved inside her sleeping bag. "You look like you are picking your nose," she said, and giggled with her tongue sticking out past her missing tooth. She knew that picking one's nose in public was taboo in my culture, though not in hers. Adults casually picked their nose in public every day in East Africa. "Are you going to eat your boogers for breakfast?" she asked, and giggled again.

"Perhaps I will put them in your oatmeal, woman," said Vijay.

"I think I will eat goat instead," she said, and rolled over.

At this stage of my life, I hadn't formed a strong opinion about eating meat. I had avoided it for the past few years, though this was due more to necessity (cost) than an ethical concern about killing animals or worries about the consequences to my health of a diet rich in animal products. I had no problem with steak when someone else picked up the tab.

However, I *was* aware of the environmental liabilities of farming animals. In graduate school, I had learned that current livestock practices are unsustainable. I had discovered that two acres of oxygen-producing, carbon-absorbing rainforest are cleared every minute to raise cattle or the crops to feed them. That it takes thirty times more water and five times more land to produce animal protein than to grow an equal amount of plant protein. That 75 percent of all grains produced in the United States are used to feed livestock. That the livestock industry is the largest user of land on Earth and occupies 30 percent of all ice-free land. That the methane produced from animal husbandry plus the carbon dioxide created by its transportation forms a substantial amount of all anthropogenic (human-caused) greenhouse gases—and so on. I knew the facts, and yet I ignored them. Besides, I told

myself, I ate very little meat, and what I did was healthy—
such as chicken, pork, and turkey.

(I did not yet know these meats are high in cholesterol,
growth hormones, antibiotics, proteins that induce blood pH
imbalances, and the adrenaline residues of suffering and terror secreted during the animals' final moments. Nor had I
considered that it is called "animal husbandry" because men
generally own animals and other resources, just as husbands
historically—and still in some places today—owned their
wife or wives.)

In any event, Mukina ate meat at every meal. She was
Kenyan, after all, and for her (as for many) eating meat meant
that one had attained a certain wealth and status. She was
also a born-again Christian. She read a tiny Gideon's Bible
each night by headlamp, and in the mornings, first thing, she
sang a song I remembered from Sunday school.

> Rise, and shine, and give God your glory, glory!
> Rise, and shine, and give God your glory, glory!
> Rise and shine and [*clap*] give God your glory, glory!
> Children of the Lord.

Vijay taught leadership and first-aid classes, Kabiru lectured on the history of the Kikuyu people, and I taught geology, map reading, and wilderness ethics (which, in essence,
meant respecting the landscape and animals around you,
thereby increasing your chances of avoiding potentially
fatal stupid decisions or accidents). As field instructors, we
were all masters of improvisation. Armed with dry-erase
markers, we duct-taped Mylar over our sleeping pads to use
as whiteboards, triangulated our position with maps and
compasses, and studied the habits of the occasional hyrax
or Cape buffalo.

We joined the Chogoria Route east of Point Lenana. At 16,354 feet, Lenana is the third-highest peak on Mount Kenya. It is a non-technical "trekkers peak," which means it can be climbed without rock-climbing gear. At dawn, our entire group hiked to the summit over rocks glazed with hoar frost and gazed down at the Lewis Glacier. I had crossed that glacier five and a half years earlier. The effects of climate change had already caused it to recede several hundred yards. On the far side of the glacier was Nelion Peak, and beyond it at 17,057 feet was Batian, the mountain's highest point. Climbing it while in the Peace Corps had been a turning point that nearly claimed my life during a full-moon rappel. That night, fissures had opened into my psyche, and I began to find a way out.

And yet, I was still here.

Mukina ate most of the goat's leg. The femur was bare, with only a knot of cartilage near the distal end on which she continued to gnaw during our last days on the mountain. I tried not to stare, but it bothered me, and I was not sure if it was because she looked so feral when she chewed on it or if I thought it was unfair to the students or to me. It was certainly unfair to the goat.

When I was young, my family had owned goats. We milked them and drank the milk and made ice cream from it. To my knowledge, we did not eat any of our goats, and I knew people who owned them as pets—and then there were the petting zoos, where kids bottle-fed goats with milk. Our keeping goats had led me to wonder why we consider some animals our pets, even members of our family, whereas we eat others or turn them into shoes and purses and belts. On what criteria did we segregate them into these categories? We also promoted or demoted some animals to different classes based on their age or value. The image of the cowboy saving the lost calf, tenderly holding her in his arms, came to my mind, as well as the Bible story of the shepherd who left his flock to search high and low for that one lost sheep. In both cases, the rescue was temporary.

Five days before pick-up, we hiked out and left the students to begin their small-group expeditions. In two groups of six, they planned to descend the north side of the mountain and join the Sirimon Route, which crosses the Equator.

By this time, we needed a break, so Mukina went to her house in the little town of Naro Moru, and Vijay phoned Moira. Kabiru had business in Nairobi and would not return to the course. Meanwhile, I checked my mail and email, but had received no report from the Kenya Civil Aviation Authority regarding my test. I also examined my bruises and lacerations in a proper mirror. They had healed, and most of the stitches in my ear had dissolved, so I stopped taping gauze over them.

A day later, Vijay offered to buy dinner for the three of us. He and I picked up Mukina in his green Jeep and drove to the Trout Tree Restaurant, where the tables are terraced at different levels in the boughs of an enormous fig tree. The restaurant is located halfway between Naro Moru and Nanyuki, so it was not far from the branch. From our open-air table, we watched golden weaverbirds flit in and out of the little holes in their nests, which faced the ground and made them seem upside-down. Mukina pointed out a flock, or a "bowl," of northern wheatears that twittered and darted about in the bushes below. Like the one that had perched on my toe at the briefing, they were dusty-red to white with a black "mask" across their face, and they flew about next to several large tanks stocked with fish. Mukina said the birds were females. Males had darker, more striking plumage.

We scanned the menus. I ordered trout, farmed in the tanks below. As another form of animal husbandry, the fish seemed packed together in stressful conditions, and many sucked at the water's surface for air . . . or help. I stopped looking. Vijay chose carrot-ginger soup, and Mukina got chicken.

"Will, did you hear the news?" said Vijay. "The Americans invaded Afghanistan."

Mukina slapped her thigh. "Good!" she said. "I hope to God they kill them all!"

I nodded. "They certainly deserve it."

"Saddam Hussein will dearly pay," said Mukina.

I blinked at her comment. I remembered the name Saddam Hussein from the Gulf War in Kuwait and Iraq, fought over ten years earlier.

"US troops have already killed one thousand civilians," said Vijay.

Both comments confused me and put me on the defensive. I wanted to correct Mukina first. "You mean, Osama bin Laden."

But Vijay jumped in. "Mostly women and children," he said. I sensed accusation in his tone. He sipped his beer and watched me.

I stated the obvious. "That's terrible."

"Yes," said Mukina, contrite. "It is very sad, and I am very sorry to hear it. But you know, sometimes these things are necessary. God sees all things, and His will be done."

The food arrived, and we forgot about the new war. I picked up my fork and knife and prepared to cut my trout. It smelled heavenly.

"How's Moira?"

Vijay smiled. "I know this is gonna sound cheesy, but I have never known a woman like her," he said, as he dipped his spoon into his soup. "She is so incredibly happy all the time and intelligent! You know, she is very intelligent."

Mukina huffed. "And she likes you?"

"She *loves* me. She told me on the phone."

A shout from a nearby table startled us. A vervet monkey had dropped from a branch onto a table at a higher terrace. It stole a fork from someone's plate, but the guests shooed it away by shouting and waving cloth napkins.

The waitress at the next table covered her mouth with her hand as the monkey raced up into the branches. I did not mean to stare, but the waitress's face captivated me. Her skin glowed almond-brown, and her smile was gentle yet bright. She returned to her customers. But as her line of sight crossed mine, she paused. I smiled at her, and she smiled back.

"Okay, I know," said Vijay. He spoke with his mouth full, as he often did. "You've been hurt really bad, both of you," he said, shaking his spoon at us. "And now you're afraid, because your love has gone array."

Once again, I did not know if he meant to say *awry* or *away*. "Dude, I'm on your side."

"I'm not," said Mukina.

Vijay ignored her.

The eye of the fish on my plate seemed to stare at me, so I flicked a basil leaf over it. "It's just that Moira . . ." I was in mid-thought, planning a pivot. "We both know, she's—"

"She's Irish, so you think she's too good for me."

"No! Come on. All I mean is she'll go home to Ireland and leave you here alone, crying." It worked. I managed to conceal my true concern that he had found love, whereas I had not.

Mukina covered her face in her hands and pretended to cry.

Vijay sipped his beer, unfazed.

Mukina put her hands on her hips. "I thought Hindus don't drink beer."

"Some do," he said. "Anyway, I'm not Hindu. You know that."

He continued to talk, but my attention wandered back to the waitress at the next table. She did not look at me again, not until she finished taking her customers' orders. As she walked past our table, she winked at me.

"Well?" said Vijay.

"Well, what?"

Mukina chuckled so that her tongue squeezed into the gap of her missing tooth. She returned to her chicken while chuckling.

"I said maybe I can bring Moira for a visit, and we could all come here for dinner."

Mukina clapped her hands and grunted agreement, but her mouth was too full to comment.

I opened my hands. "Or bring her to the branch. Introduce her to everyone."

Vijay bobbed his head, considering my idea. "I'm down with that."

His hip quip caught me off-guard. "You're . . . 'down with that'?"

Vijay's eyes brightened. "Or, you know what? They have this huge disco."

I imagined the Bee Gees, wide lapels and sequined disco balls.

"It's like a party they put on here on the last Saturday night of every month," he said. "Maybe we could all meet here after the course in December. It's mostly Europeans, but everybody comes and it goes all night. They call it the Bone Zone."

"Bone Zone?"

"Oh, God," said Mukina.

"Yeah, and there's a DJ and music, lots of dancing. Lots of chicks," he said, and winked.

I wiped my mouth with my napkin and glanced around. The waitress had disappeared.

CHAPTER 7

Red in Tooth and Claw

THE BLOOD ON my hands was my own. Several mornings, I had awoken scratching my legs and ankles until they bled. The chest-high elephant grass teemed with chiggers, and despite the heat, I switched from shorts to nylon wind-pants and slathered myself in DEET.

Transportation to Tanzania had gone smoothly, and now our group bushwhacked across the plateau above Lake Eyasi, a soda (i.e., alkaline) lake cradled by the eastern arm of the Great African Rift Valley. A sense of emptiness haunts the place, and yet it brims with life: giraffes, baboons, wildebeest, ostriches, hyenas, lions, and many others—species that coevolved with our hominin ancestors. As such, it evokes a primordial feeling of home. It was also the country in which my worldview had shifted. Returning was a sacred experience.

Near Olduvai Gorge, we rested for a day and visited an ethnic group called the Hadza, or Hadzabe. Members of this tribe are hunter-gatherers who speak a click language some linguists associate with that of the Khoisan people of Namibia. Their average height is five feet, and none weighs more than one hundred pounds, but they are expert at shooting their bows and arrows. They invited me to take aim at a leather-bound target for fun, though it may have been more for their amusement. I failed miserably, and they howled and slapped their thighs until they cried.

Vijay and the female students went with the Hadza women to gather tubers, berries, and baobab fruits, while the male students and I hunted with the men. Mukina stayed behind in camp with the elders and children.

Each Hadza man carried a bow and a quiver of arrows. They had soaked the points of their arrows in poison extracted from the *Adenium coetaneum*, or desert rose. Two of their scrawny dogs scouted in front of us. We set out at a walking pace as the men watched for spoor.

The dogs raced ahead when they found a scent. The men set off at a trot across the hard calcrete ground among the Sodom apple bushes and wait-a-bit thorn bushes that smelled of thyme or bog myrtle. They motioned for us to follow, and we ran for nearly thirty minutes in surges—some dashed ahead while others dropped behind to rest.

Everyone sprinted when we heard the shouts, but I could not keep up. I was out of breath and barely able to stand when I reached the group, which had stopped under an acacia tree. Sweat dripped off my nose onto the parched ground when I leaned onto my knees. The drops evaporated before they soaked in.

The men drew their bows and aimed at two dark forms in the crown of the tree. Several shots went off, and the creatures barked and squealed. I jumped when an adult baboon thudded onto the ground. A moment later, another fell. Four or five arrows had pierced each one, some running through like skewers, and their bodies convulsed as blood drained onto the bare, crusty earth. They shuddered and clenched their hands into fists, and so much resembled humans I cringed. When they stopped moving, we gathered close. Each might have weighed fifty or sixty pounds, and their hair was coarse and beautiful.

This was the Hadza's way of life, the endgame of the hunt. As a boy, I had hunted many times with my father, but we had used shotguns or rifles, never bows. After the kill, I would put the dead rabbit or duck or quail in a pouch on my hunting vest, and the blood always seeped through and left stains on the vest and on my shirt, even on my skin. But I enjoyed it, because it made me feel like a man, or even like the cavemen I had read about in *National Geographic* magazine. One article had quoted Lord Alfred Tennyson:

Who trusted God was love indeed
And love Creation's final flaw
Tho' Nature, red in tooth and claw
With ravine, shriek'd against his creed.
("In Memoriam," 56: 13–16)

In Sunday school, I had been taught that all the cruelty and problems of the world issued from the Fall of Man or, more precisely, from Eve's indiscretion with the Serpent at the Tree of the Knowledge of Good and Evil. By eating the fruit, Eve had disobeyed God and introduced Original Sin into the world. All women were guilty by association. The Fall led to all manner of evil, including sex, which resulted in she and Adam—the innocent bystander, under this interpretation—begetting at least three sons. No daughters are mentioned in the Biblical account. Their first son, Cain, was a farmer, who killed his brother, Abel the herdsman, because God preferred the aroma of burnt animal offerings to that of grains and veggies. The moral of the story was clear: God favored the masculine pursuits of hunting and herding to the feminine occupation of gardening. Therefore, as a boy who hunted and herded, I fulfilled the expectations of my father, my andro-centric (male-centered) society, and the uber-masculine father-God we worshiped.

However, killing had disturbed me more since I'd joined the Peace Corps. Baboons were beautiful, strong, and resembled humans much more than did rabbits and cows. Still, I under-stood the Hadza obtained their protein—that much-touted elixir of life—by eating meat. I also knew that worldwide only some 250,000 people—0.000036 percent of Earth's population—continued to live in an indigenous manner. As for the seven billion of us who were not hunter-gatherers, we had access to more than enough quality plant protein. Why, I wondered, did we continue to kill billions of animals each year if we did not need their flesh to survive? And if not strictly a physiological need, might our raising and killing of animals simply be social?

After the baboons were dead, a Hadza man reached into a small satchel wrapped around his bare torso. He took out an ember wrapped in green leaves and a short, hollow stick packed with herbs called *dagga*, a kind of marijuana made from the herbaceous plant lion's head, or *Leonotis leonurus*. He put one end of the pipe to his lips and touched the other end to the ember and puffed until the herb was lighted and a blue cloud of smoke appeared. The other Hadza men hud-dled around him and took turns smoking, while my students and I stood several feet away. The men were mostly quiet, and after a few minutes the one who had carried the pipe wrapped it with green leaves and put it back in his bag. The others extracted their arrows from the baboons.

Religiously, the Hadza are animists. That is, they believe spirits inhabit natural features, such as rock outcrops and trees, and natural forces, such as storms. They maintain a loose association with their ancestors through rituals, and they have a vague sense of their high god, who was embodied by the sun. But they are not religious zealots. When I asked, they told me they were not, in fact, propitiating their god or the ancestors but merely were taking a break. They liked to smoke and get a little high.

At camp, the men tossed the baboons onto the campfire, singeing hair off their bodies and cooking them from the outside in. Parts sizzled and popped and bubbled, and after a minute, a woman pushed the charred corpses off the fire with a stick. She allowed the bodies to cool for only a moment before cutting through their skin, muscles, sinews, veins, and nerve fibers at the joints. The elders, both women and men, received the upper legs, junior women and men got the lower legs, and children took parts on the backs and chests. Everyone shared the organs. The woman also decapitated the bodies and used a rock to knock a small hole in the top of each skull. A young mother in the group then used a stick to extract gobs of cooked and cooled brains to feed to her infant.

The Hadza offered us pieces of forearm, and most students took a bite. Mukina accepted. Vijay declined. He eyed me from under his floppy-brimmed hat. I hesitated, because these creatures were primates, and eating them felt like cannibalism. The eldest man shook a piece of forearm at me. In Swahili, he said that his people ate wild honey, tubers, berries, and fruits (around 65 percent of the time), but we had given them good luck, and this piece of meat was my reward. I took it and thanked him, and I slipped it into my mouth. It was greasy and had little flavor.

Vijay walked away.

*

After leaving the Hadza, we backpacked north into Maasai territory. Until the Germans arrived in the late nineteenth and the British in the early twentieth century, young Maasai men were feared as warriors who dominated the open plains of East Africa. Their ancestors had migrated into this region in the seventeenth century, bringing hump-backed Zebu cattle and a male-dominated monotheism with them.

Maasai of today are less nomadic and cultivate corn, squash, and beans. They do not consume wild animals and rarely eat their cattle, since more cows equals greater wealth and status. Depending on the season, up to 90 percent of food comes from cow blood—about one liter taken from the carotid artery, which does not harm the animal—and cow milk. Mixing the two in a gourd or ceramic vessel and then letting it congeal for five days produces a sort of "cheese." As for modern-day warriors, Maasai still decorate themselves with beads, red tartan fabric, and braided hair dyed red with ocher and goat fat. But instead of battle, their attention is focused on cows, young women, and cellphone functions.

We hired three Maasai to act as liaisons because we would be crossing their territory (de facto government land) and likely would encounter herders and villages. Our liaisons carried only spears or walking sticks, and we carried no weapons, not even pocketknives. I asked Mukina about our relative defenselessness, and she told me that lions and leopards seldom hunted people, especially groups of us. Hyenas, however, were another matter.

We backpacked across the Serengeti among elands, zebras, wildebeest, and Cape buffalos. Marabou storks and secretary birds stayed close to watering holes, and gray hornbills preferred the thorny protection of acacia trees. At night, elephants often approached our tents, rumbling in low, nearly subsonic tones, and lions coughed to communicate as they hunted. All the animals no doubt smelled our synthetic gear, as well as our organic, unwashed bodies, and stayed clear of the tents.

My only weapon was the hiking pole Mukina continued to call a cane. But I never felt threatened. It was as though the animals respected us as long as we respected them and their space and did not pursue them or "bait" them with improperly hung food bags. We cooked with white gas stoves and clad ourselves in nylon and polypropylene. In spite of our human trappings, however, we felt almost part of the place, partaking of its magic and rhythm and pace, seeing it on its own terms instead of from a safari vehicle or while carrying elephant guns with the intent to kill.

At the end of the section, the branch's transportation crew, who were also mechanics, drove us back to Nairobi. Bandits often raided vehicles on the road to the coast, so we flew to a small airport near the island of Lamu off the coast of Kenya. Kabiru rejoined the course for this last section.

Lamu is part of an archipelago only fifty miles south of the Somali border. The architecture is Arabian, with arches and alcoves constructed of limestone blocks cut from coral. Streets are made of sand. Islam is ubiquitous along the coast of East Africa, and we often heard the call to prayer broadcast from nearby mosques. There was only one car on Lamu. Everyone else walked barefoot or rode donkeys. At night, bioluminescent plankton in the water sparkled blue and white and streamed away like fairy dust around our dhows.

NOLS stored wind-surfboards and snorkel gear with a local man named Omari, though everyone called him Bob. He was sixty and wiry, with skin that was a wrinkled, sooty color. His fingernails were long and resembled claws. Students and instructors were not allowed to carry cellphones or other electronic devices, but Bob played by his own rules. He carried a radio-cassette player everywhere he went, and no one objected. Radio broadcasts were rare on the islands, so Bob brought a copy of Bob Marley and the Wailers' album *Survival* and often hit the rewind button to replay "So Much Trouble in the World." Omari Bob's English was rudimentary and sounded as though he may have learned most of it from his cassette tapes. I wondered if his nickname derived from his music preferences.

Bob had made the pilgrimage, or *hajj*, to Mecca and spoke Arabic, but perhaps his greatest achievement was as a master windsurfer who wore red Speedos. As for family life, he told us he had just married his fourth wife—concurrent with the other three. He boasted about having dozens of children and grandchildren, some of whom were older than his newest wife, who was eighteen. I decided now was not a good time to teach a class on overpopulation, nor to mention the inequality between the sexes that would allow an old man to marry a woman younger than his own grandchildren.

Bob got along with everyone except me. I did not know why. Perhaps he had learned I did not follow any religion, which made me the worst kind of infidel. In fact, when I asked him about the Islam practiced by terrorists, he replied, "Terrorists have no religion." It made me wonder if he lumped me with Al-Qaeda.

A more likely reason may have been that he found out I objected to chauvinism—such as having multiple wives, regarding women as chattel, child marriages, and controlling women sexually through female genital mutilation, which was illegal but still prevalent in Kenya. (FGM, or female genital mutilation, predates Islam and Christianity, but continues to be practiced in many Islamic communities and nations. According to the United Nations Population Fund,

130 million women and girls globally live with the effects of FGM. The Centers for Disease Control and Prevention estimates FGM has even been carried out on 513,000 women and girls in the United States.) I respected cultural differences, but this crossed the line.

In any event, Bob stopped talking to me, and we started to avoid one another.

One evening, I sat alone near the water's edge, where the sand is firm and wet, when Kabiru walked up behind me.

"What's up with you and Bob?" he asked, and sat down. He wore shorts and his Chicago Bulls cap, no shirt or shoes.

"What do you mean?

"The sailors were talking about you and Bob. He thinks you don't like him."

"It's not him exactly. It's his worldview and how they treat women and people who think differently." 9/11 was obvious, but I was tired of talking about it.

He nodded and pushed his glasses up the bridge of his nose. They slid down again on a film of sweat. A light crust of salt highlighted a dark band of sweat around his cap.

"It is true," he said, nodding. "Their ways are different and old, especially, like you say, with their women and their customs. They are sheltered here on these islands. Which does not make it right, I know. But they are changing, slowly, and so far they are finding, shall we say, more peaceful ways to adapt here. Yes?"

"I know. I just hope justice is served."

Kabiru stooped toward me, as if I were shorter than he was, and stared over the rim of his glasses. "Of course. But be careful. Revenge is not justice."

A breeze stirred the heat on the beach as a sacred ibis squawked, and a whole flock lifted from a copse of mangroves at the water's edge.

I nodded. Yet something about Bob had wedged itself in the middle. I looked past Kabiru and down the beach to where the dhows were anchored. Bob stood alone, watching. He shook a claw-like finger at me and skulked into the trees.

CHAPTER 8

The Canadian Quarter

THE HEAT, THE mosquitos, and Bob's aloofness toward me tested my good nature. Vijay said he was just "yanking your chain." In any event, I was relieved when the course ended and we flew back to Nairobi for the first shower any of us had taken in many weeks. For dinner, we drove to a restaurant called The Carnivore. Its menu included an all-you-can-eat meat buffet that promised guests a "beast of a feast." I had eaten baboons with the Hadza and octopus with the sailors, but zebras looked too much like the horses I had named and cared for and ridden as a boy. I ordered cow's meat instead.

After dinner, we awarded the students their diplomas, and we escorted them to the airport the next morning. On the way back to the Milimani, we drove past Uhuru Park and the place where four men had dragged me into the shadows. Mukina and I rode with Vijay. Peter and Kabiru drove the other vehicles.

"Check it out!" shouted Vijay. He pointed to a crowd of people and a news crew in a grassy area across Kenyatta Avenue.

"What's going on?"

"The woman in bright yellow, see her?"

I looked, but many women wore yellow.

"The one in the middle. That's Muta."

"Her name is Maathai," said Mukina, admonishingly. "Wangari Maathai."

"I know, but everyone calls her Muta," said Vijay.

"Who is she?" I still couldn't find her.

"She plants trees, millions of trees, all over Kenya, and she started this program called the Green Belt Movement. Have you heard of it?"

I shook my head.

"And you probably won't," said Mukina, "because she's always in jail."

"For planting trees?"

"She stirs up trouble with those big guys in government," she said.

The noise of car horns and the crowd increased as we drove past the place. Vijay shouted to me over the din. "Politicians don't like her, because they want to cut down the forests to build mansions, and she speaks up and fights against them. She also fights for women's rights, so I guess she's like an activist or something." He pointed back to the crowd. "President Moi was gonna build a skyscraper right there in the park, right where she's standing, but she stopped it. So now it's called Freedom Corner."

"That's cool." I was all for women's rights and the environment, or at least knew I should be and wanted to be. But the park on the other side of Kenyatta Avenue distracted me. I reached up to feel the place where my ear had been detached. A ridge of hard tissue ran the length of the scar above the lobe, and the cuts and bruises on my head and face had healed. I imagined someone walking around in Kibera slum wearing my North Face jacket, ring, shoes, and other things. Anxiety filled my chest and stomach, and my face blanched. I hoped the police had caught those guys and punished them.

But then I felt the talisman on the shoestring around my neck. It calmed me and revived my passion for flying and soaring above all the troubles of the world. Peter had handed out checks, and I hoped to use mine to finish training with Major Kabuthu. I had two months off before the next course started. Strangely, I never considered visiting my old Peace Corps site in Bukoba on Lake Victoria. I told myself the journey would take at least three days by bus and boat, and I would rather spend my time and money finishing flight school. The real reason I hadn't gone lurked in a fog of guilt over not having completed the transformation that had started for me there.

Mukina and Peter had business in Nairobi, and Moira was in Ireland, so Vijay and I drove to the branch together. Our shoulders and hips still showed bruises from carrying seventy-pound packs on the backpacking sections, and our muscles, while toughened, were stiff. So, we went to the Sportsman's Lounge in Nanyuki to buy a meal and use the sauna.

"That smell," said Vijay. I could tell he wanted to shout, but the slick white tiles and supersaturated air amplified the sound, so he held back. We were the only two people in the sauna.

"You mean the goat leg?"

"God, yes. It smelled worse than we did."

The steam hissed on again, and the room fogged over. I inhaled the hot, moist air, which relaxed me, but I was too tired to laugh.

"Don't get me wrong," he continued. "I love Mukina. She's a great person, a great instructor, but sometimes . . ." He shook his head.

I leaned forward on the tile bench to wipe the sweat off my face and push back my mop of brown hair, almost ponytail length. This exposed the crash scar on my forehead, though the longer scars above my hairline remained concealed.

"I couldn't believe she ate it in the tent."

"She knows better," he said, "especially how it can attract animals. But she's Christian, and Christians and Muslims— they eat so much meat. You're Christian, right? You know."

I fiddled with the towel around my hips, making sure it covered me. "Not really." I dodged half of his question. "My dad took me hunting when I was a kid, plus we had cows and chickens and goats, so we ate meat every day, almost every meal."

Vijay was familiar with the practice. Nearly everyone in Kenya ate meat. Nonetheless, its practice baffled him. "No shit? What did your dad do for work?"

"He was a pipefitter-welder, and he was good at carpentry, too. He built our house."

"Did your mom eat meat?"

"Yeah, my sister, too. She ate more meat than I did."

"No shit? Like what?"

"Oh, meatloaf, pork chops, roast, or something like that for dinner." In my mind, I could see the table set with a plastic tablecloth printed with green and yellow sunflowers. Dad sat opposite me, and it was summer, because he wore only underwear, no shirt, and it was still light outside. His forehead was white from wearing the St. Louis Cardinals baseball cap, and his chest was white, too, which contrasted with his face and neck and forearms, which were tanned reddish-brown from having worked outside every day. The aroma of pipe smoke—or later, cigar smoke from King Edward cigarillos with the plastic tip—followed him everywhere.

I chuckled.

"What?" asked Vijay.

"Oh, just thinking about dinnertime as a kid, and how much I picked on my sister."

"About what?"

"Mostly how men were better than women—the best hunters, drivers, teachers, *and* the best cooks, too, because all the great chefs were men. I remember thinking I was so glad that God made me a boy instead of a girl, because women had to give birth and take care of the kids and do housework and everything."

"What did your dad say?"

I shrugged and shook my head.

"And your mom?"

"Nothing—except once. I remember she was at the sink, wearing her yellow rubber gloves while she washed the dishes, and the rest of us were still at the table. She and my dad were arguing about something. I don't remember what. But she finally stormed into the living room and grabbed one of his shotguns off the mantle and took it out into the garage and smashed it on the concrete floor. She left the door to the garage open so we could all see. I remember seeing it."

Vijay's mouth dropped open. "Did the gun go off?"

"No, it wasn't loaded."

I replayed it in my mind. I sat on our "deacon's bench" at the kitchen table, watching my mom smash the shotgun, feeling as though she had attacked me and my dad and what we believed in, because guns and hunting were central to our lives and identity. We were outdoorsmen. And as the wood of the gunstock snapped and split over the concrete step that led down into the garage, I felt reduced, weakened.

Splinters of gunstock broke off. Some flew into the kitchen, onto the wooden floor, others into the garage. My father had cemented a Canadian twenty-five-cent piece into the step between the two rooms when he built the house. The image of a caribou on the back of the quarter faced up. The image of Queen Elizabeth II faced down.

"And your dad?"

"At first, he ignored her. Then he got up. And we had these old-fashioned scales on the stereo, like the kind they use to weigh things at the market, except these were just decorative. But they were my mom's, so he tore them apart and threw them on the floor."

"Did he hit her?"

His question irritated me. "They never fought physically, not in front of us anyway."

I stared into the steam and remembered the gun, the scales, pork chops, a caribou, and Queen Elizabeth II. A pattern of dualities emerged that symbolized violence and peace, weapons and art, meat and life, masculine and feminine. All were severely out of balance.

I blinked. My eyes filled with water, but I was sure it must be the moist heat, and I closed them. "I never thought of it like that."

"What?" he asked.

"Nothing. I just said I'm not a Christian."

I settled into my cabin at the branch that evening. I was glad the course had run in spite of 9/11, but was also relieved to take a break and relax. Matt and Kirsten were due back any day, and I looked forward to catching up with them and finding out how their course had gone.

I walked over to the lounge-admin building to use the toilet, but the electricity was out, so I put on my headlamp and went to the adjacent outhouse. A newspaper in the outhouse headlined how the Taliban in Afghanistan had been defeated and the United Nations Security Council had appointed Hamid

Karzai as the interim president of that country. It went on to say that President Bush had withdrawn the United States from the 1972 Anti-Ballistic Missile Treaty, so America could now defend itself from "rogue" nuclear states in Bush's self-declared War on Terror. The news sounded important, but it was too depressing, and I put the paper aside.

An old clipping nailed to the door caught my attention. It chronicled the wilderness experience of John F. Kennedy Jr., a former NOLS student in Kenya. In 1979, Kennedy had backpacked on Mount Kenya, sailed the Kenyan coast, and gotten lost for several days in the Maasai Mara National Reserve.

He had also been a pilot, and I remembered the crash that killed him, his wife, and their friend twenty years after his Kenya experience. I had crashed less than a year after him, yet I still wanted to fly. I needed to fly.

I went to the admin office to check my mail. In three months, I had received a birthday card from my mom, a billing statement from the hospital in Utah, and a letter from the Kenya Civil Aviation Authority. I tore it open. I had passed the written test and now knew exactly how I would spend the next two months.

CHAPTER 9

The Principle of Lift

THE "DEAD LEG" is the portion of a commercial flight flown without passengers. For small planes, this happens before picking people up and after dropping them off, rather like a shuttle service. I would soon be the dead leg pilot for Tropic Air.

Before beginning this job, I drove back to Nairobi to finish training with Major Kabuthu. Ten days later, I took my checkride (the in-flight exam), and the Major signed me off. He said nothing, no "Congratulations!" and seemed relieved to be rid of me. Having passed the written and practical tests, I now held a Kenya Private Pilot License, or PPL, which entitled me to operate single-engine planes on land in Kenya. The next step would be a Commercial Pilot License, or CPL, where I could not only fly but earn wages for doing it.

Tropic Air, Incorporated was located on Nanyuki Airfield, a thirty-minute drive from the branch. Dark wooden planks and a green metal roof housed the office, and a fence helped keep large animals off the runway—most of the time. The rural airport evoked a more romantic era of flight, of Charles Lindbergh and Amelia Earhart, in spite of a modern Beechcraft King Air parked on the apron. A third-generation British-Kenyan named Jamie owned and operated the air charter service. Kabiru had called him a Kenya Cowboy. In his late forties, Jamie lived on a nearby estate that resembled a British colonial manor straight out of a novel about the old empire and the African bush. His wife was also a white Kenyan. She was in her mid-thirties, and they had a toddler.

White people in the Kenya Highlands traditionally cultivated *qat*—or *miraa*—an herbal stimulant taken as a remedy for hangovers. *Qat* contains an amphetamine-like narcotic that induces mild euphoria. For this reason, Islamic courts in Somalia had banned it in the 1980s. Jamie said he used to smuggle bales of it to Mogadishu in his plane. His stories reminded me of those told by Commander McBragg, a cartoon character I watched as a child on *The Bullwinkle Show*. McBragg stereotyped a retired British colonial officer who wore tweeds and smoked a pipe and spun tales of adventure from his drawing room.

Jamie had been a pilot for decades, but he flew less often since becoming the owner-manager of Tropic Air. A commercial pilot named Steve now undertook most of the contracted flights. British, blond, and in his late twenties, Steve was the chief pilot at Tropic Air. Now that I had my Kenya PPL, Jamie invited me to fly dead legs with Steve in a Cessna 182 and a Cessna 206.

The flights themselves were spectacular. At dawn, taxiing onto the runway, I called my departure on the common traffic frequency, and in fewer than a thousand feet, the plane floated into the sky. Lift is the key aerodynamic force of flight. It opposes weight and gravity. Two or three seconds of it were enough to elevate us above the mundane world and fill the panorama with Mount Kenya, the Aberdares, and the endless plains to the north. Most days we flew north over herds of giraffes, elephants, and Thomson's gazelles, which appeared larger than life and older than history in the early morning sunshine. The landscape emanated such power and drama I was certain it would bear us up should the engine fail. It evoked scenes from *Out of Africa* and that book's opening line: "I had a farm in Africa at the foot of the Ngong Hills." The author, Baroness Karen von Blixen-Finecke, wrote her memoir in 1937. However, she published under the pseudonym Isak Dinesen because men wrote and purchased most books in her day. Female authors were largely ignored.

Still, I imagined the romance of a time when aviators like Beryl Markham and Blixen's lover Denys Finch Hatton flew bi-winged "aeroplanes" over Kenya's Mau Forest and the Ngong Hills. They and the other white colonists played cricket with Lord Delamere at the Muthaiga Country Club and took their thoroughbreds to "race meetings" in Nairobi. "Kitchen boys" served tea at four o'clock, supper at seven, and sweetmeats with local coffee for dessert.

Now I, too, flew planes over the savanna, and more than ever such fantasies populated my plans for a life in Africa. Like Peter Pan, I was carefree, and this was my Neverland. Yet, even a flying boy has to come down to earth and not fly too near the sun. I could see that my romance with Britain's colonial past perpetuated the vestiges of chauvinism, violence, and exploitation that had kept my vision for my life aloft. Deep inside, I like to think, I sensed my error and longed to let go. But fear stopped me—fear that letting go would weaken me and make me fall. Flight kept me safe and uncommitted, up in the air for a few more seconds.

The first leg of morning flights lasted about an hour. When we spotted our destination, I radioed our intentions to enter downwind, base, and final. This is a standard practice at uncontrolled fields in case other planes are approaching or taxiing to takeoff. But before entering the pattern, we always flew low over the runway to drive off wildlife and to check surface conditions, especially during the rainy seasons.

We typically flew to tourist lodges at Ol Malo, Lewa, Sangara, or Loisaba. After landing on the red murram field, we would cut the engine, hop out to meet our passengers, load their luggage, and fly them to another lodge, or back to Nanyuki, or Jomo Kenyatta International in Nairobi. Steve took the controls for this leg of the trip.

Jamie said business was growing. He hinted he might need another pilot in a year or two and invited me to a Christmas party with his friends and family in the grassy courtyard of his home. Several employees from Tropic Air were present, including Steve. I noticed that black Kenyans were conspicuously absent.

After dinner, Jamie introduced me to Bongo Woodley. Bongo had flown the white plane over the branch on the day I arrived.

"You're with NOLS then?" Bongo asked.

"I'm a field instructor."

"Bloody good," he said, and shook my hand.

Jamie stepped in and handed me a tumbler with a half-inch of clear liquid in the bottom, no ice. "Brandy?" he asked. "It's South African."

I hesitated. I had never tasted hard liquor but was curious and thought Christmas might be the perfect time to try. I also wanted to fit in and become one of the boys, so I took the glass. Bongo exhaled cigar smoke into his snifter. The smoke overflowed the rim like dry ice in water, which impressed me. It seemed like a fitting thing for a man to do, to smoke and drink, especially in this almost magical fashion.

He lifted his smoky glass. "To flying in smooth air."

"And to women with smooth skin," said Jamie.

We smiled and clinked glasses. I sipped the brandy. My lips and face flushed hot, and I tried not to cough. It tasted like kerosene siphoned through a hose, yet I detected a note of grapes, and the second sip was less foul. The third was almost enjoyable. It reminded me I needed to talk to Vijay about the big party scheduled at Trout Tree. It reminded me of the waitress who worked there.

Chatting with the Kenya Cowboys, I learned that Bongo was a British-Kenyan and the chief warden of Mount Kenya National Park. He flew a white Piper Cub on poaching patrols, and said he could use my help sometime if I were interested.

After Christmas, I continued to fly dead legs with Steve. The routines and landscapes became familiar, but I was never blasé about flying in the way Kabiru had mentioned, and I always watched for potential landing sites in case of emergency. Thoughts of my crash mingled with those of the assault in the park, my fall on Grand Teton five years earlier, and even the attacks on the Twin Towers. We were at war, and almost overnight the world seemed to have become a less compassionate, more malevolent place. The combined effect was to uncover a latent madness in the human condition. To combat such thinking, I distracted myself with flight. This and the talisman lifted me above it all, so I could feel safe, like nothing could go wrong now.

Tourism slowed down in January, so I only flew about once per week. The rest of the time I ran errands for Peter in Nanyuki, did calisthenics, and jogged the trails. I also prepared to lead my next NOLS course, scheduled to start in February. Enrollment had recovered, and twenty-two students were signed up for each course.

Matt and Kirsten were in Lamu, taking a personal trip, and Vijay had not contacted me in weeks, not since he drove to Nairobi to see Moira. I had hoped we could meet at Trout

Tree at the end of December, but the restaurant was closed for the holidays. With or without him, I decided to go to the next scheduled party at the end of January. It interested me for two reasons. First, I was now thirty-six, and while I had sipped a beer or two and now a brandy, neat, I had never experienced the much-lauded state of drunkenness. I wanted to see what all the fuss was about and to find out what it meant to be thoroughly sloshed. I considered it an experiment.

The second reason was less concrete. I was attracted to the young Kenyan woman I'd seen waiting tables there in October. I thought she was attracted to me, too, but nothing guaranteed she would be present or interested. She was pretty. She no doubt had a boyfriend.

At nine o'clock in the evening on the last day of January, I checked out one of the Land Rovers. No street lamps or reflectors lighted the road, and only the odd kerosene lamp glowed from a grass-roofed home along the way. Whiffs of wood smoke seeped into the vehicle's cab and vanished again. At least the sky was clear, and a full moonrise poured light as pale as milk over fields of tea and corn. I could have easily driven with the headlights turned off.

The restaurant was impossible to miss. Land Cruisers, Peugeots, and BMWs packed the gravel parking area and lined the highway, and colored lights festooned every branch of the great tree. A temporary sign hung over the entrance. The letters of the words "The Bone Zone" were sketched to resemble long bones.

I parked and paid a two-hundred-shilling cover charge, about two dollars. Tables, stools, and an open-air bar lined a concrete dance floor at ground level, and a DJ tested his sound system with "The Gambler" by Kenny Rogers. Most patrons were white and forty-something. It was still early, and the floor was empty, except for a few black girls who danced in a tight huddle. The waitstaff were also black, but I did not see the woman I remembered.

Steve stood at the bar and waved. I walked over.

"Hey, Willy! Let me buy you a beer!" he shouted over the music and held up a glass.

"What are you having?" I shouted back, though I had already read the label on the bottle in front of him.

"Primus!"

I ordered one. The beer was dark and came in a pint. A waitress poured it into a glass, and I started my experiment.

"Here's to bloody Kenya!" he yelled.

We clinked glasses and drank. The beer tasted bitter and was not to my liking, but I did not grimace. The music changed to "Oh, What a Night" by The Four Seasons. I had not heard that song since grade school, but after only half a glass of Primus, I started to tap my foot and felt myself smile. Suddenly, the music was not so old and the place no longer a sad collection of middle-aged whiteys trying to recapture their youth. When I finished my Primus, I ordered from the liquor selection behind the bar. I pointed to a bottle of Zima, the brand of Kenyan cognac I had seen the Major drink at Wilson Airport. The bartender poured a shot and pushed it out to me. Cautiously, I sipped. Nearly as sweet as pancake syrup, it brightened my eyes, so I quaffed the rest and ordered another.

Steve laughed and slapped me on the back. "Easy tiger!"

"Don't Stop Me Now" by Queen was playing when I went to the dance floor. By then, several couples danced freestyle, which was the only style I knew. I danced alone. I danced with strangers. Everyone came out on the floor when the DJ played the Bee Gees' "Stayin' Alive." I twirled, I leaped, I did "The Hustle." When ABBA's "Dancing Queen" ended, I returned to the bar and ordered another Zima, which in Swahili means "extinguish" or "put out." A full moon soared high overhead, and I felt anything but quenched.

That's when I saw her. She glanced at me and smiled as she poured a drink for a patron at the end of the bar. My mind spun. After returning the bottle to the shelf, she came to me with a smile that could not wait.

She leaned over the bar, and I lifted myself halfway across to meet her. In English, she spoke softly but close to my ear. I felt her breath on my skin.

"You are a very bad dancer."

I giggled more easily than I expected. My nose brushed her cheek, and she smelled like jasmine and gin. The drinks and the music had given me confidence, yet I knew the moment was wild and unpredictable. Anything could happen.

"Maybe you can teach me."

She reached across the bar and held my hand. My body was on fire.

"What is your name?" she asked.

I stuttered, like I had forgotten.

"You look like Jesus," she said.

My hair was long enough to tie back, and I had not shaved in a few days. I rubbed the whiskers on my chin. "Except, my eyes are brown, not blue."

She blinked and studied me, but did not appear to get the joke. As a Jew from the then-Roman province of Judea, Jesus almost certainly had a dark complexion. However, most renditions, especially older ones, portray him with light skin and eyes and, sometimes, blond hair.

"What's your name?"

"Rachel."

I stroked her hand. She had carefully shaped her finger-nails and painted them deep red. I recalled how my ex-wife had painted her nails, but since our divorce nearly ten years previously, none of the women I knew in outdoor education attended to such physical adornment. I preferred the organic look, but Rachel's allure eclipsed any social scruples I may have had.

Customers wanted her attention for drinks, so she stood up from the bar and shouted to me, "May I bring you another drink, sir?"

I studied the shelf of liquor behind her. My eyelids felt heavy and slow to blink. "I'll try the red one!"

She pointed to The Hammer, a whiskey drink. I nodded. She filled a shot glass to overflowing and handed it to me with a smile before going to other customers.

I downed the shot of whiskey and slammed the glass onto the wooden bar as I had seen cowboys do in the movies. Steve had disappeared, so I stumbled back to the dance floor. My legs felt wobbly, and the floor seemed an unreliable surface, as if I floated a little above it. This was a new application of the principle of lift. It influenced the three axes of flight—pitch, yaw, and roll—though I took care to avoid the last.

Two of Steve's friends, Esten and Louisa, danced in a group of whiteys. They were the son and daughter of an American doctor who lived nearby, and they invited me to dance with them. Louisa was about twenty and danced close to me, bumping me and shaking everything she owned at me. However, I could think only of Rachel. I was drunk, and everything felt wonderful, so I discoed like a fool, and I didn't care. Nobody cared.

I glanced at the bar but did not see Rachel. The clock above the shelves of liquor read three in the morning. A meek place at the back of my brain, dressed like a librarian and wagging its fingers in my direction, warned me not to drive back to the branch.

I stumbled to the bar. Rachel was back. I asked her for a bottle of water and a bag of peanuts—called groundnuts in the Commonwealth. If I did not return the Land Rover before dawn, Peter and Charlotte would be worried and might search for me and call the police, a sobering thought.

"Will, it is dangerous for you to drive," said Rachel. "I live just there, behind the restaurant. You should stay with me."

CHAPTER 10

Predator and Prey

A HAND STROKED my hair, and I awoke. With eyes still closed, I wondered if it had all been a dream—the dancing, the drinks, the beautiful woman—because now it was so quiet I could not move. I did not want to move.

The hand stopped, and teeth began to gnash at the ends of my shoulder-length hair. My eyes snapped open into darkness.

I gasped and shook my head, and a rat dug its claws into my scalp. Jumping to my feet on the bed, I smacked my head into a wooden joist in the low ceiling as the rat leaped to the wall and scurried around a ledge. Pain from the impact and the hangover shot through my head, and I fell to the floor. I crawled across a grass mat to a broom in the corner and used it as a cane to help me stand. I flicked on the light. The rat scurried around the ledge between wall and ceiling, so I slapped at it with the broom, loosing debris from the tin ceiling, but the rat escaped.

The headboard of my bed touched the south wall of the cabin, which was also the north wall of a bulk-food supply room. Eighty-pound sacks of flour, rice, and cornmeal were stored adjacent to my sleeping quarters, and every night the creatures next door scuttled and munched—hyraxes, rats, and God knows what else. This was the first time one of these animals had opted to sample fare in the adjoining room.

I dropped the broom. Pressure swelled at the top of my head, and my stomach twitched. I wore only underwear briefs, but I threw open the cabin door and sprinted across the yard in broad daylight toward the instructors' lounge and bathroom. My stomach churned and squeezed, so I dived into a bed of roses outside Peter and Charlotte's house. The flowers fronted their living room window, and I hoped they had either slept in or gone to church. Thorns lanced my arms and legs, but I hardly noticed. Crouching between bushes, I vomited what felt like liters of bile, stomach acid, and all my internal organs, in the process coating my talisman and the ends of my hair in lumpy brown goo.

I glanced through the window. Peter and Charlotte's son, Miles, stood in their living room, staring at me, eyes wide with wonder. I heard heavy footsteps inside, and Miles pointed at me with an outstretched arm, as if identifying the guilty party in a police lineup.

I sprang out of the bushes and dashed across the lawn to the bathroom in the admin building, where I vomited again. This time, I was empty and could only dry heave.

Tap water cooled my face, and I rinsed out my hair and the talisman in the sink and put on a gray cotton robe that hung on the door. My reflection in the bathroom mirror revealed bloodshot eyes, pasty skin, and a haggard face. I turned away.

Food was the last thing on my mind, but I was parched, so I shuffled to the kitchen. The room smelled like grease and Clorox, which almost made me sick again, but I swallowed hard and filled a glass of water from the ceramic filter on the kitchen counter. I drank it in sips and refilled the glass.

TV did not interest me—another plane crash, bombing raid, or "collateral damage"—so I went to the library with my glass and sat down. Sunshine beamed through the windows and soothed me. I stared into the yard and listened to the warble of gamble birds and the bleat of a neighbor's goat, before a familiar *chat-chat* sound caught my attention. A wheatear jumped into the grass from a bougainvillea shrub next to the cookhouse. Sunlight highlighted the shrub's pink flowers, which cascaded onto the green grass and formed a colorful backdrop for the bird's acrobatics. In this light, the wheatear's mask resembled an aviator's goggles, and I admired its ability to leap into the air and fly wherever it chose, whenever it pleased.

The bird hopped toward me. Could it see me, I wondered? Could it be the same bird that perched on my toe? It hopped again, then stopped, looked askance, and flew off in a great hurry. A skinny dog scampered across the yard with its nose down. It had spooked the bird but did not notice it and continued on its way, hot on the scent of my vomit.

The yard was then empty, and I remembered Rachel—the smell of her hair, the smoothness of her cheek, and the glint in her eyes. "You should stay with me," she had said. I may have grinned, but my mouth had been numb, and I could not be sure. In the same moment, a yellow flag had hoisted itself in my consciousness and signaled caution with this beautiful African woman from the Bone Zone. After an hour of nibbling groundnuts, sipping bottles of Glacier water, and making trips to the men's room to pee, I felt less wobbly, steady enough to drive. Rachel winked and waved. That one memory was worth every fluid ounce of misery I experienced the next morning.

The library was small, perhaps 150 square feet, and held reference books on Swahili, East African wildlife, geology, coastal ecosystems, and human prehistory. But the telephone on the table interested me most. It was an old-fashioned corded phone like the one at the flat in Nairobi. I picked up the receiver. It had a dial tone, and I remembered taking Rachel's phone number, which was the restaurant's, and telling her I would call.

I put the receiver down and returned to the kitchen for more water. In bare feet and a gray robe, I carried the glass of water to my cabin, and on the way noticed the skinny dog nosing around the rosebushes. It was gross to think, but I hoped the dog lapped up my puke before Peter or Charlotte discovered it.

I dressed, walked back to the library, and called Rachel. She sounded different on the phone, less confident, and I wondered if she had not expected me to call her after all. Yet within a few minutes, she had loosened up and sounded interested. We even shared a laugh regarding my white-boy dance moves. By the end of the call, we agreed to meet Friday for dinner.

The notion of forbidden love tasted sweet. However, I did not examine this impulse too closely, afraid of what I might discover. My father had verbally and socially discriminated against ethnic, racial, and religious minorities when I was a boy. In the Peace Corps, I saw how his worldview had impacted me, and how I relinquished it. Rachel was certainly pretty. But I had to wonder if I liked her merely out of spite, opposing what my father stood for, or whether I was genuinely attracted to her. Perhaps, I thought, the only way to find out would be to pursue her and attach myself to her and her needs, as I had tried to do with Amy.

By afternoon, the headache and nausea had subsided, so I donned my running shorts and tied my hair into a short, high ponytail. Hopping over the fence behind the branch, I skipped across the stream and took the trail that bent into the forest.

Halfway there, the path recrossed the same stream, but here it flowed through a ravine thirty feet deep. The only way to the other side was over an enormous yellowwood tree that someone had felled to create a footbridge. Like a child, giddy with adventure, I tiptoed across and raced on. The rhythmic slap of the talisman against my sternum reminded me I was a bush pilot in Africa and as free as a bird.

The trail wound through meadows of golden cassia flowers and long-bladed grasses that smelled like pumpkin, all lazy and buff in the evening sun. I bounded over a stream that ran through a grove of cedars. The air here was damp with resin, and the mountain's bouquet was as cool and fresh as water. I breathed deep and gained speed on the incline.

In a little while, the grade leveled out, and I came into an open area perhaps fifty feet across. Eucalyptus trees grew around the perimeter, and vines covered several rotted stumps in the center. I stopped and breathed hard, happy to have pushed myself. To the west lay the broad valley floor, tawny and somnolent. Blue ribbons of smoke snaked into the sky from a hundred cooking fires, and I caught the scent of onions simmering with roasted goat. It reminded me of Mukina's goat leg, and I smiled and shook my head.

I lifted the shoestring necklace over my head and laid it on a stump so it draped over the edge. Lying down in the grass, I clasped my hands behind my head and admired the talisman in the glow of the setting sun. Then I closed my eyes. I saw myself earning my CPL in Kenya and exploring this land of adventure. I might even settle here, I thought: maybe Kenya, maybe Tanzania. Maybe Rachel.

A twig snapped. My eyes popped open. Bushes rustled behind my head, and I heard a snort. My face blanched, and my heart thumped against my sweaty T-shirt, but I lay as still as stone.

A wheatear landed in a tree where I could see it and focused on the creature behind my head. My father taught me to sit for hours without moving a muscle when hunting some animals. With others, the intention was to flush them out and make them run so they'd provide a clear running shot. I wondered which rules applied when I was the prey.

The heavy creature pushed aside brambles and moved closer. Turning my head as little as possible, I searched for a big stick to use in defense or a tree close enough to climb but found neither. The sound was almost on top of me. I swallowed hard.

A deep rumble vibrated through the ground and turned the air moist with the smell of rotten cabbage: signs of a forest elephant. Less than half the size of their relatives on the open savanna, forest elephants still weigh four thousand pounds and stand seven feet tall. They are herbivorous, so they would not consider me food, but if I jumped up and surprised one, it might deem me a threat, especially if it had young nearby. It could easily outrun me and trample or gore me to death.

I watched the wheatear. It bobbed its head, focused on the creature I could not see, and flexed its knees to jump and fly. But I did not wait. I leaped up and ran as fast as I could. I heard a snort behind me, and I ran faster. I sped out of the forest into the first meadow and vaulted one stream and then another. A small animal scurried under a bush, but I did not turn to look. I raced over the tree-bridge into the lower meadow, and the thorns of wait-a-bit bushes lanced my shins until they bled. The elephant could not possibly be chasing me, I thought, or it would have caught up to me by now.

But adrenaline bathed my muscles and compelled me to run lest my heart explode. I raced across the lower meadow, where the trail vanished under a mat of long grasses, moist and slumped like pasta in a bowl. I plunged into it, but the grass concealed divots. My right foot sank and rolled hard to the outside and made a great popping sound like a rifle shot.

I howled and crashed onto my side, rocking and holding my leg. I pulled down my sock, and before my eyes, the ankle swelled and turned purple and carmine. I did not dare take off the shoe for fear it would not go on again.

The elephant had not pursued me, but I was still two miles from the branch and could not walk. No one knew I had gone for a run, and the brightest stars already twinkled over the African bush.

CHAPTER 11

Empires of Blood

VINES OF THE Saint Thomas Bean plant had climbed the plastered cinderblock walls to twine themselves around French patio doors and square-paned windows. In the yard, eucalyptus trees dappled the grass with shade, and the flowers of a purple bougainvillea bobbed in the slightest breeze as if waving hello. A gray hadeda ibis perched on the tin roof and squawked.

The Nanyuki Cottage Hospital survived from colonial days. The grounds reminded me of a scene from an old movie, though I could not remember which one (was it *The Devil at Four O'Clock* with Spencer Tracy and Frank Sinatra, or *Born Free* with Virginia McKenna and Bill Travers?). Both films portrayed European heroics and possessed a nostalgia for the glory of the former empire.

But I was in no mood for nostalgia. The night before, I had hopped and crawled back to the branch and knocked on Peter and Charlotte's door around ten o'clock. They were still awake and had given me an ice pack and an old pair of crutches. I did not mention the elephant.

"I can't believe you went for a run after that. After this morning, I mean," Peter had said, motioning to the rose bed outside their bay window.

Vijay arrived from Nairobi the next morning and drove me to the hospital, and now Dr. Bhatt, the chief physician, applied a plaster cast to my lower right leg and foot. However, he prescribed no pain medications. He said drugs were in short supply and were dispensed only for those in dire need, such as when an elephant—or whatever animal—actually ran the person down, and the person lived.

I paid the nurse at the front desk eight hundred Kenyan shillings and hobbled out on my crutches. Vijay leaned against his Jeep, enjoying the sun. He straightened when he saw me, and walked over.

"Dude, that's fucked up," he said, pointing to my cast.

"That's basically what the doctor said."

"Is it bad?"

"He said it's an avulsion fracture on the right distal fibula, I think?"

"Your ankle."

"Yeah, and he said the ligaments and muscles are shredded."

"Fuck. That is fucked up."

"Yeah, but no surgery."

"No?"

"The ligaments weren't completely severed, so they'll heal, but it will take time, like eight weeks before the cast comes off, twelve before I can carry a backpack."

We worked our way over to his Jeep. He opened the passenger door for me.

"We're gonna miss you on the course," he said.

Vijay's use of informal contractions and slang annoyed me. I had kept quiet about it but was not sure how much longer I could hold my tongue. I wished he would not try so hard to sound hip. I wished he could be himself.

I lifted myself onto the seat. "Yeah, it sucks. And I really need the work. Not that this cost anything." I motioned to the cast.

"Can you fly?"

"I doubt it. I'll have to call Jamie and tell him what happened."

Vijay started the Jeep, which still lacked a muffler. "You know, it could have been worse!" he shouted. "You could be dead!" He laughed.

The purple bougainvillea waved goodbye. Part of me longed to stay a moment and bask in the memory of old fables, thrilling yet cozy—at least for white boys like me.

Peter reshuffled instructors for the upcoming semester courses, and I called Jamie at Tropic Air to give him the news. "Gotta watch those damn jumbos," he said, using the Kenyan term for elephants. "They'll run you flat to bits! I've seen it happen."

I called Rachel, too. The broken ankle was of little concern to her. She had known many people with serious physical deformities, injuries, or illnesses. This was nothing. She was more disturbed by the thought of an elephant and what could have happened. The worry in her voice pleased me.

We went ahead with our date. Unable to dance, I suggested dinner at the Naro Moru River Lodge on Sunday night. The rudder pedals in an airplane might be difficult to operate, but the cast was not as bad as I had imagined, and I thought I could drive a car.

I had access to three Land Rovers at the branch. One of them had a sluggish takeoff, which meant it decelerated more slowly, too. This gave me an extra half-second to switch my left foot from the clutch to the gas and back again. Still, it was impossible not to jerk the vehicle when shifting from first gear into second, and it stalled several times.

I shaved my face extra-close and took a shower in the instructors' bathroom with a plastic bag tied over my cast. I owned two pairs of Levi's and cut the right leg off at the knee of the older pair so it would fit over my cast. I topped off my outfit with a red short-sleeved polo shirt. I had always been told that red was my power color and looked good on me, and I wanted to impress Rachel. I fantasized we might hit it off and get serious. Maybe she and I would move in together, I thought, after I earned my CPL. Maybe I could fly for Tropic Air, or AMREF (African Medical and Research Foundation air services) in Nairobi, or some other international aid organization. Maybe it was fate.

My foot throbbed by the time I pulled into the parking lot at Trout Tree. I had unrolled a sock over my exposed toes to keep them warm, but the sock had fallen off. After I parked, I found the sock crumpled on the floorboard and rolled it back down over my toes. I grabbed the crutches from the passenger seat and checked my hair and teeth in the rearview mirror.

It was difficult to use crutches on the gravel. But none of that mattered when I saw Rachel. Her smile, her body, her mystery enchanted me and made me feel strong and confident.

She pointed to my shirt and then to hers. "We are the same," she said in English. We both wore a red shirt, though hers was blousy and hung loose and looked smart, casual yet chic. She also wore khaki slacks and black pumps. As before, her hair was straightened, and she had combed it down to a point on the left side of her face. "Except for that," she said, pointing to my cast.

"Yeah, no dancing tonight."

"Oh, I am sad," she said, and we laughed.

I opened the passenger door for her, but she stopped and squinted at my neck. "Will, where is your charm?"

I wished she had not remembered the talisman. My heart sank when I pictured it on the stump.

"I lost it."

She clicked her tongue. "That is too bad. I liked it."

The Naro Moru River Lodge was built in the 1940s and refurbished in the 1980s. It retained elements of both decades. Dark wood paneling, photos of hunters and climbers, and an impala's head mounted over the bar catered to manly interests. Michael Jackson's "Black or White" provided counterpoint over the Bose sound system. Tourists reclined at the pool.

The maître d' seated us in the dining lounge and informed us they normally served barbeque on Sundays, so I ordered mashed potatoes with prime rib cooked medium rare. I told Rachel that dinner was my treat and to get whatever she wanted, so she ordered tilapia with French fries (or chips, in former British colonies like Kenya). Our dinners came quickly.

"How's your meat?" she asked.

"It's good." My fingers dripped with sauce. "Bloody, just the way I like it."

"You Americans! You eat so much meat, isn't it?"

"I guess. But Kenyans do, too." I thought of Mukina and her goat leg.

"Yes, sometimes. But you know, we Kikuyus did not eat so much of it before the British came."

"Because hunting is hard? It was hard to get meat?"

"No, because it was holy. It was our religion. But now we are Christians, so we can eat meat every day. Like it says in the Bible, 'One man's faith allows him to eat everything, but another man, whose faith is weak, eats only vegetables.' But not every day, because it is too expensive."

I nodded and chewed my prime rib and kept chewing so as not to start a conversation about religion. Like most

Kenyans, especially in the country's interior, Rachel probably observed a Protestant denomination of Christianity similar to the Assembly of God Church of my youth. However, since my time in the Peace Corps, my worldview had evolved. With Rachel, I hoped to find common ground before broaching something as pivotal as religion.

I pointed to her plate. "Is it okay? I'm paying."

"I know," she said, and smiled and winked, as if I were the man in the family.

More white men came to the bar, but also Indian men who wore white shorts and T-shirts and terrycloth sweatbands on their wrists and foreheads. The River Lodge had racquetball courts, and Indian businessmen loved to play. Some glanced at us. Others smirked. I imagined they assumed I had bought dinner for my evening's entertainment. The thought made me uncomfortable and a little irritated, but I could not help also wondering if any of them had ever bought dinner for Rachel.

"You know, you were so drunk that night," she said, giggling.

I smiled, glad for the distraction. "I know. I just wanted to know what it was like to be drunk. That was my first time."

She laughed. "Yes, I am sure of it."

I could have argued my point, but I decided to let her think it was a joke and continue to pretend I was an adult.

Over dinner, she told me more about her Kikuyu heritage. I learned that Kikuyu is the largest of dozens of ethnic groups in Kenya. Her people historically lived near the Aberdare Range and south to Nairobi and the Ngong Hills. They were at one time sworn enemies of the Maasai, though old hostilities had mostly cooled.

When I asked, Rachel said she was twenty-three and studying to become a secretary in Nairobi but had run out of tuition funds. She worked as a waitress and bartender at Trout Tree to save money for school. With subtle flair, I told her I guided wilderness expeditions and flew bush planes, too, which was my next career. I expected her to be impressed, but she only nodded and asked how much money I made.

"Very little." To me, forming relationships had never been contingent on wealth. In fact, I avoided those that were. But here, for the first time, I felt nervous. I grinned over the bloody ribs on my plate and followed up my answer. "Pilots earn more."

She nodded, satisfied.

After dinner, I paid the check, and we played a game of pool, which I won, and a game of darts, which she won. The sun had gone down, but it was still light outside, so we descended the stairs into the backyard of the restaurant. The Naro Moru, or Black Rock, River was no more than a stream and flowed in a narrow channel around the edge of the yard. A wooden footbridge spanned the stream, and a path led into the trees on the other side.

"I think it can be difficult with crutches," she said, "but would you like to try?"

We crossed the bridge. The path was well maintained and wound through dense patches of forest. Frangipani trees grew nearby, and we smelled their sweet licorice scent as frogs croaked along the stream. We came to another footbridge, and halfway across Rachel leaned over the rail and gazed into the water. I set my crutches against the rail and leaned over, too. The water was lower and quieter than normal. The long rainy season spans March to June in Kenya, and the short rains come in October and November. Both had disappointed farmers since the 1970s, and the cycle of drought increased with each passing year. We saw no fish in the stream.

"Hah!" she shouted, and pointed to a meadow through the trees. A red Boran bull with short spiky horns and a shoulder

hump grazed in a clearing thirty yards away. Nilotic ancestors of the Maasai developed the Boran breed from Zebu
cattle in Ethiopia around 1500 CE.

The bull raised its head. Long stalks of vegetation drooped
from the sides of its mouth, and a wheatear perched on its
hump.

I had just eaten a piece of a cow for dinner, and now my
body was in the process of literally incorporating its flesh.
I liked the thought of the cow becoming me. It resonated
with the great cosmic cycle of birth, death, and rebirth, and
reminded me of the Way of Nature spoken of in Daoism.

I also knew I could have chosen something else from the
menu. I could have ordered rice with beans, or plantain soup
with yams. I could have allowed the cow to continue to
be a cow—or at least voted toward such an outcome with
my wallet—and still recognized my part in the grand cycle.
Instead, a trusting creature like this bull had ambled into
a stall following its keepers, who had fed and watered and
protected it all its life, and with its harness drawn tight, its
keeper had plunged a knife into its carotid artery, and blood
had poured out as the cow struggled and bellowed in confusion and terror.

I had a choice.

Rachel pulled the collar down on my red shirt.

"A bird," she said, "a beautiful bird."

I was nervous, but I pulled my collar down farther to
expose the colors of my tattoo. Rachel stroked my neck.

"What does it mean?" she asked.

"It's a phoenix, which is like an eagle—"

"I know the phoenix. It is Greek from the time of Christ."

I stood up from the rail, wobbly on my cast, but Rachel
held me around my waist and steadied me. I stood four or
five inches taller, just over her head, and her hair smelled like

jasmine, and her cheeks glowed like honey. I held her around her waist.

"Well, Christians adopted it from pagans, but—"

"Why do you have it?"

"I was in Mexico a few years ago, working for NOLS. There was a big party at the beach. Someone else got one, and I had been thinking about getting one—"

"Will," she said, staring up at me with her face a few inches from mine. I had avoided her deeper question.

I smiled at her and bobbed my head side to side. "It symbolizes change."

"Change from what to what?" She studied my eyes, my mouth.

I felt hot and turned to look at the cow. It grazed in the same place as before, and now two wheatears perched on its hump. I wanted to tell Rachel more—more about who I had been as a boy and how much that had changed in the Peace Corps. I wanted to tell her about the crash and needing to return to Africa to fly and to live, and that I wanted her to be part of that. I needed for her to be part of that.

She touched my cheek and chin. I turned back to her, and her face was very close, so close we blinked and touched noses, and I felt her breath on my lips. My heart pounded so hard it caused the skin of my chest to rub against my red shirt. It throbbed in my ears. I closed my eyes, and her lips were warm and soft, moving so slowly I forgot.

We opened our eyes, and she studied my face. She reached up and ran a finger over the scar on my forehead, the red notch on my ear, down along my tattoo, and patted the place where my necklace had been.

"I want to learn your secrets. What do you want from me?"

I felt hot. I looked at the cow again and tried to make a joke. "I don't think there's a safe answer to that question."

But the urge to disclose my life to her, to someone, to the right one, was powerful. I needed to attach myself to her and her needs and for my life to become hers.

We continued on the path to the lodge, and I drove her back to Trout Tree. A new female employee at the restaurant had moved in with her, so she did not invite me in as she had after the party. But standing on the stoop outside her cabin, she told me she would like to see me again and suggested Sunday for church.

"Can you come with me?" she asked.

My mind raced. "I'm afraid I'll be coming back from Nairobi that day with Peter. It's for work. Maybe next time?"

"Okay, but I want you to come with me to church sometime. Then maybe I can come with you to America."

She caught me off-guard. I immediately wondered if her interest in me was merely to get a ticket to the United States, or if she was that serious about starting a relationship. Would it matter if she knew I wanted to stay in Kenya?

My emotions were in turmoil, so I did not answer her. Instead, I suggested dinner at the branch on Sunday evening. I would cook. I would also clean my cabin and put fresh sheets on the bed.

As for the rat, I hoped it returned before Sunday. I had put a shovel next to the door for just that occasion.

CHAPTER 12

Executions

I DID CHIN-UPS from the rafters of the gazebo in the yard behind Peter and Charlotte's house, push-ups, too, and sit-ups for those all-important abdominal muscles. Then I swept the cabin floor and hand-washed the sheets and pillowcases in the outdoor sink using OMO Fast Action detergent powder. Everything was set.

On our next flight to Loisaba Lodge, I operated the controls and radio communications during flight while Steve handled takeoffs and landings. Along the way, I told him about my date with Rachel.

"I know the one," he said, over the headset intercom. He wore sunglasses, so I could not see his eyes, only his grin. "She's a dish, that one—watch your altitude, old boy." He pointed to the altimeter, but it was unchanged, and he laughed.

I smiled and nodded, even though his remark made me uncomfortable. "So, you know her?"

He shrugged. "All I know is—" His transmission crackled, and I didn't catch what he said, but his movements were hasty and his manner sharp, so I was reluctant to ask him to repeat. "Anyway, you do what you want," I heard him say when the transmission became audible again. "In fact, if you're interested, there's a ranch west of Naro Moru. It's owned by an elderly chap, an American named Ray. He owns stables and horses, and he guides tourists on safari, on horseback, you know. Women love that shit," he said with a smile that suggested experience.

I liked the idea. I had grown up around horses and knew I could impress Rachel with my expertise.

The plane droned on, and we flew over a thousand zebras that fanned out across the red savanna. It was a raw spectacle of nature, but I hardly noticed. Thoughts of Rachel consumed me.

"She told me about these old Kikuyu traditions and religious customs."

"Who?" asked Steve.

"Rachel."

"Right. You mean their hocus-pocus, their myths."

"Yeah, of course they're myths. But they tell you a lot about how they view the world. Culture is contained in its stories."

Steve stared out the window. We had passed over the zebras, and the savanna now consisted only of dry yellow grasses and bare earth and the occasional baobab tree.

"Did you see the paper?" he asked.

He was not interested in the philosophies of culture, but the abrupt change of subject did seem odd.

"It said Al-Qaeda captured some American bloke," he continued, "a journalist, in Pakistan."

"Yeah?"

"Yeah! And they chopped the poor bastard's head off! Fucking shit! Can you believe that shit?" He was referring to Daniel Pearl, the South Asia Bureau Chief for the *Wall Street Journal*.

My body stiffened, and I stared at Steve. I had read accounts of beheadings and stonings that occurred long ago in Europe and Asia, and hangings in the Old West, but I assumed humans had progressed beyond such barbarity. I could not have been more naïve. Although uncommon worldwide, decapitation is routine in nations that base their laws on monotheistic worldviews, such as Saudi Arabia, Yemen, and Qatar, as well as in many terrorist organizations. Other methods of execution are legal in Afghanistan, Somalia, Iran, Pakistan, China, Indonesia, and the United States, among other places. (As of 2017, methods of execution in the United States included lethal injection, electrocution, the gas chamber, hanging, and firing squad. The United States is the only industrialized Western nation with a death penalty, and was ranked fifth in the world for total executions in 2015.)

"That is beyond fucked up," continued Steve.

I could not help but imagine the scene—hands tied, made to kneel and bend forward, a man in a black *dishdasha* robe wielding a shining scimitar, the onlookers horrified but silent.

I swallowed hard and stared ahead through the Plexiglas. I felt nauseated, even though the air was smooth. But more than a mere queasy stomach, it was the sadness, the senseless loss, the violence toward humanity and life itself that shook me to my core. This was pure evil.

"Good thing old Bambi's sending in the Royal Marines to help you Yanks, eh?"

"Who?"

"Bambi. Tony Blair. America's Poodle."

"Poodle?"

"You know, like he's on a leash. And I guess that's a metaphor for Britain being America's bitch!" He smiled and pointed at me. "But don't get cocky. 'Cause we're in this together, right, mate?" He punched my shoulder.

I did not pursue the topic, or talk more about Rachel. The way Steve talked about both made me consider how

America courted Britain for reasons similar to those for which I courted Rachel, for self-interest to help us control our world and achieve our ambitions. However, I did not yet see that we did so to avoid growing up.

Peter later confirmed Steve's description of the stables and said the owner, strangely enough, had emigrated from Lander, Wyoming. He drew a map with directions to Ray's house, and Sunday afternoon I picked Rachel up and drove us out to the ranch.

A girl was bent double over a hand-broom, sweeping the dirt yard in front of the house, when a white man with white hair stepped out and greeted us. He introduced himself as Ray. "Peter just called," he said, "told me you were coming." We shook hands, and I introduced him to Rachel. He was delighted we had come and did not seem skeptical of my African date.

I guessed Ray was in his seventies. He wore cowboy boots, Wrangler jeans, a snap-button shirt, and a huge oval belt buckle etched with cowboys and broncos and the words "Cheyenne Rodeo Days." He also wore a Colt .357 Magnum revolver on his hip.

Ray said he sold his ranch in Wyoming and moved to Kenya because he preferred the mild climate and friendly people. He also said he liked to hunt, mainly the "big five"—lions, elephants, Cape buffalos, leopards, and rhinoceroses. On a tour of his home, he pointed out the heads mounted over an enormous stone fireplace blackened with soot. So far, he had killed a leopard, a lion, a buffalo, and several Thomson gazelles, but no elephant. It was illegal in Kenya, and he said he'd have to go to Tanzania to get one.

"No rhino, either," he said. "Damn tags are too expensive."

Rhinos, I knew, were critically endangered, and three subspecies were on the brink of extinction. I asked myself why anyone would want to kill an endangered animal, especially a remnant of prehistory and an herbivore that hurt absolutely no one. Rhinos were nearly blind, and a person could practically walk up to one and shoot it.

I stared at the heads over the stone fireplace, and it struck me how similar this practice was to how Al-Qaeda dealt with infidels. The main difference was that the animals were shot before being decapitated. Terrorism and manliness, it seemed, applied similar methods.

But Ray was elderly and had no doubt hunted and trapped and ranched all his life. Like my father, this was how he viewed himself in the world, and now he hunted so he could continue to feel manly and dynamic.

Ray walked us to the stables, where an organic, almost tangy funk of manure, horse sweat, and saddle-leather saturated the air.

"You familiar with horses?" he asked.

"We had some when I was kid."

Rachel shook her head.

Ray calmed Rachel's nerves and told her she could ride Sundrop, a chestnut mare that was gentle and easy to control. Because of my cast, he gave me an older gelding named Maximilian, also easy to ride. All of his horses were thoroughbreds, descendants of those owned by British colonials a hundred years earlier. They were long and sleek and built for speed, though ours had seen faster days.

We walked into the corral, and two Kenyan boys saddled the horses.

"This must be very dangerous," said Rachel. She was nervous yet plucky and climbed onto Sundrop on her second attempt.

I swung my casted leg over Max's saddle with little difficulty and felt like a kid again in rural southern Illinois. My cast was too big to fit in the stirrup, so I wedged it between the leather straps holding the stirrup. One of the stable boys slid my crutches into a rifle scabbard on my saddle, in case I had to get down to pee or something, though dismounting was discouraged. On horseback, we had some degree of protection, and the horses could sense when a predator might be near. And Ray had his revolver, just in case.

One of the stable boys brought Ray his gray Stetson cowboy hat. A stain of dried sweat ran around the band. Ray saddled his own horse, and in five minutes he guided us onto the savanna. Cumulonimbus clouds piled up over Mount Kenya, but the rest of the sky was clear, and the sun shone brilliant and hard on the tall grasses. I was excited to get close to some of the wildlife. Ray explained that as long as we rode on horseback, the zebras, giraffes, and other ungulates would perceive us as other herbivores and, therefore, not as a threat. Shortly thereafter, he led us into a herd of plains zebras. We rode close enough to touch them, and we did, though they could smell we were different and slowly moved off.

"I did not know this could be possible," said Rachel, and she giggled.

I rode close to her for a moment and held her hand. I knew it was far too early to ask, but I wondered if she wanted children. She was Kenyan, so I assumed she did—several, no doubt. The question was more for me. As a child, I had never questioned the traditional order of life events, which meant having children of my own one day. By high school, I was engaged to marry (this was long before the Baptist woman), and we had even chosen names—Jacob for a boy and Stephanie for a girl. But since my divorce (from the Baptist woman) and my experiences in the Peace Corps, I had questioned the custom of having children.

I knew people in the United States, especially young parents, who accused childless couples of being selfish. Yet, the world's human population had nearly doubled since I was born, which stressed every natural system to its breaking point. I knew that if I did have children, I would love them and educate them to my best ability. But I had to ask if the world really needed more mouths to feed, especially in the most consumptive, profligate country on Earth. I could tell myself that having kids was a means to help shape the future, give life to new beings, as well as ensure my genes were passed on—an egoic insurance policy. But to me, all of those reasons seemed far more selfish, indeed.

I smiled at Rachel. She smiled back, and in that moment, I fantasized: What better way to bind our lives together than to create a family?

We descended a trail into a dry ravine. A dozen wildebeest followed each other single-file in the streambed like zombies, and we rode alongside them for a short distance before climbing another trail back onto the plain.

Ray stopped his horse and motioned toward Mount Kenya. "Clouds are moving this way," he said. "We best head back." The sky to the east had turned black. Lightning flickered, though it was too far away to hear the thunder. "It's a straight shot from here back to the barn," he said, pointing in the opposite direction. "Max and Sundrop know the way."

"Where are you going?" asked Rachel.

Ray turned in his saddle, causing the leather to squeak like an old door. "I've been meaning to check on a water tank up the way. It keeps the wildlife coming around."

"We'll be okay." I sounded confident. I wanted to impress Rachel.

"Yes, you will," he drawled, and then clicked his tongue so his horse started to walk. "Get some refreshments when you get back to the house," he shouted, turning his head halfway around. "Just ask Juliet, my house-girl." He spurred his horse to a canter.

Riding side by side, we started back to the barn. "Did you finish your work in Nairobi?" asked Rachel.

"Yeah. It was fine. How was church?"

She grinned at me, glad I asked, glad I sounded interested, even though I said it to deflect further questioning. "Will, I think you should come. Our church is in Nanyuki, and we are not too big, and we sing praises to Jesus Christ. You should come with me next Sunday."

I half-shrugged and made a face but did not answer as we rode through the tall grass, nearly as high as my cast. I imagined a black congregation, singing, swaying, and clapping hands, like one I had visited shortly before joining the Peace Corps. I had gone for a run and happened to jog past a black church. Knowing I was headed for Africa, and at the time still a Christian, I walked into the church, sweaty shirt and all, and began to sing and clap with the assembly. The pastor invited me to the pulpit to tell people how I would soon live in Tanzania, God-willing.

"Will?" she asked again.

"I would like to. I should. But—"

"Are you not Christian?" Her voice carried a note of concern, as if she had suspected it and discussed it with friends. "In school, I learned that most Americans are Christians, so I am hoping you can take me to your church in America someday, isn't it?"

Her comment surprised me. It was fraught with complications and assumptions, but it created an opportunity to confess. It was time to tell her.

"Maybe you should know that when I was a boy, my family went to an Assemblies of God church, and later a Baptist church. But not anymore, not in a long time."

"Oh, that it is okay. You are only a backslider. I have known so many, and in time they are coming back to the church. They see the Light of the Lord."

I smiled with sad understanding. She saw I was not like one of the friends she described and drew herself up straight in her saddle. "Do you mean . . . are you saying you are Muslim?"

"Ha! No. And I know this might be hard to understand, but I don't believe in any gods."

She blinked and leaned away from me in her saddle. "You mean, an *atheist*?"

My views aligned with much of atheism. However, I considered myself closer to the tenets of pantheism—from the Greek word *pan*, which means all or everything, plus theism from the Greek word *theos* for god. Pantheism holds that all is divine and immanent.

"Not exactly. See, it took a long time, but I learned that people basically create their gods in their own image, because they're lonely or they feel sad or they need to justify their own personal agenda."

"Agenda?"

"Yeah, like Al-Qaeda bombing New York last year or Nairobi in 1998. Remember that?"

She did not answer.

"Or like George Bush's war in Afghanistan." I chuckled and shook my head. "I cannot believe he called it a *crusade* and told the French president the war was *necessary* to start the Second Coming of Jesus and the Rapture. It's a political-religious agenda, and it doesn't hurt that Southwest Asia just happens to have enormous oil reserves.

"But that's just one example. People interpret whatever they want from their holy books, right down to what they eat. What did you say last week? Meat is for Christians and vegetables are for pagans, something like that? These are all legends and stories from Bronze Age tribes that owned slaves and treated women like property to be bought and sold and stoned to death if they wore cotton and wool at the same time."

She was silent and stared ahead. Max and Sundrop made swishing sounds as they waded through the grasses, and now the barn was in sight, so they walked faster. My casted leg throbbed. Thunder rumbled behind us.

"I cannot have dinner with you tonight," she said.

I knew it. I had said too much.

"Instead, I want you to come to church with me next Sunday."

She saw something in us and wanted our relationship to grow, and that pleased me. But the gulf between our worldviews was formidable. And there was something else, too, something she had not told me.

Like Peter Pan, my optimism was boundless. I swallowed hard, as if my head was on the chopping block. "Okay."

She beamed at me. "Yes?"

"Yes. But I have to warn you. I cannot change who I am."

"I know. But Jesus can."

CHAPTER 13

The Quagga

THE ELECTRICITY AT the branch often failed, and the solar battery-bank lasted only a couple of hours, so frozen foods had plenty of time to spoil. The old hunk of unclaimed sausage I found in the freezer tasted fine after I fried it for breakfast, although the milk—unpasteurized and delivered weekly—had smelled a bit sour.

Whatever it was, a fever and chills came over me by noon, so I wrapped myself in blankets on the couch in the instructor's lounge and did not stray far from the toilet. I watched a VHS of *Blair Witch Project* and then Swahili soap operas all afternoon. Programming broke away every seven minutes to an Eveready Battery commercial of exploding stars behind D-cell batteries that zoomed into the foreground. Tina Turner's "You're Simply the Best" provided musical context.

My lower back stiffened and cramped after the third or fourth time I retched. It had given me problems since I'd fallen while climbing Grand Teton five years earlier. I had fractured my sacrum and herniated an intervertebral disk that prevented me from sitting or driving or even reaching my feet to tie my shoes for six months. A Native American woman on the Wind River Indian Reservation administered acupuncture, massage, and chiropractic adjustments. By the end of her treatments, I could carry an eighty-pound pack on a NOLS course for weeks at a time. As a follow-up, she recommended I do a "sweat" at a lodge with an Arapaho man named Stanford, saying it would help relax the muscles in my back, as well as the ones between my ears. Wry humor like that was her specialty, and it always held a ring of truth. Unfortunately, I did not take her advice, not until after my crash three years later.

I wrapped ice cubes in a hand towel for my back, pulled a sock over my toes below the cast, and hobbled to the toilet every hour or two. It was Saturday night, and I knew I would not be strong enough to meet Rachel for church the next morning—a fate I could live with.

Before it got too late, I limped into the library and phoned her.

"Oh, Will, I am so sorry. Do you have Bovril?"

"What?"

"Bovril, a beef broth. But maybe you should drink *chai* instead. Yes, try black *chai*, no milk, just sugar."

"Right. I'll make some." I paused. I regretted having lectured her on religion. "Rachel, about the—"

"Will, you are sick. You must rest. I will pray for you and call you as soon as I return from traveling."

I searched my memory. Had she mentioned a trip? The plane crash had compromised my short-term memory, but it seemed to have improved. "You mean, from church?"

"No, no. I must visit my mother in Nairobi. I have been away too long." I heard hesitation in her voice.

"Your mother, is she okay?"

"She is fine. I only want to see her and talk to her."

"Talk to her?"

"Yes, about you, and us, and everything."

"About me?"

"Yes. Maybe you can come and meet her sometime."

"I would like that very much, if you think it's okay."

"I will talk to her and see."

I imagined their conversation would focus on religion and my lack of it. At the same time, I could not help but wonder if my American citizenship—which equaled wealth and power in the eyes of many—would work in my favor. Perhaps, I thought, being an American might substitute for my not being religious, or even figure as a kind of religion itself. Either way, it delighted me to know she wanted to discuss us with her mother and introduce me to her. I was certain she would love me and find me a charming match for her daughter.

"When will you return?"

"Not long. Only four or five weeks."

"Weeks?"

"Will, you must rest. I will call you as soon as I return. I promise."

After we hung up, I made a cup of black *chai*. I sat down at the computer in the library and wrote an email to Rachel. It was schmaltzy and tedious and filled with verbal hearts and flowers that expressed as much as possible without sounding lewd or telling her I loved her, which I did not. I wanted to love her, and with a little time it seemed possible, even likely. But I needed her to love me, too. And before any of that could happen, we needed to spend as much time together as possible so we could open up and tell each other our secrets—because there was something mysterious about her I could not put my finger on.

Religion and god were important concepts to both of us, though for very different reasons. If only I could talk to her, I thought, and tell her what I had learned about religion and patriarchy and racism and how they were interrelated, maybe her worldview would transform as mine had. The

Africa explorer Sir Richard Burton summed up my views on the matter: "The more I study religions, the more I am convinced man never worshipped anything but himself."

My finger hesitated over the computer mouse. Then I clicked it and sent the email.

Peter had rescheduled me to lead a sailing section in April. In the meantime, I studied sea life, tides, and Swahili coastal cultures. I tried not to think about Bob, but knew that he and I were destined for a showdown.

A title in the wildlife section of the library caught my attention. A book called *The Quagga*, by Tamara Green and Tony Gibbons, described a subspecies of zebra that was smaller than a plains zebra and colored with brown and white stripes, though much of its body hair was solid brown. European colonials had hunted them for their meat, their exotic hide pattern, and to open grazing lands for livestock, mostly cattle. Small isolated herds roamed the South African veldt into the nineteenth century, where the last wild individual was shot in the 1870s. The last captive quagga died in an Amsterdam zoo in 1883.

The book's conclusion asked why people love some species, eat others, and exterminate many more they consider nuisances. The culprits, it said, were cultural inertia and ignorance: we have always done it this way, so it must be right. These struck me as simplistic answers to a question so deeply rooted in the human psyche that hardly anyone noticed, let alone argued about. Or rather, everyone, including me, indulged in the mass denial of an issue central to the way we live, which bases our very existence on violence.

I grew up hunting and fishing, enjoying the life of a "sportsman." Game—that is, wild animals—should be managed and contained, I learned, because a healthy environment is a place where men and women (but mostly men by nearly 10:1, and white men to black men by 35:1) go to recreate by affirming their masculinity. I was told to eat animal meat and animal fat because "it'll put hair on your chest."

The traditions of my country and the religion of my youth were founded upon hunting and keeping livestock. Heading into the wilds to test one's skill against Mother Nature was a time-honored enterprise that reconnected us with our Stone Age ancestors. As a boy, I fantasized about living as Neanderthals did fifty thousand years ago. In a similar vein, I identified with the militant gorillas on *Planet of the Apes*, who carried guns and looked tough and kept their human subjects in pens like animals. I did not know that real gorillas are herbivores (plant eaters).

A seminal moment came the first time I helped slaughter a bull. My father guided me through the process. As usual, he wore cowboy boots, jeans, a denim jacket, and a red, high-crowned baseball cap with a St. Louis Cardinals logo. A toothpick was inserted through the cap's mesh. He flicked off the safety on a .22 caliber rifle and laid the gun's muzzle between the eyes of a brown-and-white Hereford. The bull could not comprehend its fate and only blinked and stared out the back of our horse trailer at the people who had fed and watered him and kept him warm in the barn through the winter. The horse trailer shook when the bull dropped. Luckily, a second shot was not necessary. I helped secure chains around the bull's hooves to winch it into the air on a rack like those I had seen used on prisoners during movies and TV shows about the Spanish Inquisition. Then my dad sharpened a butcher's knife on a leather strap and split open the bull's stomach, allowing the internal organs to flop into a large steel tub. I helped slice the hide away from the muscle with a Buck Knife he had given me.

When we butchered on cold days, I warmed my hands by folding them into the bloody hide, steam rolling off, while my father divided the carcass down its backbone using a chainsaw. He warned me not to look, because tiny flecks of bone and spattered blood could lodge in my eyes. I was nine or ten years old.

I did not look forward to slaughtering and butchering animals. Yet, when it happened, it excited me. The ritual of dissecting and consuming animals implied more than simply stocking the freezer with provisions. It gave me power over life and death, and the pursuit of wild animals contained qualities of adventure that deemed me the top predator, not in a web but in a chain. It made me a man.

Most hunting seasons occurred in the fall, which is when my father and I hunted geese and ducks on the Mississippi River. We drove our johnboat to brush-covered blinds in backwater sloughs and stood in the cold and stared into the sleet for hours. The blinds were not ours. We borrowed them, and on one occasion my father fell asleep on the bench and began to snore. I knew his snoring might frighten the ducks, so I went to nudge him to stop. When I did, I noticed a magazine wedged among decoys and floats under the bench. I pulled it out to discover a copy of *Playboy*. The hunters who owned this blind, I thought, hunted more than just ducks and geese, and it reified the notion that hunting was a manly man's game. With my dad still asleep, I stuffed the magazine into my gun case and smuggled it home.

Sex was never discussed at home, and I did not receive a "facts of life" talk from either parent. Studies in psychology indicate such prudery tends to yield higher rates of teen pregnancy, abortions, and sexual exploitation and repression, including pornography, prostitution, and violence against women. A lesser-known byproduct is the violence inflicted on "absent referents," such as animals (meat) and the Earth itself. Hunting was my primary outlet.

By the time I was twelve, a cousin and I made a game of playing with squirrels we had killed as if they were puppets, punching, kicking, and talking in falsetto voices. On another occasion, he and I discovered a hatching of baby frogs and sat them on firecrackers and lit the fuses. It was violent and mindless and made me feel like a man. Yet, I also knew it was absurd, and I laughed at my barbarity for reasons I did not fathom.

As I grew older, I replaced the absurd with the sporting. I recognized that nature must be respected as well as controlled. So, instead of killing five squirrels per day, which was the legal limit, I restricted myself to three. Instead of using a 12-gauge shotgun to fill the air with lead shot and make the game less "sporting," I preferred the challenge of a rifle.

Mine was a Winchester 94, lever-action .22 with open iron sights, so it had no scope. It was a beautiful weapon. The steel was blue-black, and the stock was polished cherry wood that glowed with gun oil. When hunting with it, I never took an old or a young animal, only adults in their prime. I had perfect vision and could shoot the primer out of an empty shotgun shell with my rifle at thirty yards. When I hunted squirrels, I could hit one in the head—usually in the eye—on the first shot every time.

Late in August when I was twenty, I walked into the forest behind our pasture to hunt. At dawn, I sat in camouflaged clothing at the base of a hickory tree. Sunbeams filtered through the leaves, and spider webs sparkled with dew. The wind was light, but it strengthened as the sun rose, which made tree branches sway and creak. A flock of blackbirds landed in the crown of the hickory, screeching and cackling, so it was difficult to listen for squirrels. It was not a good day to hunt.

I heard a thud on the ground but did not move. Twenty yards up and to my left, an adult fox squirrel munched on hickory nuts and dropped the shells onto the dry leaves of the forest floor. It was an easy shot.

In tiny, incremental movements, I turned on my hips and brought the rifle up to my left shoulder. As a left-handed shooter aiming left, I squeezed my torso and muscles tighter than if I were aiming right. But I was strong and able to compensate, so the awkward position would not affect the shot.

I sighted in as I had a thousand times before and found the furry head of the squirrel as he feasted, content and oblivious. I took a deep breath and slowly exhaled. When I had exhaled half my air and my aim was dead-on, I squeezed the trigger and heard the familiar *pop*. The blackbirds took flight, and I looked. The squirrel sat on the branch as before but did not move a muscle.

The sight startled me. I cocked the lever-action .22 and took aim and fired again. The squirrel lost footing for a second but regained balance and scrambled back onto the limb. I cocked and fired a third shot. This time I heard a high-pitched squeal, and the squirrel spun. One of his back legs dangled from his body, but he managed to run and leap to an adjacent tree. I jumped to my feet, cocked, and fired again. I was no longer trying for headshots: a body shot, anything would do, and I pulled off one after another as fast as I could, and for the first time in a long time my heart pounded as if I were a neophyte in the woods.

Then I stopped. Specks of blood on dry leaves sparkled in the sun. I held my breath and listened but heard only the wind in the trees. I searched around the area where I'd shot the squirrel, and after several minutes with no luck I returned to the first tree and leaned against it. A knot of guilt swelled in my throat. I wanted to cry, but I was too old for that now and too strong.

It came to me that I had caused the suffering and eventual death of a perfectly sentient, fully functioning being. And to what end, I wondered? If I had found the squirrel and taken the body home to eat, as I normally did, would that have made it okay? Would I have felt better? My father had divorced my mother and taken most of his income elsewhere years earlier, but my mother, sister, and I were not starving. We did not need to hunt to survive. So why did I do it?

Wind roared through the trees. The beautiful rifle in my hands felt cold and dead.

I never hunted again.

Eight years later, I lived in Tanzania. When I arrived, the meat I encountered was quite bland without the seasonings, gravies, and special sauces I was accustomed to in America. Besides taste, the meat in Africa was rubbery and rendered in unsanitary conditions. So due to merely gustatory reasons, I experimented with vegetarianism.

After the Peace Corps, I again shopped in the frozen foods section of supermarkets for meat. The packaged flesh was convenient and far removed—in time, space, and representation—from the creatures grown for slaughter and their lives of misery. It was easy not to think about how they had been turned into meat.

As I sat in the library reading *The Quagga* and reflecting on all these masculine pursuits, I wondered if our food habits were more complex than any cultural preferences or taboos or even blood types. What if the institution of eating meat was linked to more than just heart disease, environmental degradation, and the inhumane treatment of animals—and women? What if it was an index of everything gone wrong in the world?

CHAPTER 14

Poached

"JUMBOS!" SHOUTED BONGO. He sat behind me and pointed over my right shoulder. I searched for the elephants through breaks in the forest canopy but saw none. The plane's cockpit had tandem seating—one behind, one in front—and each compartment had a set of controls, so he slowed the plane and pointed to a copse of bamboo two hundred feet below. Four elephants moved.

"I see them!" They were magnificent, and the impulse to shout was natural, though it was also necessary, since the plane was loud and not equipped with headphone jacks.

Jamie had told Bongo about my leg, and even though Steve helped me fly the planes for Tropic Air, it was still painful and difficult for me to operate the controls, and I flew less often. The tourist season was slow, too, probably because of heightened tensions and global instability. As one pilot helping another in need, Bongo invited me to fly with him on a poaching patrol around the mountain.

Like a barnstormer, Bongo swung the plane around and made another pass low and slow over the treetops. The forest elephants flared their ears and waved their tusks as they headed for cover. My foot throbbed in its cast, and I was happy to view them from the air.

"That's good!" Bongo shouted. "We'll leave them alone now!" He pushed the throttle forward, and the horsepower pressed me into my seat as the nose of the plane tipped up.

Bongo's given name was William. His nickname referred to a type of forest antelope. He said he was happiest in the wilderness, and in 1989 he had joined the Wildlife Conservation and Management Department (WCMD), then under the stewardship of Richard Leakey. (Richard was the second of three sons of famed paleoanthropologists, Louis and Mary Leakey. In 1990, the WCMD was renamed Kenya Wildlife Service.)

Bongo had been the senior warden of Mount Kenya National Park since 1990, fighting to protect wildlife and wild places. He recounted many close calls with poachers. Elephant tusks weigh up to two hundred fifty pounds each, and the ivory can fetch up to $1,500 per pound on the black market. The poachers, who do the actual killing, earn an average $25 per pound.

Bongo also hunted, but he had a license and bought tags, so it was legal. His father and grandfather had passed down this tradition to him from a time when the country was ruled by Britain.

I respected Bongo and his way of life, but his stories—similar to those of Ray, the cowboy—caused me to question the ethics of hunting. How was what Bongo did so different, I wondered, from poaching? Certainly, one was legal and regulated while the other was not. Beyond that, differences were a matter of interpretation. I supposed that while poachers killed for food or profit, hunters killed primarily for "sport" or status, though many also ate parts of their prey's body and displayed other parts in their home. In this case, they might hire a taxidermist to mount the trophy in such a way as to depict its most fearsome behavior, baring teeth and claws, or presenting horns or antlers. And for all exhibits, size mattered.

According to ethologist Marc Bekoff, writing in *Psychology Today*, and Bruce Wood and David Petersen in *Mother Earth News*, hunting serves two psychological functions. First, hunters subconsciously believe they will appropriate, or poach, an animal's power when they kill and perhaps consume it, thus assuaging masculine insecurity. The duration of this power is extended when hunters display parts of animals as trophies in their home. In so doing, argue the writers, hunters assert egoic control over themselves by ritually "killing" feminine aspects of their psyche (empathy, altruism, nonviolence, etc.). Although the number of American women who hunt increased during the first decade of the twenty-first century, 91 percent of American hunters are male.

Second, Wood and Petersen suggest the hunt is replete with sexual symbolism. A predatory sexual act is reified when a hunter draws "first blood" by using a phallic-shaped weapon to "penetrate" prey.

For instance, in July 2003, a business venture called Hunting for Bambi came to public attention. In the desert near Las Vegas, Nevada, men dressed in camouflaged fatigues wielding paintball guns were filmed "hunting" women who wore nothing but tennis shoes. This was the promotional advertisement. Prospective "hunters" soon contacted the business willing to pay $5,000–$10,000 to stalk and shoot women like animals. The "hunt" combined sex and mock violence, guns and red paint. The story swept across 24/7 cable news channels and the Internet—the thought of men pretending to kill women for sport may have been reprehensible, but it was entertaining and profitable, too.

A few weeks of mad publicity passed before Hunting for Bambi was exposed as a hoax. The promoter, Michael Burdick, had staged the entire event in order to sell a few videos—no actual "hunts" took place, other than in the promo ad. Most people were relieved. But the question remained: How could so many men be willing to pay thousands of dollars to ritually "kill" women? What sort of worldview incites this brand of misogyny? And finally, what led Burdick to choose the name Bambi for his venture, presumably after the Walt Disney cartoon?

In a wider context, Hunting for Bambi was not as outrageous as it appeared. Ten thousand pornographic videos are produced each year in the United States, nearly all of which degrade women, physically and socially. According to a 2009 Harvard Business School study, the number of Christian Americans who view online pornography is at least as great as those who professed another faith or no faith: 65 percent of Christian men, and 18 percent of Christian women. (Among those who self-identified as "fundamentalist" Christians, the number of those who consumed pornography increased to 95 percent.) According to the same study, most viewing occurs via free-access sites. Paid subscriptions are more common in religiously conservative states, where a higher percentage of people say they agree with the following statements: "Even today miracles are performed by the power of God," and "I have old-fashioned values about family and marriage," and "AIDS might be God's punishment for immoral sexual behavior."

In 2013, the best-selling video game in America was *Grand Theft Auto: Vice City*, which allowed players to have virtual sex with a prostitute and then beat her to death. Another video franchise that featured male violence with guns, *Call of Duty: Advanced Warfare*, was most popular in 2003 and remained in the top ten for video sales through 2015, racking up over $11 billion in profit for its developer, Sledgehammer Games; its publisher, Activision; and other affiliates. Bearing this in mind, it is no accident the military uses violent video games to train soldiers. Studies show that children who play violent video games become less sensitive to pain and suffering, more fearful of the world, and more likely to behave aggressively toward others. Culture and media target boys with games that involve womanizing, hunting, killing, firing guns, joining the military, and pursuing wealth and power.

Over 16 million people in the United States—5 percent of the nation's population—hunted animals in 2016. Nearly all did so with guns, as opposed to traps or bows. The total number of legally owned guns in 2016 in the United States was well over 300 million—or 112 guns per 100 people, far more than any other country on Earth. (In 2016, males in the United States committed 95 percent of homicides and 94 percent of mass shootings there.)

I was not aware of the sheer amount of violence committed by men with guns in 2001. However, that obscure little book, *The Quagga*, had caused me to ask what made so many people, mostly men, so insecure and afraid they felt compelled to act out and dominate, often with deadly force.

I still owned five guns, stored at my mother's house. What was I so afraid of? Was it women, or what I perceived as becoming soft, dependent, and vulnerable? Was it a feeling that my identity was so tied up with my being an American, and that being an American meant being forceful, decisive, dominant, and in control—that to allow the "feminine" to emerge would mean not merely emasculation, but that the United States itself would be diminished and open to attack or assault? Had the mugging in Uhuru Park and the groping to which I'd been subjected given me an insight not only into what women might undergo when men sexually assault them, but also into my own unease at how readily I, too, had been willing to stalk, attack, and assault defenseless creatures minding their own business? Events from the present and the past intermingled in my mind, pointing to my complicity in violence that was predatory and rapacious and served my purposes as an American man.

The mental friction of hunting, violence, and sexism disturbed me, so I gazed down at the cloud forest, the trees and vines, and living things. The landscape was beautiful and sublime, and the plane's engine loud. With little effort, I forgot, or at least ignored, such dangerous ideas.

Bongo's plane was a white, Piper J-3 Cub, a tail-dragger built in the 1940s. The instrument panel was simple: altimeter, airspeed, magnetic compass, and engine temperature and pressure. Most curious was a control stick instead of a yoke. Everything worked, except the cabin heater. The air grew colder as we climbed and the wind whistled around the windows. I was glad I wore a fleece pullover and a warm hat.

"Will!" he shouted.

"Yes!"

"My boys are on the north side! Lots of poaching up here, so we'll fly low! Bastards will shoot if we fly too high!"

I gave a thumbs-up.

"Watch for smoke!" he added, referring to poachers' campfires.

We flew a wide arc around the north side of the massif at two hundred feet off the ground, although the altimeter read ten thousand feet above sea level. At this elevation, goat's beard moss and liana vines hung from black cedars and jasmine trees, all speckled with white flowers. We flew at sixty knots, or about seventy miles per hour, and the ground passed quickly underneath.

In a few minutes, Bongo pulled the power back, and the plane slowed. A spiral of smoke wound through the canopy ahead, and we flew toward it. I saw a camp in a clearing.

"Our boys!" he said. "Hang on!"

I grabbed the longerons in the fuselage next to my seat as he rolled the Cub hard left, then right, then left again, waving the wings. I saw two canvas tents and five or six men in army fatigues. They waved as we passed over.

Bongo contacted the men on the ground using a handheld mike. Poaching patrol was serious business, and poachers and park rangers alike were shot and killed on a regular basis. Kenyan rangers used G3 battle rifles, and some wore a sidearm as well, but poachers were much better financed and normally outgunned them. Many weapons used by poachers in East Africa were first issued to combatants in the sixteen-year civil war in Mozambique. When that war ended in 1992, the Mozambique army's guns disappeared into the hands of people in the bush. Since then, .458 Winchester Magnums, .378 Weatherby Magnums, and hundreds of AK-101s and AK-47s had been confiscated from poachers in the Serengeti and Tsavo national parks. New rumors had it that poached ivory was sold to help finance Al-Qaeda.

Bongo took us to the east side of the massif. He added power and we flew to sixteen thousand feet over the headwall of the Lewis Glacier. This was as high as he dared fly the Cub, so we descended the glacially carved Mackinder's Valley to the west below the tree line. In a few minutes, we landed on a grass airstrip next to the park headquarters.

After logging the flight, we drove into Naro Moru and had beers at the River Lodge. I liked Bongo. He seemed levelheaded and down-to-earth, dedicated to conservation. He suggested that if I wanted to fly in Kenya, I should talk to Jamie at Tropic Air, because as an American I could never hope to fly for the Kenyan National Park System. Besides, he said, it was a lot safer carting people to and from tourist lodges than dodging bullets from poachers' guns.

The cast on my leg was due to come off soon. I thought less and less about the elephant who nearly trampled me and the men who had jumped me in Uhuru Park and more about flying bush planes and finding a home in Africa, maybe with Rachel. Flying helped me forget about reckless decisions I had made, as well as some I refused to acknowledge.

Surrounded by the ghosts of the old empire, I leaned against the mahogany bar in the River Lodge and pretended I was a conservationist and a Kenya Cowboy, if only an honorary member. For a little while, I forgot about being politically correct regarding guns, animals, food, the environment, and even women. I was, after all, my father's son.

Bongo and I each ordered a steak with baked potatoes and Tusker Lagers. The slogan on the beer label read MY BEER. MY COUNTRY, a sentiment I imagined for myself. After dinner, I bought a box of matches and a box of cheroot cigarillos and shared them with Bongo. They reminded me of the ones Clint Eastwood smoked in the film *High Plains Drifter*. Sitting on the veranda above the grassy backyard and the Naro Moru River, I lit my cigarillo, shook out the match, and blew smoke at the purple ramparts of Mount Kenya. Dark clouds gathered.

CHAPTER 15

Conjunction

DR. BHATT USED a hacksaw to remove my cast. When he'd finished, he placed the saw on a steel cart and took a handkerchief from his white lab coat to pat the perspiration from his forehead. Nearly bald and with intense eyes, the doctor reminded me of actor Amrish Puri, who played the pagan high priest in the film *Indiana Jones and the Temple of Doom*.

Dr. Bhatt tucked the handkerchief back into his pocket and crouched to study my ankle. The calf muscles had atrophied and all the hair had rubbed off, so my lower leg resembled that of a young boy, except it was yellow and smelled like sour milk. He poked it with his finger, squeezed my feet and toes, and flexed the foot to test its range of motion. My skin was hypersensitive, and I jerked my leg.

"Hmm," he said, and stood to cross his arms. I imagined him wearing a headpiece made of water buffalo horns like the high priest.

"You cannot and should not go running or climbing for at least one month," he said. Instead of deep and resonant, Dr. Bhatt's voice was high-pitched, like the boxer Mike Tyson's. "Because if you do, it will make a very bad problem with arthritis. Very bad." His frown morphed into a smile. "So. Okay?"

The fracture had healed, but the ligaments and muscles were stiff and weak. Dr. Bhatt advised me to use crutches for a few more days, and said that if I was careful I could ride a bicycle to help restore the joint's range of motion.

I had written my mother about the injury, though I'd neglected to mention the elephant—or the mugging. She wrote back, saying she would send a gel ankle brace. I hoped to receive it any day, since I was scheduled to join Vijay and Mukina on the coastal section of their course in two weeks.

Peter let me use his bicycle for my ankle. I could soon walk without the aid of crutches and decided to hike up to Eucalyptus Point. I was certain the wheatear had found my necklace and either used it to build a bower or taken it to Alaska to attract a mate. When I reached the Point, I spotted the stump. All of the foliage was trampled or eaten. I watched and listened for elephants, but heard only birds.

A reflection of light next to the stump caught my attention. I hesitated, then stooped, and to my astonishment spotted the talisman. I snatched it up and held it to the sun to admire, as if I'd discovered a treasure or a pearl of great price. I slipped the necklace over my head and pressed the talisman against my sternum. Relief washed over me. I sat on the stump and gazed over the valley and imagined the look on Rachel's face when she saw me wearing it again. I could not wait to show her. I could not wait to see her.

The next day, I flew a dead-leg with Steve. I operated the rudder pedals, but it was painful to hold the plane steady during our final approach to land. Throughout the flight, I had tried to talk about Rachel, but Steve deflected the conversation to Afghanistan and suicide bombers and the price of fuel.

Back at Tropic Air, we were walking to the office, when he pulled me aside.

"Listen, Willy," he said, and exhaled and rubbed his forehead. "I don't mean to be a spoilsport . . . with the girl, I mean."

"Rachel."

"Right. It's just, last year before you came, she dated a white chap from Australia who worked out at Lewa Conservancy. I saw them together a lot."

I shrugged, knowing I might not be the first foreigner she had dated.

"Anyway, he paid her tuition to some school in Nairobi and told me they were talking marriage, but something happened. I don't know . . ."

My forehead wrinkled, except for the scarred area.

"I just thought you should know."

"Thanks. But it's not like that. We're good."

Steve nodded and went to his car. I was about to leave, too, when Jamie stepped outside and called me into his office.

He bit the end off of a fresh cigar, a South African cheroot, and spat it into a trash can. As he took a seat on the corner of his wooden desk, he motioned to my leg. "How's it doing?"

"Not bad."

He grunted and struck a match to light his cigar. He took several short puffs before shaking out the match and examining the smoldering end of the cigar, pleased with his work. "I'm sure you'll be fighting fit in short order."

I nodded and inventoried his office. This was only the second time I had seen it, the first being when he asked me to fly dead-legs. Aeronautical charts of East Africa covered one wall and a whiteboard with the flight schedule took up another. The names of pilots and support staff were scribbled into blocks of time on the schedule, but my name did not appear. I prepared myself to receive the bad news.

"Will," he said, between draws on his stogie, "Steve tells me you're a solid pilot, and I've watched you. You're careful. You fly steady." He picked a piece of tobacco off his tongue and flicked it aside. "Of course, he's the only pilot I need right now. Esten's interested, but he's a few years off.

"The fact is, pilots are hard to find, especially ones who know the country like you do; especially Tanzania, which is where we'd like to expand. So, when you get your CPL, here or in the States, wherever, you let me know. Things could change, of course, with fuel prices and all, so I can't promise anything, but we might have work for you, if you're interested."

I exhaled harder than I expected, as if I had held my breath for the past minute. Jamie chuckled softly. I thanked him and told him that, yes, I was definitely interested. He shook my hand and offered me a cheroot, and I took it. For me, things were settled. After my next field course, I would return to Wilson Airport and train to become a commercial pilot, news I could not wait to share with Rachel.

I imagined she had already convinced her mother that I was the one for her, and now she was eager to move in with me at the branch or perhaps into our own cottage in Nanyuki or Naro Moru. I was not concerned with our differences of opinion regarding religion. With time, I knew we could work the problem out and move beyond it, especially after I explained to her the history of the Church and how it had joined with the imperial goals of the colonizing powers to extinguish her own people's religious beliefs.

I could not wait to tell her.

The transmission speed at the Internet café in Nairobi was slow but bearable. I had still not heard from Rachel, but I was so excited to earn my CPL in Kenya and work for Jamie that her silence did not concern me. I wrote an email that described all my plans and wrapped it up by asking Rachel to wish me luck so the sharks at the coast did not eat me. I closed with, *In Love, Will.*

Mukina, Vijay, and Kabiru had just finished leading a hiking section in the Maasai Mara. I met them in Nairobi. With a glint in my eye, I told them about Rachel and me. Mukina giggled and sighed. Kabiru glanced at me over the rim of his glasses and grunted. Vijay gave no reaction. Their collective indifference disappointed me, to say the least, and I did not bring it up again. It felt as though they knew something I didn't, and I did not want to press the issue.

Before we flew to the coast, I went to a barber at the Sarit Centre. From a catalog, I chose a hairstyle called The Great Gatsby, because it had that classic aviator look—short on the sides and back with a flop of longer hair on top. Kabiru thought it should be called The Kenya Cowboy.

Omari Bob had been on my mind, and I did not look forward to seeing him again. The situation was strange. He was jovial and cracked jokes and enjoyed teaching students how to windsurf and snorkel. He was a great guy. Yet his worldview and mine were diametrically opposed.

Or were they? His way of life centered on a patriarchal god that granted him superiority to all other worldviews, women, animals, and the Earth itself. Although I had let go of Christianity, I ignored how it continued to affect my everyday perceptions and interactions, including those with women. So, perhaps Bob reminded me of myself—the worst parts of myself—parts I loathed yet feared to let go of. At the same time, I may have envied the certainty he had of his own masculinity, virtue, and superiority. Perhaps part of me wished I could be more like Bob.

When we arrived at the coast, the Swahili sailors teased me about my weak ankles and the tattoo on my neck, and I laughed with them. We got along well together. But Bob avoided me and always boarded one of the other dhows for the day's sail. Likewise, I did not seek him out.

Nonetheless, Bob surprised me after dinner one evening when he walked over and sat next to me on the beach. He pointed to the waxing crescent moon and the planet Venus in the same quadrant of the sky. They would soon pass within a few degrees of one another in a celestial event called a conjunction.

"It is a very good sign," he said in Swahili.

Guilt washed over me. I had considered him an opponent, if not an outright enemy, and now he was offering me an olive branch. "Yes, it is beautiful."

Using a stick, he drew the letter C in the sand and put a dot in the center. "When they come together like this," he said, slowly, like a grandfather, "so the star is inside the moon, ah, then it is as the Prophet said—may God praise him—and all people will know peace."

He was trying to tell me about his religion in a way that included everyone, even me, but I refused to forgive his celestial error.

"You mean, like this." With my finger, I drew another C and dotted the sand just outside and to the right of it.

His coal-black, leathery forehead rumpled under his white Muslim *kofia* hat. "No, like this," he said, and stabbed a dot inside the C that I had drawn.

His misunderstanding of basic astronomy struck me as heresy, and I was in no mood to tiptoe around cultural sensitivities. I turned to him with my hands open. "*Baba* [father], the crescent moon is still a whole moon, and that star," and I pointed to it in the sky, "is a planet, millions of kilometers farther away—"

"Will," said a voice behind me. Vijay leaned down and put his hand on my back. He indicated he wanted me to follow him.

"But he—"

"I know. Come."

I got up.

He turned to Bob with a smile, and said in Swahili, "Forgive us, *baba*. The heat has affected this one. He needs water."

Bob nodded and waved us on.

Wearing shorts and Teva sandals, no shirts, we shuffled over to a derelict building made of coral blocks with large openings that had likely never held window glass. The structure had no roof, and sand had blown in to form deep mounds on the floor. Birds roosted in the ruins.

"Will, I know you only want to educate him. I understand. But try to remember he's old, and the way he sees the world is never gonna change."

"I know. I'm sorry."

"He's Muslim. And I think right now, he's trying to reach out to you, to a—whatever you are. And to do that, you might need to let go of the details, some of the little things that don't really matter."

"I know. It's just . . . things only improve when we let go of old ways of thinking and old ways of living, because the world changes. It needs to change."

He turned his head and winced, as though he had bitten his tongue, or sweat had dripped into his eyes. Something I said hit a nerve.

I retreated to my trump card. "For example, 9/11. I don't know why that happened or what those people were thinking, but my guess is it had a lot to do with old ways in the face of new ways, and the old ways felt threatened, so they attacked."

He bobbed his head, smiling, almost laughing. His silence made me uncomfortable, so I stammered on. "Of course, not all changes are good. I realize that." The heat was suffocating.

He continued to smile, but his eyes were red. "Will, you sound like the pot is calling the kettle black."

I almost laughed at the idiom, but I kept quiet.

"Americans," he said, "believe they are *so special*, they freak out whenever they are attacked, because it means they might not be so special and so strong after all. Do you know how many people die from attacks every day in Pakistan or India or Sudan? *Thousands!* But America is attacked, and the whole world has to stop. Especially when they're attacked by Muslims, because that means Armageddon and the end of the world is at hand, according to some desert tribe in Asia thousands of years ago." He squeezed his eyes shut and pinched them with his fingers. He opened his eyes as he slapped his thigh. "Christian extremists are no different from Islamic extremists! And none of them can *let go* of anything!"

Tension was building fast. We stood about ten feet from one another and knew better than to move any closer.

"I know. I agree."

"And that necklace, and that stupid bird!" He pointed at my tattoo with an open hand. "They make you think *you've* changed, that *you've* let go! But you haven't. And now you have a Kikuyu girlfriend to help you be someone you're not, to make you feel superior like a Kenya Cowboy or something!"

"Do you hear yourself?" I responded, my temper rising. "Do you need me to draw a picture for you? Because for some reason, you feel shitty about yourself, and so your girlfriend—your *European girlfriend*—makes you feel better about yourself, like you've traded up on the social ladder. But hey, at least you're better than Kikuyus, right? Does Mukina know you hate Kikuyus?"

Vijay erupted. "*Really? Is that* what you think? You must think you're better than all of us. And now you just told poor Bob to let go of *his* world because it's ancient, because *you're the savior* who's gonna save him, and you know the right way. But you don't, do you? And you know you don't. Is that what you're so afraid of?"

Visions of Stanford and the sweat lodge and my crash rolled through my mind. I thought I wanted to grow up, and then I had unwittingly sabotaged that end, just as America had unwittingly played a part in creating 9/11. We had basked in a fantasy of immortality and superiority, and now our magic flight was over.

I stomped out of the ruins, and my sandals made no sound in the sand, which made me angrier. *How dare he talk to me about letting go!* I thought. *He* was the one who should let go of his Irish girlfriend and get a real life.

I turned around and marched back to the ruins. "I'm telling Peter not to schedule us together again."

Vijay stood there with his arms hanging at his sides.

My mind raced. "*And your slang sounds stupid!*"

I stomped off again. Vijay called after me once, but I kept walking. I went to the beach where the dhows were anchored and the water was peaceful, and I stared across the dark channel toward the mainland. No one was on the beach. Bob was gone. I touched my necklace and focused on Rachel and flying airplanes. Nothing else mattered.

CHAPTER 16

Empty

A HAND STROKED my hair, and my eyes opened into darkness. When the petting stopped, tiny teeth gnashed at the ends of my hair, though woolen blankets muffled the sound.

This time, I jumped to the floor and shook the rat from my head. Groping for a headlamp, I knocked over the books on my desk but managed to find the light and switch it on. The rat had grown fat on cornmeal and rice and was stuck in the gap under the door. As it struggled to escape, I grabbed the spade from the corner and raised it over my head like the three-pronged gig I had used for spearing bullfrogs when I was a boy. I brought the blade down hard and fast into the rat's back, into the Earth, with more than enough force needed to kill, yet not enough to crush a pang of conscience, and I winced. The blow nearly severed the body in two. Black blood spurted onto the door, sprayed across my feet, and pooled in a divot on the threshold. The rat did not squirm. It did not flinch or show signs of suffering, and I was glad for that, though I shuddered with regret. Instead of feeling manly as I had when killing animals as a boy, I felt like a hypocrite, a coward, and my lips quivered.

The blade of the shovel would not dislodge from between the rat's vertebrae, so I scraped its pudgy body across the doorjamb. A kidney fell out, and the smell of feces stung my nose—its intestines were severed. Using the shovel, I scooped up the rat and its bowels and tiptoed around the cabin through black grass wet with the night's dew and flung the corpse past a thicket of wild olive bushes. I heard it thud on the ground. A hyrax stopped its raspy cry, but only for a moment.

I shook out my bed sheets and brushed my hair and went back to bed. But I could not sleep. The rat's bloody death had shaken me, and the more I thought about it, the more I thought of violence, food, Rachel, my talisman, and flight.

"I have to say, I'm kind of surprised," said Peter. We sat at a picnic table in the cookhouse pavilion at the branch. "After your thing in Nairobi, and then the elephant, I didn't think you'd want to stay any longer than you had to. And now there are rumors of a terrorist cell in Somalia. NOLS might close this branch next year."

"Somalia?"

He nodded. "People are lining up to fight." He pulled a sheet of paper out of his satchel and handed it to me.

It was a copy of an article from the *Washington Post* that said that Pat Tillman, a safety for the Arizona Cardinals, planned to give up his career in professional football to join the Army and train to become a Ranger. As an American, said the article, he felt it was his duty to fight and kill the enemy. The public was shocked, yet praised his decision and called him a patriot, especially after he turned down a $3.6 million offer to play for the Cardinals and postponed life with his new bride.

I did not know what to think about the Tillman story— surprised, maybe, or afraid for him, or jealous. To my mind, the rationale for sending the American war machine to

Afghanistan had begun to sound dubious. Was the sole purpose of the US-led coalition—a massive military force—simply to kill a few hundred rag-tag guerrillas in one of the poorest regions on Earth? The 9/11 attacks were horrific and demanded retribution, no doubt. But was this the best way? The wisest way? Whatever Bush's intent, any decision to jump in and start shooting struck me as impulsive.

I was suddenly unsure if our kneejerk response to 9/11 could be termed a "fight" or a dysfunctional form of "flight." What were we so afraid of?

Yet, what did I know? Surely, the US government and the American people were privy to more information than an expatriate like me holed up in the African bush. So, I looked the other way.

"But we're glad you want to stay," continued Peter. "It makes it easier for us on this end. I'll draw up the paperwork, and you can sign it after you finish in Tanzania."

My original NOLS contract expired in two months. Until I earned a CPL and flew planes for Jamie, I would need to find an income and a way to extend my work visa. Peter solved both problems by offering me a contract for a second year, and to me this meant the cosmos had approved my decision to stay in Africa.

"We can work around whatever happened between you and Vijay," said Peter. He smiled, but his forehead wrinkled with confusion. I was unsure, too. Maybe Vijay was right, and the heat of the coast had compromised our patience with one another. When Peter debriefed our course, I had asked him not to schedule us together again. Vijay had not spoken to me since.

"We'll schedule you on separate sections," he said. "Are you okay with that?"

I nodded as a small bird landed at the end of our table. It hopped and chirped and picked up a crumb in its beak.

"Wheatear?"

"No," answered Peter. "That's a little bushshrike, a female. But you don't see them around here much. They like it out in the open on the plains."

"It looks like a wheatear."

"A little, but they're gone now. They left for Alaska months ago."

A week later, Mukina and I and several other instructors drove Land Rovers to Tanzania. We would meet our students at Kilimanjaro International Airport in a few days. I rode with Kabiru.

"Tell me," said Kabiru, the ex-pilot. "What do you see in it? Flying, I mean. I do not understand your interest." He repeated his question in various forms throughout the drive. "All you do is sit there and look around. So boring!"

None of my answers satisfied him.

"Very well," he said finally. "But why is it you want to fly in Kenya? Why not go back to America and do it there? It is much safer, and cheaper, too."

"Maybe it's my history with the Peace Corps. I like it here."

"Mmm-hmm." He glanced at me over the rim of his glasses, askew on the bridge of his nose. "Could it also have something to do with your Kikuyu woman?"

I smiled and arched my eyebrows.

"Do you love her?"

"Oh . . . maybe. We'll see."

"Hmm. Or are you avoiding something in the USA?"

I felt the skin knot between my eyebrows, but I tried to relax. "What do you mean?"

"I mean that it seems to me you are trying to escape from something or someone—always resisting, struggling—very polite, but impulsive. And a Kikuyu woman, even a pretty one who likes you, she cannot solve a problem like that. She is—how do you say?—a crutch."

My eyebrows knotted again. A ball of hot vitriol swelled in my head, but I contained it and forced a happy face. "No. I'm here because I want to be here. I'm very careful about choices like that."

"Yes. You are very careful."

We rode in silence for a moment across the Athi plains, yellow and hot.

He waved his hand over the steering wheel. "All I am saying is that everyone manages certain issues in their life. Your issues, whatever they are, will not be solved here in Africa. Because whatever we avoid or fight against, we end up becoming that thing. Do you see?"

I felt like a little boy being lectured by his father. I did not know how to respond, only to smile and nod and be polite.

We drove on in silence. I did not know what he meant— avoiding issues, becoming what we fight against. And I did not appreciate his comment about Rachel. I had begun to depend on my fantasy of us, and how I needed her to need me.

A Tanzanian who had been my friend during the Peace Corps once told me she thought people took themselves too seriously. At the time, we had been discussing religion, so maybe this was different. I certainly took Rachel and myself seriously. *Could this mean it might be love*, I thought? Would that make it okay?

We stayed in the border town of Namanga that night and continued south to Tanzania the next day. At the town of Usa River, we pulled off the main highway and climbed a dirt track toward a compound called the United African Alliance Community Center, or UAACC. The Center would function as the staging area for our course. It was owned and operated by an African American couple, Pete and Charlotte O'Neal (another Peter and Charlotte). Pete kept his hair tied back in graying dreadlocks, and he had a short, graying beard. He and Charlotte had lived there since 1970, when Pete fled the United States after being accused of transporting weapons across state lines for the Black Panther Party.

Pete and Charlotte were gracious hosts. In addition to their home, the UAACC grounds included four rondavels with bunk beds, a main building with additional bedrooms, a library, showers, a full-service kitchen, a detached computer lab, a classroom, and a pavilion called the Red Onion used for group meals and meetings. A mural of Martin Luther King, Jr., Malcolm X, Harriet Tubman, and other African American leaders was painted on a water tank in the center of the compound. A concrete wall eight feet high encircled the perimeter and was guarded day and night by *askaris*.

Most of the books in the O'Neals' library were by Africans and African Americans. One, called *Reinventing Africa: Matriarchy, Religion & Culture*, caught my attention. Its author, Ifi Amadiume, wrote how imperialism, violence, and patriarchy were social structures that colonialism had imposed on Africa. But her main thesis held that prior to European contact, many African societies were matriarchal, horticultural (garden cultivation), and egalitarian.

According to Amadiume, the monotheisms of Judaism, Christianity, and Islam were by-products of a series of attacks led by peoples that worshipped sky gods. They also usurped the goddess-centered cultures in many regions, not only in Africa. Because these religions contend that Satan was banished to Earth, women and the feminine were construed as corrupt due to their association with Earth's natural cycles and generative powers. In Genesis, this feminine principle was called Eve, the ruin of all humanity and a theological justification for the subjugation of women.

Reinventing Africa made a great impact on me at the time. And though it does not tell the whole story, it added an important new dimension to our understanding of the complexities of the world prior to the expansion of patriarchal religions and societies. It also provided a counterpoint to the male-biased perspective on the history of civilization.

The library also had a Bible, so I skimmed it to verify Amadiume's claims. Sexist scriptures litter the Old Testament, and while the New Testament is arguably less misogynist, it is clearly gender-biased.

Women should remain silent in the churches. They are not allowed to speak, but must be in submission, as the Law says.—1 Corinthians 14:34

A woman should learn in quietness and full submission. I do not permit a woman to teach or have authority over a man; she must be silent.—1 Timothy 2:11–12

There I saw a woman sitting on a scarlet beast. . . . This title was written on her head: MYSTERY\BABYLON THE GREAT\THE MOTHER OF PROSTITUTES\ AND OF THE ABOMINATIONS OF THE EARTH. —Revelation 17:3b, 4b, 5b

Now I want you to realize that the head of every man is Christ and the head of every woman is man. . . . —1 Corinthians 11:3a

The apostle Paul wrote 1 Corinthians. As a Jew who persecuted and condemned Christians to death, his given name was Saul. However, after he experienced a vision of Christ on the road to Damascus, he converted to the new Christian cult. Other than this report, he never met the person called Jesus, and yet he is credited with writing at least half the books of the New Testament.

As a citizen of the Roman Empire, Paul was no doubt influenced by Greco-Roman social roles as well as Jewish customs, both of which were misogynist. Paul's writings are fraught with this gender imbalance, which would go on to shape Christendom and its colonial footprint through to the present day.

The connection between scriptures and Amadiume's thesis did not surprise me. They did, however, remind me of Rachel's remark on food and faith.

> One man's faith allows him to eat everything, but another man, whose faith is weak, eats only vegetables.—Romans 14:2

I was well aware that hunting and raising livestock often ended in violence, but was it somehow connected to broader forms of violence? Amadiume's book spoke of a warrior culture and a pantheon of vindictive gods. Did a connection exist between religion, misogyny, and eating meat?

I jotted down the note in my journal and returned the book to its shelf. It was dinnertime, and I was hungry. The food being served at the Red Onion smelled heavenly—tilapia with baked potato and rice—and I wanted to make sure I got my share.

After picking up our students at the airport, we backpacked from Lake Eyasi to Ol Doinyo Lengai, an active volcano considered holy by the Maasai. A scene from *Lara Croft: Tomb Raider*, starring Angelina Jolie, had recently been filmed at the summit. We again hunted with the Hadza but were unlucky (or lucky, depending on your perspective) and killed no baboons. However, our liaisons organized a feast with local Maasai, who led two live goats to our camp.

According to Maasai tradition, blood is sacred and cannot be wasted, so the goats had to be killed by suffocation. The Maasai would later collect the goats' blood and drink it.

We were invited to help, and several of our male students held the goats to the ground, clamped their mouths shut, and covered their nostrils using their bare hands. The goats struggled and squealed until their eyes rolled back and they either vomited or shat themselves. The Maasai men made quick work of bleeding, gutting, and butchering them and then stretching their meat out on sticks to be roasted over the campfire. I did not know why, but I decided not to eat the meat.

After three weeks, we returned to the UAACC to gather rations, and then climbed a buffalo path on the southwest side of Kilimanjaro. The students were keen to summit the mountain with Mukina and Kabiru, but I hiked out with a student who came down with dysentery. We descended the north side of the mountain, called for pickup, and drove to see a doctor in Arusha. The doctor prescribed medications, and I drove the student to the UAACC compound to recover.

That evening after dinner, I went to the computer lab to check my email. Rachel had written back.

My Dear Will,

   I apologize to be taking so long to send this message. I have a new boyfriend. But he is not new. His name is Steven. He is an Englishman and he flies aeroplanes like you. I think you may know him, yes? We were not together for a year, but he has come back to me and we are happy. In a fortnight, he wants to take me to his home in England. Therefore, I cannot see you again, especially since you are not Christian. My mother is agreeing with me.

Thank you for the riding horses, the dinner, and the darts.

Rachel

Blood drained from my face and arms. A searing pain pierced the top of my skull like a long, thin blade. I had fooled myself. Africa was no magic kingdom. It was not my island of adventure, and now it had robbed me, beaten me, and rejected me. I was overcome with desperation to escape. I had to fly far away to some lonely corner of the globe.

I ran out of the computer lab, through the main gate, up a hill, and into an empty soccer field. A blue clapboard kiosk sat vacant at the corner, its Pepsi sign reminding fans, reminding me, *chaguo ni lako* (The Choice Is Yours). I had made a choice but ignored its consequences. I continued to resist.

Lightning arced across the night sky over Kilimanjaro and Mount Meru. I touched the talisman on my necklace and remembered what Stanford had told me that night at the sweat lodge: "There's something you've been avoiding. . . . You gotta let it go."

Guns and war, killing and food, the Earth and women: it was all connected, but I could not see how. I was too afraid to see how. Full of rage, I curled my fingers and clawed at the night sky, struggling to scream, trying to stay aloft, but I was empty.

Fireflies pulsed and blended with the lightning. The bugs flickered like sparks from a fire wafting into the sky, like particles of those moments before the crash, when the engine had sputtered and stopped. *"Mayday! Mayday! Mayday!"* shouted my copilot over the radio. I switched a lever to activate the other fuel tank. The gauges read one-half full, but both tanks were empty.

BOOK TWO

The Last Frontier

CHAPTER 17

Migration

"DRINK THIS," SAID the man. I sat cross-legged on a square of carpet in the dirt, and he handed me a bucket with a ladle. I glanced at Stanford. His expression was solemn, and I could feel the weight of everyone's gaze on me. I dipped the ladle into the bucket and sipped. The cold sweetness of the water surprised me, and I drank every drop.

People chuckled, and an old woman clapped her hands and laughed until she broke into wheezes and coughs. Stanford's stare melted into a toothless grin.

Stanford's helper, Marty, collected the bucket after it had circled the room. He ladled water onto the floor in the shape of a cross and scattered more water over the hot rocks. Steam hissed and the rocks cracked. To trap heat and moisture, Marty lowered the canvas flap over the doorway to the lodge, sending us into complete darkness.

At six o'clock on a December evening, the temperature outside the lodge was already zero and falling fast, but it sweltered inside. I had brought a Nalgene bottle of water, a towel to breathe through, and a sheet to crawl under in case the moist heat became unbearable. Meanwhile, the Arapaho and Shoshone smoked Camel Blue cigarettes, which made it even harder to breathe.

Stanford began singing. He chanted solo in Arapaho, which I did not know. The words sounded like long, plaintive vowels moaned in repetition in a minor key rather than words. To the Arapaho, however, they held great meaning: *Forgive us, Creator. Our life is our prayer.* His song lasted only a minute. Then he coughed several times and spoke.

"You there, Marty?"

"I'm here."

"Maybe you oughta sing from now on." Everyone chuckled.

"I'm not old enough to sing that song."

"Maybe I'm too old," said Stanford, and everyone chuckled again.

A long pause followed before Stanford broke the silence. "Maybe we can start now."

I had returned from Africa four months earlier with enough cash to buy a 1996 Ford Escort LX Wagon with a hatchback. It was painted brownish-tan—the color of dirt—and got 30 mpg on the highway. This was better than the national averages of 23 mpg in 2002 and even 28 mpg in 1990. America's love affair with oil, most of it from the Middle East, had only intensified since 9/11. And for reasons I could not fathom, the Bush administration had expanded its target beyond Afghanistan. Iraq was now in our sights, and the idiom "blood for oil" seeped into the American vernacular. Once again, we were reminded that "freedom isn't free," and to secure our liberties and comforts we must control the lion's share of oil, weapons, and power. It was, after all, a man's world, and America had the most powerful men who wielded the biggest guns.

While I was staying in Lander, I had gotten a second tattoo, this one a flower placed over my heart, just below where the talisman hung on my necklace. On the surface, it symbolized my love for the mountains. More profoundly, I sought the pain, blood, and violence of that tattoo as a punishment for my failures in Africa. I had learned the bitter lesson that being white, male, and strong was not always enough. Like the United States, I was not invincible. I did not have control over my destiny.

As the tattoo healed, I read *Pioneer Bush Pilot: The Story of Noel Wien* by Ira Harkey. The author described Wien's adventures of flying medical evacuations from remote Eskimo villages and delivering babies in flight, all in such frigid conditions that he was forced to build fires under his plane's engine so it would start. Cold was a constant theme. But Harkey also described the magic of the Northern Lights, the threat of wolves and grizzly bears, throngs of caribou, and mosquitoes so big, he joked, they appeared on airport radar.

I had read Jack London's *The Call of the Wild* as a boy, and Harkey's stories rekindled my imagination of the far north. I needed only a little more training to earn my CPL, and if not in equatorial Africa, then perhaps I might do so in the Arctic. The population density in Alaska was less than one person per square mile. With such enormous tracts of roadless, empty land, people flew bush planes to town for groceries and to take their kids to school, or so I had heard.

The Great North appealed to my sense of adventure and isolation. Perhaps there, I thought, I could extend my escape from reality, suppress my nascent transformation, and float in boyish limbo indefinitely. But it was a big change, a big challenge, and I needed to be sure. Going to a sweat, I thought, would help clear my mind. So, I had called Stanford and introduced myself as "Lisa's friend, Bill." He paused before blurting, "Hey, you're that guy who flies planes, yeah?" It surprised me to feel such comfort at being recognized by my old name.

The Wind River Indian Reservation is surrounded by three snow-capped mountain ranges. At twice the area of Rhode Island, the reservation occupies the windswept plains of

Western Wyoming and embodies a grandeur both beguiling and severe, almost melancholy, but too tough to admit it. The landscape is vast and open, yet it gives the impression of being inside of something, the dimensions of which are too immense to comprehend. It grants insight into one's soul the farther out one strains to see, which is forever.

Everyone in the sweat lodge was Native American except me. The men sat on the north side of a pit filled with hot rocks, which was in the center of the lodge, and the women sat on the south side. Stanford reclined at the west end, opposite the door.

One by one, people talked about how they suffered in their everyday lives. My new tattoo was still healing. The salt from my sweat made it sting, which preoccupied me. We took breaks every hour from the heat and emerged into the dry winter air. Steam wafted from everyone's body under a constellated sky and the dusk-to-dawn light next to Stanford's doublewide trailer.

Stanford puzzled me. He was easygoing yet blunt, almost secretive, and he kept me a little off-balance, as if he knew more about me than I knew myself. I had left my talisman in my room but still wondered if he would notice that I had not taken his advice to return it to its rightful place.

By midnight, everyone had confessed something to the group—everyone except me. It was unbearably hot inside, and I draped a sheet over my head so I could breathe.

"Does anyone else wanna say anything?" asked Stanford.

I knew he meant me. I longed to confess and tell him I had not given back the talisman. Sweat rolled off my body and soaked my hair. A knot in my throat surprised me and tears formed and streamed down my face. However, I kept quiet and knew the darkness and the sweat would hide me. My heart pounded as it pushed the thick, heated blood through my dilated vessels, creating a pressure that was barely contained by my skin. It was too hot. I wanted out, so I imagined myself in a cooler place—a frigid, austere place—where no one knew me, and I could start over.

I did not stay for the midnight feast or talk to Stanford that night, and the next morning, I phoned the NOLS Alaska branch. I was referred to a man named Greg, who rented a cabin in the woods near the town of Palmer. The same town supported a small airport with a flight school called Mustang Air. I called the school, and the flight instructors told me they could use my help in the office.

On New Year's Day 2003, I packed my Ford Escort LX Wagon with everything I owned and drove north. Lyrics on a cassette tape of John Denver's album *Autograph* excited me about my adventure to Alaska, especially songs like "American Child":

> Going up to Alaska
> Up to the north and the pioneer life
> Where courage and strength still survive
> And a man can be free
> Men can be free!

The theme of this song was hard to reconcile with that of another on the same album called "You Say That the Battle Is Over":

> And you say that the battle is over,
> And you say that the war is all done.
> Go tell it to those with the wind in their nose
> Who run from the sound of the gun.
> And write it on the sides of the great whaling-ships,
> Or on ice floes where conscience is tossed.

With the wild in their eyes, it is they who must die,
And it's we who must measure the loss.

Parts of me agreed with each perspective. American culture stressed the value in both. The first song equated the concept of freedom—a vague yet loaded term—with resilience, manliness, and the pioneering spirit that (as embodied by someone like Theodore Roosevelt) also entailed hunting, killing, and the white man's manifest destiny to rule all peoples from sea to shining sea. Denver's second song reminded us of the hypocrisy that attended too much of what passed for conservation, hunting, and the same do-or-die braggadocio in the wilds of nature. One was narcissistic, the other ethical. Their combination was antithetical and suggested delusion, mental fragmentation, and withdrawal from reality—symptoms of schizophrenia.

As ever, I ignored any such relationship and looked forward with relish to the freedom that came with icy temperatures, which steadily decreased through Montana, Alberta, and British Columbia. Nighttime lows hit -40°F by the time I reached the Yukon Territory, and snow was piled ten feet high along the sides of the two-lane highway. This was the farthest north I had ever migrated.

Towns in northwestern Canada were sparse, so I packed a five-gallon can of gasoline. Nonetheless, I was careful to gas up at every station along the way and arrive in a town by eight or nine o'clock in the evening. I would look for a Subway sandwich shop or a truck stop that sold hotdogs and nacho chips or some other cheap food. After I filled the tank, I parked in a hotel lot and pulled my backpack out of the back of the Ford Escort and sat it in the driver's seat. This left a hole in the back where I could curl up inside of two sleeping bags—a North Face Blue Kazoo, rated to 10°F, nested within a Mountain Hardware 3D bag, rated to -30°F.

I slept with a water bottle to keep the water from freezing. On two or three nights, I slept in the parking lot of a Holiday Inn Express. In the morning, I walked inside like I owned the place, grabbed a continental breakfast, and caught up on CNN's Headline News. I learned that Al-Qaeda had issued a *fatwa* for Muslims to kill all Americans, and the FBI reported that a significant number of US military servicemen were ex-gang members. They had joined the military either to escape the gang lifestyle or to expand gang membership into the military and gain access to weapons. I was relieved to be a world away from that madness.

After six days, I pulled into Palmer, Alaska, and called Greg from a pay phone outside the Carr's Grocery Store.

"Damn foolish to try it in the middle of winter," he said. "But glad you made it."

An hour later, I met him at the end of a snowplowed road in a spruce forest. We used a post-hole digger to make our way in knee-deep snow to the back door of a two-story rental cabin he had built the previous summer. It had four hundred square feet of floor space—two hundred up, two hundred down. The upstairs ceiling was A-framed and would make a nice bedroom, though I would have to buy a mattress from the thrift store in town. From the bay windows, I could see the entire Palmer Valley ringed by rugged mountain peaks. The view was breathtaking, but most importantly, the cabin was surrounded by pristine nature. This was the solitude I craved.

The cabin had electricity for lights, propane for the oven, and Greg had recently installed a phone line. However, the floor was bare plywood, and a woodstove provided the only heat. The cabin had no running water, and an outhouse forty feet away was the only toilet. The driveway stopped 150 yards away, where Greg was building another cabin. Mine was second to the right from the road.

I moved in and drove down to Palmer Municipal Airport to meet the staff at Mustang Air. They did not mind I was a *cheechako*, a Chinook term for newcomer or greenhorn, and they immediately put me to work at the front desk. Harley was my first flight instructor. He had flown every bush plane known—Super Cubs, Beech 18s, Twin Otters. He was experienced, but my learning style differed from his teaching style.

"Goddamn it, boy! Set your flaps! Pull your power back!" he shouted.

I sat in the left seat of a Cessna 172 as Harley "coached" me on the approach to land at Anchorage International Airport. Lucky for me, he was in a good mood that day. Harley was the classic Alaskan sourdough, and at seventy-one had survived longer than most of his ilk. The hood on his CPO parka, or "parky," as he called it, was lined with wolverine fur because "the hairs don't break off when they're frosted." But I never saw him pull the hood up over his blue US Navy Veteran ball cap, which he always wore, even in the dead of the Alaskan winter. He rarely wore gloves, preferring instead to expose his shriveled, arthritic hands to the elements, which made for an unforgettable handshake.

"That seven-four-seven's gonna run up our ass if you don't get this ship down, pronto!" he shouted over his headset.

"I got it." I pulled the throttle back to idle, pushed the left rudder pedal, turned ailerons full right, and pitched the nose down, waiting to lower flaps. In this configuration, called a sideslip, we lost fifteen hundred feet per minute and increased speed to eighty knots. Major Kabuthu had used this maneuver in Nairobi when I overflew the approach.

Harley adjusted his glasses and scrutinized the instrument panel. He quieted down but remained skeptical. "Easy. Easy," he said, barely audible over the mike.

We were fifty feet high when we crossed the threshold on runway zero-niner, and I increased backpressure on the yoke. This caused the plane to flare, lifting the nose slightly above level flight to slow the aircraft. Our airspeed fell to sixty-five knots, and I set flaps at ten degrees. This increased drag on the plane, which slowed it further. I lowered the flaps to fifteen degrees, then twenty, and all became quiet as we floated into ground effect—the cushion of air created by the wingtips. In a few hundred feet, the main wheels touched down, and we barely noticed when the front wheel floated onto the runway seconds later.

I grinned at him. "Like butter."

His arms were folded across his chest. "You're gonna miss your taxi."

I stomped on the toe brakes. The plane bucked and squealed around a corner onto the taxiway.

Harley was an old-school, by-the-book Navy vet, and I was not. He once asked, "What's that thing crawling up your neck?" and was left unimpressed by my phoenix tattoo. I soon decided to fly with a different instructor. Harley disapproved of me from that day on, and I was sure he thought I was soft and effeminate.

I arranged to fly with Jacquie, the flight-school chief. A tall woman of about fifty, Jacquie's complexion suggested a mixture of European and Native ancestry. She smiled easily and was always helpful, but she had grown up in a man's world, the Alaskan world, and knew when to be tough. When necessary, she transformed into a gritty pilot with a deadpan stare that warned any potential adversary to beware. This alter ego surfaced most often when she dealt with chauvinistic tourist–hunters, who assumed their guides would be grizzled men, and who quickly turned humble and contrite when Jacquie turned her steely glare on them.

I opened a bank account at First National and a box at the post office. I also joined Peak Fitness Health Club. After workouts, I showered at the club and filled four three-gallon water containers—totaling about 100 pounds—loaded them into my backpack, put them into the Ford Escort, and brought them up to the cabin. Twelve gallons covered my domestic water needs for three or four days.

Propane was expensive, but I used very little in cooking frozen pizzas or spaghetti. For protein, I sometimes stopped by Carr's to pick up a box of wild Alaskan sockeye salmon. Manufactured by Peter Pan Seafoods, Inc., the packaging assured buyers their product was WILD, NATURAL & SUSTAINABLE, and eating it always made me feel like a real Alaskan.

Greg had piled firewood behind the cabin. I used it to start a fire in the woodstove every morning before I left and rekindled it in the evening. After dinner, I liked to sit next to the fire while I smoked a Swisher Sweets cigarillo and studied for my flight exams. (The local Carr's store did not sell cheroot cigars.)

Since arriving in Alaska, no rats had nibbled my hair nor any elephants charged, and I could now continue my vague pursuit of freedom. Underneath this veneer lurked a quiet desperation, as if an elephant had, indeed, followed me to Alaska and was in the room with me, waiting to run me down.

Sitting next to the glowing woodstove, I rubbed the talisman on my necklace. It eased my worries yet aggravated my guilt. By coming to Alaska, I had raised the stakes, and I knew I must go forward and win. With sheer force of will, I thought, I must hold onto my youth and stay in the air—no matter the cost.

CHAPTER 18

The Farm

THE THERMOMETER ON the back stoop read -18°F. Sunrise at ten o'clock was still four hours away, so I put on my boots, polar fleece gloves, a warm hat, and a down coat to use the outhouse. My breath floated like smoke in the light of my headlamp. Halfway there, I stopped and switched off the headlamp to behold a night sky so clear and powdered with stars that I had to squint.

A great snort startled me. I held my breath and switched on my headlamp to illuminate a mass of hair between the outhouse and me. Two pairs of eyes reflected red-gold— one pair five feet high, the other pair seven feet. I immediately thought of grizzly bears—or elephants. Neither was realistic, since bears hibernated, and nothing resembling an elephant had roamed Alaska since the Pleistocene Epoch, twelve thousand years ago, when prehistoric tribes hunted woolly mammoths.

The mass of hair moved. A female moose and her calf stood twenty feet away, and the mother grunted and stomped at me, preparing to eliminate the perceived threat. Without a thought, I sprang back onto the stoop and into the cabin, switched off my headlamp, and stayed quiet. The mother moose circled the cabin several times, holding me hostage for the next half hour before she and her calf ambled away in the dark. Unable to wait, I peed in the kitchen sink.

I called Mustang and told Jacquie why I would be late. She chuckled and told me not to worry, to wait and make sure the moose had gone before I hiked through the woods to my car. My story impressed no one at the airport, and tales told by other employees soon evolved from encounters with moose to those with wolves and grizzly bears. Harley described a creature that sounded like Bigfoot.

Although I'd hired Jacquie as my instructor, the ignition key to the trainer-plane often came up missing, reappearing only after it was too late to fly. I did not accuse him and never had any direct evidence, but Harley was the only person around when it happened.

Most days, I worked at the front desk taking rental fees and posting weather reports. However, I knew very little about airplane mechanics and could offer little advice to other pilots. I wanted to learn more, so I started helping a young man named Ben work on his tandem tail-dragger, a Bellanca Model 7 Champion, or Champ for short. Ben had just turned eighteen, and his dad—a pilot for Alaska Air— had purchased the plane for him. Ben showed me how to change the Aeroshell W80 oil in his Champ one afternoon, when he noticed my talisman.

"Cool necklace," he said, as he fastened his plane's cowling over the engine. He took a rag from his back pocket and wiped a drop of oil off the fuselage.

I touched the talisman where it rested on the collar of my T-shirt and looked down at it, although the shoestring was short like a choker, and I could not see it very well.

"Looks like aircraft aluminum," he said.

I could have told him the story. As a pilot, he might have admired me for it. The talisman made me feel like a real aviator, a real man, even as I floated between childhood and adulthood. Without fully understanding why, I cherished the talisman, although it embarrassed me that I had taken it and (more so) had not returned it as promised. Beyond that loomed an inconvenient truth I could not face.

I slipped it under my collar. "It's just something I found."

"Well," he said, brighter and motioning to my neck, "that's a cool tattoo. It must have hurt."

I was happy to change the subject and talk about Mexico, Carnival, and leading wilderness courses in Baja.

Other than Greg and the people at Mustang, I knew no one in Alaska. I was there to become a bush pilot, as I slowly separated myself from NOLS. But I still wanted to meet people at the branch and perhaps make friends there.

After helping Ben with his Champ, I drove five miles north on the Glenn Highway, looking for the branch. Along the way, I tuned in to 91.1 KSKA, the local affiliate of National Public Radio. The news summarized how President Bush had established the Office of Homeland Security immediately after 9/11 and signed into law the Homeland Security Act of 2002. The administration had now created the US Department of Homeland Security, which had the ostensible goal of protecting Americans. Part of the agency's directive included monitoring Americans' emails, web-browsing habits, and telephone communications in order to profile people and create watchlists. Together with CIA data and military kill lists, the DHS could potentially detain, torture, and kill American citizens with impunity.

It all sounded Orwellian to me, but its advocates quieted opponents by emphasizing how the United States was in permanent and ever-present danger of attack. They produced a "terrorism threat advisory scale," which consisted of five colors that ran from green to red, indicating low to severe levels of threat. With the exception of green, all colors expressed a heightened level of risk, and the level seemed to always be orange, which conveyed a "high risk of terrorist attacks."

As for the war itself, by March 2003 forty-three US soldiers had died in Afghanistan and, according to a University of New Hampshire study, 3,300 Afghani civilians had died in crossfire, bombing raids, and air-to-surface missile attacks. This was just the beginning. Over the next ten years, the death toll in Afghanistan and Iraq would reach 6,923 US soldiers, 1,442 coalition soldiers (minus US casualties, based on data from iCasualities.org), and approximately 210,000 Afghanis and Iraqis—three-quarters of whom were civilians. The estimated number of war orphans would approach 800,000. In ten years, these children would be vulnerable to radical Islamism and Jihadism. We were creating the enemy we imagined.

The statistics and insanity sounded unreal, as if it were happening on another planet. I lived amidst the natural splendor of Alaska, so the violence was easy to ignore. I turned the radio off and immediately felt better.

Musk oxen huddled around a pile of hay opposite a scenic overlook of the Matanuska River and the spectacular Chugach Mountains. Glaciers carved this landscape during the last ice age. The Cordilleran Glacier Complex reached its maximum extent fifteen thousand years ago to cover the Alaska Range, the Talkeetna Mountains, the Chugach Mountains, and the Matanuska Valley. To the southeast, it extended over the Canadian Rockies and the Cascade Range. During the same period, a second and much larger complex, called the Laurentide Ice Sheet, covered the Brooks Range, most of Canada, and reached as far south as Rhode Island. However, the region between the two glacial systems, as well as the North Slope of Alaska, remained ice-free.

When the glaciers receded from the Matanuska Valley, they left behind loess soils the color and texture of cocoa powder. They also sprinkled the valley with glacial erratics (boulders deposited by melting glaciers), which have not stopped farmers from taking advantage of the area's fertile soils. During the Great Depression, the US government persuaded farmers from Wisconsin, Minnesota, and Michigan to migrate to the Matanuska Valley. Each family received forty acres. After initial failures, many established successful farms. Farmers today cultivate carrots, beets, rhubarb, spinach, broccoli, Brussels sprouts, and zucchini in abundance. Seventy-pound cabbages two feet in diameter are not uncommon. Even so, agriculture contributes an insignificant amount to the Alaskan economy, and nearly all food is imported from Washington and Oregon. In 2003, transportation costs added at least fifty cents per pound to the price of food items.

I parked my Ford Escort in the branch lot next to a maroon Toyota 4Runner with a dreamcatcher hanging from the rearview mirror. An old farmhouse, a barn, a newer home, and several one-story buildings dotted the grounds, and sled dogs barked and yelped from a kennel behind the home. Someone had recently shoveled a snow-path to a warehouse, so I followed it. The door was unlocked.

Sleeping bags were suspended from the ceiling in the first room. In the next, outdoor clothing hung on racks, and hiking boots lined the shelves. I called out. My voice echoed, and I heard keys jingle and footsteps approach on the concrete floor. A man walked over who was slender and slightly taller than I was. He wore a Leatherman pocketknife on his belt and had clipped a large ring that held a bundle of keys to a belt loop on the side of his jeans.

"Can I help you?" he asked, smiling as he straightened his dark-rimmed glasses. I told him my name and explained that

I was a NOLS instructor but was not there to lead a course. I was working on my CPL in Palmer and had just driven over to say hello.

"Cool. I'm Kurt," he said, and we shook hands. "I mostly do maintenance around here. But let me take you to the office. I'll introduce you to the boss."

He put on his coat, a military-style CPO with wolverine fur around the hood that reminded me of Harley's. We walked over to a singlewide trailer, climbed the wooden steps to the door, and wiped our feet on a metal grate. Inside, a man, nearly bald, and a woman with shoulder-length salt-and-pepper hair sat at computers that faced away from the door. A calendar hung on the wall between them. The square allocated to each calendar day prior to the current one was crossed off. It was a practice that had always irritated me, like the past was no longer important, and today was a countdown to destiny.

"Guys, we have a visitor," said Kurt. "An instructor."

The man swiveled around in his chair, the woman a moment later, and Kurt introduced us.

"Hey, stranger!" said Don. I was surprised he recognized me. I took off my polar fleece gloves when he stood to shake my hand. "What brings you north in the middle of winter?" We had once met at the headquarters in Lander. His attire had changed little—blue jeans, a turtleneck sweater, and a cream-colored down vest.

I had never met Donna. She smiled easily, and when she half-stood from her chair to shake my hand, I noticed one of her eyes was brown, the other dark blue. I had never known a person with two different eye colors and did not know it was possible in humans, only in some dogs, like the huskies chained behind her and Don's house.

She sat down again and swiveled back to her computer.

His task complete, Kurt smiled and nodded and left the trailer. The keys jingled on his belt, and his boots squeaked in the snow as he marched away.

I explained to Don and Donna that I had moved to Alaska to become a bush pilot, but I was curious to see the branch, too. Don said there were no instructors currently in town, but I should feel free to look around. He suggested I check out the Lower House, where instructors bunked between summer courses.

I thanked them, put on my polar fleece gloves, and walked down to the older two-story home. A family of farmers had lived in it before NOLS purchased the property, which is why the branch was sometimes called The Farm.

Bare beech trees lined the boundary between yard and field, otherwise hidden by snow. Undulating bands of clouds threatened more snow, and at two o'clock the sky grew dim in twilight. The air suspended tiny crystals of ice that smelled clean and glittered in a dusk-to-dawn light. The combination of these effects convinced me that fate had brought me to this exact spot for some divine purpose.

I knocked on the back door to the Lower House. No one came, so I opened the door. It squeaked loudly in two spots at different pitches.

"Hello?"

No one answered.

Ski boots, skis, and bulky coats hung on hooks along the wall of the entryway that led into the kitchen. I wiped my boots but kept them on.

A picture of Denali hung on a wall between the kitchen and the living room, which was furnished with couches, a recliner, and a TV. A quote on the picture read, "Those who defeat others are strong. Those who defeat themselves are mighty." The saying was attributed to Laozi (Lao Tse), author of the *Daodejing* (*Tao Te Ching*), an ancient book of Chinese wisdom. I had read this book during my time in the Peace Corps. My worldview had just collapsed, and I was hungry for information that might shine light into the void that had opened in my soul. I did not understand many verses in the book, though they were beautiful and pure and spoke to my subconscious.

The picture frame hung crooked, so I straightened it.

In the living room, a cat with medium-length gray hair jumped down from the couch and stretched.

"Hey, buddy." I knelt down, and the cat walked over and rubbed against my leg. I petted it and scratched it behind the ears, and it purred. I picked it up and stood and continued to pet it, coaxing it to purr louder, when I heard the crunch and squeak of someone approaching in the snow beyond the door. The knob turned. A person bundled in a parka walked into the entryway and saw me holding the cat. The hooded stranger stamped snow from their feet, tossed back the hood of their parka, and smiled.

"I see you've met Lucky," she said, pulling off a glove and putting out her hand. "I'm Penny."

CHAPTER 19

Protein

THE MOVIE WAS called *Atanarjuat: The Fast Runner*. Produced in 2001 by a Canadian film company, it was named for the protagonist of an ancient Inuit-Yupik myth of jealousy, murder, and love.

When Europeans arrived in the eighteenth century, they suppressed Native traditions and stories under the rubric of god, gold, and glory, a policy that intensified when gold was actually discovered near Juneau in the 1870s. Alaskan statehood in 1959 and the discovery of oil in 1967 further eroded traditional lifestyles. The director of *Fast Runner*, Zacharias Kunuk, summarized the effects this way: "Four thousand years of oral history silenced by fifty years of priests, schools, and cable TV." Kunuk and the film's producers sought to revive a fragment of Inuit pride by portraying their traditions in a positive light.

Penny called and asked if I wanted to see the movie with her. It was showing in Anchorage, fifty miles away, and we wanted to eat dinner first, so we left by four o'clock in her maroon Toyota 4Runner. It was dark and snowing, but we were in no hurry.

"What's the tattoo on your neck?" she asked.

I had not lived up to my reason for getting it, and Vijay's rebuke lingered.

"Oh, it's just a . . . long time ago."

She sensed my unease. "So, you're a pilot?"

"Yes. I'm working on my instrument rating and commercial license. I should finish by summer, and then I'll look for work at air charter companies and see what happens." I lied to her. Companies rarely hired pilots with fewer than eight hundred hours of flight time, and I had less than half that number. With my income, it would take at least ten years for me to accumulate that kind of experience. Still, as an American and former Christian, I had an almost pathological ability to deceive myself about my own virtue.

"In Alaska?" she asked.

"Definitely. Maybe Talkeetna or somewhere farther north."

"Or Palmer?"

I read her question as a hint, and it pleased me. The green glow of the dashboard light obscured facial expressions, though enough light reached the steering wheel for me to notice she kept her fingernails trimmed short and did not paint them—quite the opposite of Rachel. This, too, pleased me. "I don't see why not."

I played with the black strip of rubber around the windowsill on the door, not able to see it, only to feel the cold penetrate when I pushed on it. It was a convenient way to spend nervous energy as I contemplated Penny and Palmer and what it might be like to live in one place for more than a year or two and actually settle down.

"How about you? How long have you lived in Alaska?"

"Nine . . . nine years," she said. I saw her forehead wrinkle in the wan light, and she shook her head. She had pinned her shoulder-length hair back to expose as much as possible of her small face and pretty smile. The light illuminated only the blackness of her hair, not the strands of gray. At forty-two, she was five-and-a-half years older than I was, had never been married, and had no children, nor did she want any. She emphasized that point.

She had also worked in Antarctica, or "on the ice," as she put it, and described emperor penguins, mind-numbing cold, and the emptiness. Every horizon cut a clean line between white below and blue above. The isolation, she said, was cathartic but made it difficult to reintegrate into quasi-normal society. We had that in common. Both of us floated between places and gravitated to lonely corners of the globe, where we could either puzzle out our lives or avoid the matter entirely.

She'd grown up in West Paterson, New Jersey, but her ancestors were Greek, hence her black hair, cream-colored skin, and family name. Her father had died, but her mother still lived in West Paterson, and her brother and his wife and family lived in London, England. In the dim light, I thought she resembled a dark-haired version of Jennifer Aniston, whose father was Greek.

"Your family?" she asked.

"I have a younger sister, divorced, and she has two kids, a boy and a girl."

"Parents?"

"They divorced a long time ago. I was in my teens. I didn't see my dad much after that, not until after the Peace Corps. But we talk more now."

"That's good. Did he help? With college, I mean?"

Her question caught me off-guard. I watched the dream-catcher sway under the rearview mirror and remembered the summer after I graduated from high school. My father had mailed a packet to me that contained everything I needed to enlist in the National Guard. Inside the front cover, it advertised how I could earn a tuition waiver toward a four-year college program after I completed thirty-six cumulative months of service. I had played war as a boy, but for some reason, if only because I resented him for leaving us, I threw the packet out.

Rumors of his bar fights and sleeping with women angered me as I navigated my teens. When I got my driver's license, he gave me his '69 Chevy short-bed pickup truck. Its motor was a rebuilt 350 Target Master fitted with Glasspack Cherry Bomb mufflers. It had a gun rack in the back window. I painted the truck Marlboro maroon with silver flecks and proceeded to drive recklessly, often over one hundred miles per hour, collecting speeding tickets, having two wrecks, and watching for animals on the road, dead or alive, that I could aim for and run over.

In the summer after high school, my mother helped me apply for a student loan to take classes at a local community college.

"Bill?" Penny snapped me out of my trance.

"Yeah?" I remembered her question. "No, he didn't help with school; college was never a thing in my family. My dad was a pipefitter. My grandfathers were steelworkers, welders, blue collar."

"You said that was in the Midwest?"

"Southern Illinois."

Revisiting my past made me uncomfortable. It reminded me I had not completely let go of it.

I asked her about college. She said she was studying online to earn her master's in nutrition and expected to graduate in December 2004.

"How about you?" she asked.

"My undergrad was in biological sciences."

"You mean like health?"

"Biology, physiology, nutrition—"

"So, health."

"Yeah."

"I thought you said you taught geography in the Peace Corps."

"I switched to geography in grad school."

"I see. But you know about healthy foods, and you eat healthy, right?"

I fiddled with the windowsill. "Pizza and pasta, sometimes a cheeseburger."

Her smile faded. "Well, you know, red meat, it's not so good for you. It's not healthy at all."

I knew she was right, but I had grown up eating red meat nearly every day, if not at every meal. It was a habit that came from decades of conditioning, and the smells that floated from a steakhouse made me drool.

"Are you vegetarian?" I asked.

"Ha!" She was surprised by her response and covered her mouth for a second. "I mean, I eat fish and chicken and maybe mutton—rarely mutton. But I stay away from most red meat, the mammal meats, you know. How about you? Do you eat fish?"

"I eat salmon, tuna. I grew up fishing in the Mississippi River, catfish mostly."

"Like Tom Sawyer."

"Straw hat and everything."

She smiled, but I knew she wanted to say more and she was leading me somewhere, so I waited.

"Do you work out?" she asked. "You look like you work out."

I was happy she noticed, in spite of my winter clothing.

"Because if you're concerned about getting enough protein without red meat, it's really not an issue. One of the things

I've learned in my program is that the high-protein craze is a billion-dollar propaganda scheme."

"Like that?" I pointed to a billboard alongside the highway. It showed a side of ribs on a grill with flames, and its caption read, BEEF. IT'S WHAT'S FOR DINNER.

"Yes! Or, MILK. IT DOES A BODY GOOD. It's all propaganda! The USDA spends half a billion dollars a year on ads that convince people to buy more meat and milk. And the government spends something like $38 billion each year to subsidize those industries. Fruit and vegetable farming get less than one percent of that amount.

"But we go on eating it, because it's normal. It's what we've been told and what we've done our whole life, and now every man, woman, and child in this country eats *two hundred pounds* of meat each year! It's the highest average in the world, and because of it we have rates of cancer, diabetes, and heart disease that are two to three times higher than anywhere else in the world. We're killing ourselves with what we eat. Not to mention obesity—nearly two-thirds of all Americans are either overweight or obese. Can you believe that?"

I was not sure I did. "But we have to eat protein, like 35 percent of our diet."

"The actual number is 10 to 15 percent, and we can get everything we need from plant foods, like rice and beans, barley, quinoa, lentils, nuts, corn—there's a million things, even pasta and potatoes have protein. And I say that, but I'm just as bad, because I still like fish and sometimes chicken and cheese."

I did not eat much meat anyway and could give it up entirely for Penny, because she knew who she was and where she was going in life. This quality attracted me to her even more, and if my airplane ambitions fell through, I could attach myself to her world and her needs and further avoid confronting my own. The age difference made me feel younger, too.

My breath fogged an elliptical spot on the window. Lights along the highway grew stronger and more frequent, and clouds of steam boiled up from vents around buildings. We would arrive in Anchorage soon.

I turned toward her. "How about I cook dinner for you at my cabin next Thursday?" We had not even seen the movie, and I had already proposed our next date. But our conversation had piqued my interest, and I wanted to learn more. I wanted to hear about her views on religion.

She clicked her tongue. "I'd love to, but I have an online discussion with my professor that evening. How about Friday night?"

"I'm scheduled to fly my long cross-country that day, and I might not be back until late. And Saturday, I work the evening shift at the airport."

She chewed her lip. "Sunday?"

"I'm free all day."

"Then Sunday it is. But two things."

"Okay."

"First, before dinner that day, I want to take you to a special place I know."

"Okay."

"And second, dinner's on me at The Farm."

"Okay."

"And one more thing. Do you ski?"

CHAPTER 20

Into the Wild

I HAD FLOWN small planes over the mountains of the American West and the savannas of East Africa, but this time it was different. Never before, not even in Kenya, had I flown over such a vast wilderness. After leaving Palmer-Wasilla airspace, I would see no roads or other signs of human activity until arriving at my first destination four hundred miles north.

According to FAA regulations, a solo cross-country flight must cover at least 150 nautical miles and include three stops. However, I aimed to push the plane's limits and cover 700 nautical miles—over 800 statute miles—in less than eight hours of flight time. Penny asked me to be careful. I had not yet told her about the crash, perhaps because I needed her to trust and support me instead of introducing doubt.

The next day was the spring equinox, though winter remained firmly in control. Plows had piled snow along the sides of the airport runway, and morning temperatures hovered near zero. The only significant change was the number of daylight hours. Equinox is one of two annual celestial events in which the amounts of daylight and darkness fall equally across the globe—twelve hours of each. After the spring (vernal) equinox, regions in the high northern latitudes, such as Alaska, race into summer, while those of the southern hemisphere hasten into a long, frozen night that lasts six months at the South Pole.

Most stars had vanished by six in the morning. The plane I rented for the day was a Cessna 172, call-name 868 India Uniform. I had scheduled to fly a different plane, in case the key went missing, but all keys were present that morning. I unplugged the electric blanket that covered the engine cowling. It felt warm through my gloves, so I held it for a moment, then folded it and put it in the back seat of the plane.

To eliminate any condensation or sediment in the tanks, I strained fuel from a valve under each wing into a Pyrex tube. The 100-octane, low-lead fuel glowed a transparent blue. No particulates were present, and it smelled sharp yet clean— good signs. I inspected the ailerons, elevators, and rudder, and then climbed onto the wing struts to visually check that my tanks—one per wing—were topped off.

Checklists recommend pilots visually inspect their tanks before takeoff, a precaution I normally followed, although I did so with greater attention since the crash. It had been nearly three years, and while the physical scars had healed, holes still punctuated my memory of those final moments. Three of us had agreed to fly to two nearby airports, each pilot taking the controls for one leg of the trip. I would fly the last leg from Rangely, Colorado, back to Vernal, Utah—our point of origin. Before our initial departure, I started to preflight the plane, but the man flying the first leg instructed me to abort the check. As pilot-in-command, it was his job to review the checklist, but the sun was low, and he wanted to finish the flight before dark. He may have been negligent, but I was foolish. Against the odds, I lived to practice greater caution.

For emergencies, the *Alaska Airmen's Guide* recommends pilots carry dried food, water, extra clothing, a sleeping bag, matches, and flares. I packed them all. The requirement for a loaded firearm had been rescinded, though a fishing line and hooks were still advised. I could not imagine trying to ice fish, and all my guns were stored at my mother's house. A pocketknife and faith in my talisman would have to do.

I planned to fly north over the Alaska Range, across an untamed expanse of boreal forest to a town on the Yukon River called Galena—or Notaalee Denh, to the Koyukuk people of the region. It was as far as I dared to fly without refueling. The flight would take almost five hours, so I had packed a lunch, which I would eat at the Galena air terminal before flying southwest to an even tinier outpost called McGrath. After refueling again, I would ascend Grasshopper Valley through a labyrinth of glacial peaks that culminates at Shellabarger Pass. Perfect weather is required to fly this route. I double-checked the NOTAMs (Notices to Airmen), and the forecast promised clear skies and calm winds.

I untied the plane, pulled the chocks, and settled into the creaky aluminum cockpit. The small plane reacted to my every movement like a canoe, and the Plexiglas window distorted outside shapes like a mirror in a funhouse. The combined effect made my stomach queasy, and the hypnotic green-white pulse of the airport beacon accentuated both the cold and my nerves.

I pulled my SoftComm headset down over my fleece hat and plugged it into the console. I toggled the battery switch, hit the directional lights, set the carb heat and throttle, shouted "*Clear!*" out the window, and turned the key. The propeller lurched and spun, and the gauges on the instrument panel jumped to life.

Palmer Municipal Airport was wrapped in a bubble of Class E airspace. This meant it had no control tower, and pilots were advised to self-announce their position and intentions. I pressed the push-to-talk button on the yoke and identified my aircraft. No one responded. Alone on the tarmac, I taxied for takeoff.

By sunrise, I had leveled off at eight thousand feet and plugged my Sony Walkman into the comm system. Penny had been on my mind all morning, so I inserted a cassette tape of the Sugar Ray album *Floored* and queued up the song "Fly." The lyrics expressed my feelings about her and flying at the same time:

> I—just wanna fly
> Put your arms around me, baby.
> Put your arms around me, baby.

We had not kissed after our first date in Anchorage, though the energy was palpable. Our body language made it clear we liked one another, maybe a lot, but we would delay the mutual gratification of a kiss—for now. The anticipation made it difficult for me to focus on flying.

I soon approached the Alaska Range and Denali, the highest point in North America at 20,320 feet. The mountains ahead reminded me of *Into the Wild*, the book by Jon Krakauer. Krakauer describes how in April 1992 a twenty-four-year-old named Christopher McCandless abandoned his car, gave his savings to charity, burned what remained in his wallet, and hitchhiked to Alaska. With only a .22 rifle and a bag of rice, he backpacked into Denali National Park and camped in an abandoned bus. An intelligent young man, he nonetheless made a series of small errors that were tragic in combination, and by August that year he had starved to death. A moose hunter discovered his body a month later.

McCandless has been described as a high-minded adventurer and a suicidal fool. In his book, Krakauer quotes an observer: "Sometimes [McCandless] tried too hard to make sense of the world, to figure out why people were bad to each other so often." Another added: "That's what was great about him. He tried. Not many do."

McCandless may have been high-minded, or a fool, or both, but one thing is certain: the discord between the world at large and the world he glimpsed within himself profoundly affected him. He felt it intensely enough to embark upon a journey that tempted fate.

His story struck a chord. I, too, left everything when I joined the Peace Corps to puzzle out not only the flaws in my life but those in the world, as well. Like McCandless, I sought to comprehend these truths through spending time in wild nature, free from the fetters of money, power, and material possessions. McCandless had not finished his journey. Perhaps his story impacted me most on this visceral level, because if I did not fully embrace the ramifications of change, I was headed for a similar fate.

Clouds gathered over the Alaska Range, so I increased altitude until I reached the plane's service ceiling of 15,000 feet. Sharp granite spires punctuated the icy mist below. If the engine failed now, there would be no escape.

Beyond the peaks, the country dropped into an almost endless forest of lanky spruce, resembling the tree line in the Rockies. However, this limit on woody vegetation was due to latitude rather than altitude. Trees here become shorter and grow farther apart until the tree line descends, in effect, below sea level. North of the Arctic Circle, the landscape is composed of muskeg bogs, tundra, and ice and snow.

The Yukon Flats contain over 36,000 lakes. In the summer months, they teem with geese, canvasbacks, scaup (a kind of duck), cranes, swans, teal, widgeons, and mosquitoes in quantities that only a theoretical physicist can appreciate. For now, the lakes were frozen, and winter stretched to the horizon. I had it all to myself, and the purity and loneliness of it was spectacular. At the same time, the sheer scale of its monotony demanded vigilance. Wilderness does not forgive mistakes.

All morning, I sipped water mixed with fruit punch Gatorade from my Nalgene bottle. Now I had to pee, but I was still one hundred miles from Galena. So, I slowed the plane and operated the yoke with my knee as I pulled down my pants, turned sideways in the cramped seat, and peed into the water bottle. It provided great relief, and almost all my urine went into the bottle. I promptly emptied it out the window.

The airfield was on the north side of the frozen river. After landing, I taxied onto the snow-packed apron, tied down the plane, and hustled into the wood-paneled air terminal to warm myself next to a propane heater. I found a table and chair and ate my lunch. The only other person present was a Koyukuk woman, who sat at the front desk reading a year-old copy of *Cosmopolitan.* The cover title read, FUN, FEARLESS FEMALE OF THE YEAR 2002: BRITNEY SPEARS. The woman never looked at me or acknowledged my presence, not even when I greeted her. I did not know if she was afraid of me or if she loathed me as a representative of the "white man's world."

I checked my map, and after lunch I refueled the plane and flew southwest into Deg Xit'an country on the barren northwest edge of the Kuskokwim Mountains. Snow and rock dominated the terrain. The town of McGrath was established there in 1906, when prospectors discovered gold. Deposits dwindled by the 1930s, though hermits continue to dig there today, using everything from pans and sluices to hydraulic miners, dredges, and D9 Caterpillars that can move over 40,000 cubic yards of streambed gravel in a single season. By the end of summer, a latter-day sourdough might extract enough yellow powder to fill a Peter Pan peanut butter jar. More than gold, the prospectors' efforts liberate sulfides and create heavy metal tailings that pollute stream water and harm the animals that depend on it.

Since the 1980s, McGrath's primary function has been as a resupply station for the Iditarod dogsled race. In towns and villages in the interior, winter temperatures can reach -70°F, conditions that freeze gasoline. Engines are kept running until spring, and if a vehicle idles too long in one spot, the flattened side of the tires on which it rests will not rebound. This produces a helicopter-like sound when the vehicle is driven over snow-packed roads.

A few hundred people lived in McGrath. I saw only bearded men in fur-lined coats with rifles slung over their shoulders. They reminded me of creatures from the bar scene in the original *Star Wars* film. In contrast, I wore a Patagonia down coat, but no one paid too much attention to me. I used the bathroom, gassed up the plane, and took off.

Thousands of caribou fanned out across Grasshopper Valley. I flew low enough to make them gallop, and I could see the white hair flare on their rumps and necks. They ran fast, and I saw their shadows run with them against the auburn lichen tundra and thickets of dwarf willow and alder. The view was pristine.

I flew past them, over valleys scoured by glaciers ten miles wide and two miles deep. At the top of the pass, a herd of bighorn sheep scrambled up a rock face I could not have scaled even with all the right technical climbing gear. In Alaska, caprids are known as Dall sheep. They are fearless climbers, though they feared the sound of the plane. As a boy, I dreamed of traveling to Alaska to hunt Dall sheep and caribou. My father inspired me to hunt nearly every species of wildlife, and I remembered musing about future hunts with him in Alaska.

The sheep below were magnificent, and the power of the scene was raw and emotional, yet I still felt the impulse to kill. The discrepancy was undeniable. These creatures did not threaten or bother me. I was not starving, and according to Penny I did not need their meat for protein. In fact, their mere presence uplifted me, and if I never visited this place to see them, just knowing they were here would provide a deep satisfaction.

I wondered if the temptation to kill was an inborn human trait. As a boy, I had wanted to mount all manner of animal heads on a wall. How might killing them have benefited me personally, and was this boon greater or more natural than allowing them to live, wild and free? The thought of killing bothered me. But in a superficial way, it bothered me that it bothered me.

The sun had gone down, but it was light enough to see when I landed in Palmer. At the refueling area, I killed the engine and climbed onto a wing strut with a gas hose. I squeezed the trigger, and as the 100LL gasoline filled the tanks, I noticed an old Douglas DC-3 parked next to a hangar. Snow had drifted around its deflated tires. Built in the 1930s and '40s, DC-3s were sleek and powerful and among the first airliners to provide commuter service across the United States. They conjured a more romantic era of flight. I considered the DC-3, the Canadian Otter, and the Lockheed Electra the most beautiful planes ever built.

DC-3s were converted to military planes during World War II, when bases were built across Alaska. More bases were established and nuclear missile silos installed during the 1950s and '60s, but most were abandoned after the Cold War ended in 1991.

As the tanks filled, I felt the talisman on my necklace. I slipped the necklace over my head and held it up to the DC-3 behind it. The big plane and my talisman were made of the same material. Like a rabbit's foot, the talisman ensured me Penny's love. I could fly and avoid growing up.

But Stanford's memory interrupted: *You gotta let it go.* I pushed it out of my mind and slipped the necklace over my head.

Back at the cabin, I watched for the moose and her calf, but they were not around. I started a fire in the woodstove and heated a pot of water to make dinner—mac-and-cheese with mushrooms and frozen peas. I also washed the Nalgene I had peed in that morning. Then I washed it again.

I had purchased a Philips radio-cassette player at a Fred Meyer store—Alaska's version of Wal-Mart—and tuned it to 91.1 KSKA while I chopped mushrooms for the pot. I sliced my finger when I heard the news. Blood was everywhere.

We were at war in Iraq.

CHAPTER 21

The Principle of Power

AT THE AGE of nineteen, I visited an Air Force recruiting office. Posters of smartly dressed young men covered the walls. The soldiers in the pictures were adorned with medals and swords, and the pilots flew their jets through lightning storms, where they dueled with demons.

I had spent a year at a community college studying music, but I was restless and regretted not taking my father's advice to join the National Guard. I longed to see the world—the world portrayed in these images—and the military promised to grant my wish.

"Welcome!" A man in dress blues rose to attention from behind a desk and put out his hand. He told me his name, lieutenant so-and-so, and said how excited he was I had decided to join the Air Force, a very intelligent decision. We sat down, and he explained my options. I could become a career-enlisted rank, take the four-year college benefit after serving, or train to become an officer while in college by enrolling in ROTC (Reserve Officer Training Corps). Whichever option I chose, I could earn a good living and make my family and country proud.

At the time, I was a Christian and found great satisfaction in the notion of defending our Christian nation against

the godless Soviet Union, what Ronald Reagan declared the
"Evil Empire" in an address to the National Association of
Evangelicals in 1983. I had heard similar sermons preached
from the pulpit as far back as I could remember. As with
most teens, but especially poor ones whose fathers had left
the family, I was confused and adrift. Like a surrogate father
figure, the military promised to tell me who I was and what
I should fight for. People would respect me and honor me as
a hero when they learned I had served to protect them and
what they believed in and what they consumed. As a veteran,
I would receive benefits that included lifelong preference
points on all job applications, housing allowances, health
care (albeit inadequate), pension, full college-tuition reim-
bursement, free passes to national parks and some museums,
and discounts at restaurant chains, just to name a few—apt
rewards for having served my country. (Ten years later, in
1996, I would finish my service in the United States Peace
Corps. As a Returned Volunteer, I received a readjustment
allowance of $4,600; Perkins Loan forgiveness, comprising
7 percent of my student loans; and noncompetitive status in
applications for government jobs only. This status expired
one year after I completed service. No matter the rhetoric,
Americans value war much more than they do peace.)

The lieutenant was confident he had me. A stack of
official-looking papers with lots of blank lines to be filled in
and boxes to be checked rested on the desk between us, but
he pushed them aside and pulled a three-ring binder from a
drawer. It contained a photo album, and he opened it to a
collage that showed a modern two-story home with a green
yard and trees and sunshine. A red convertible corvette
was parked in the driveway. Its owner leaned against the
driver's side door with his feet crossed and his arms folded,
smug and cocksure. His hair was buzz-cut, and he wore

blue jeans, a white T-shirt, and a smile. He was muscular and handsome.

The lieutenant told me the man in the photo was an Air Force airman—an enlisted rank. "This guy played football in high school," he said. "Did you play football?"

I shook my head.

In Western civilizations, contact sports that emphasize size and power have long been recognized as a prime venue through which to prove one's manhood. In contrast, I had expressed interest in becoming a dancer or a gymnast as a small boy. Undeterred by my preferences, my father enrolled me in Little League and bought me a weight bench. As I entered high school, he hoped I would play football, in part because his parents had not allowed him to play, but also to help "make a man out of me," since he and my mother were separated and he was no longer around. My mother insisted I join the team, but I didn't want to; it was not in my nature. One morning before practice, I ran away from home. The next day, she let me turn in my helmet.

"Well, that's alright," said the lieutenant. He returned my attention to the album. Next to the guy in the photo stood a woman with blonde hair. Her skirt was short, but her blouse was not too revealing. She leaned against the man while smiling up at him, and her skin had an artificially dark tan that contrasted with the diamond ring she wore on her left hand. The ring was near the center of the photo, where the woman rested her hand against the man's powerful arm.

The photos on the next page showed more enlisted men, who wore tuxedos and lifted drinks in a kind of toast to me, the viewer, as they sat in their Porsches and smoked cigars. The women who invariably sat next to them in the passenger seats wore less clothing and had more hair. The lieutenant was making clear to me, man to man, just what kind of status, sexual desirability, monetary wealth, and prestige awaited me if I joined up. Combat, danger, and killing literally never entered the picture.

The lieutenant continued to talk, but I no longer heard him. I had seen movies like *Red Dawn* and *Uncommon Valor*, and regardless of the death and carnage they portrayed, I knew they were only movies. Maybe it was the Iran–Contra hearings or the Reagan-backed massacres in Guatemala that struck discordant notes with the vainglory presented in the photo album. Or maybe it was my memories of executing cows and chickens when I was a boy, or tearing through the bones and muscles and organs of so many animals I had hunted and killed. Whatever it was, a light flickered in my consciousness that day, and the lieutenant began to sound like a used-car salesman, a flimflam man. It seemed to me he was attempting to fool me into using my blood to lubricate the machinery of an ideology beyond our comprehension. He promised me these enviable trappings if I would sign a paper and relinquish any further critical thoughts.

Buried in the fine print of the contract were less frivolous matters that disclosed I might be required to kill people or help my fellows kill them on my behalf. Boot camp would help desensitize any misgivings with chants such as RAPE, KILL, PLUNDER, BURN! RAPE, KILL, PLUNDER, BURN! And in the finest print of all—so small it did not even appear—was the reality that I, too, might be shot at, tortured, and killed. Enlisting was less a ticket to freewheeling hedonism than a commitment to become a slave—a willfully ignorant, even proud one—to the American imperium.

The lieutenant saw he was losing me but did not know why. So, he turned the pages faster, talked more, and laughed more often. When he finished the album, he pushed a paper with official-looking letterhead across the desk and handed me a pen. I took the pen and rolled it between my thumb and index finger. Then I laid it on the desk and told him I would think about it.

We shook hands and I walked out of the recruiting office. I never returned.

"Look!" shouted Penny, pointing her gloved hand at the horizon. A ski pole dangled from her wrist, but it did not break her rhythm in the parallel tracks we followed. I had focused on the ground for the better part of an hour, tracing our tracks back to the 4Runner, so the scene on the horizon caught me by surprise.

"*La Luna*," she said, breathless over the slicing, rasping sound of our skis in the snow and the nylon shells of our pants and shirts. The sun was gone, yet the sky grew both darker and brighter at the same time. This new light was soft, as if conjured by the snow.

Two people skied toward us on Archangel Trail, and I signaled Penny. "Sweetness, up ahead!" Over the past month, I had used different terms of endearment for her and had settled on *Sweetness*. Nicknaming her made me feel more confident about our relationship, like she belonged to me. She did not seem to mind. She had not chosen one for me.

"Hey!" she shouted ahead. "Who let you guys up here?" It was Don and Donna. As we came together, we skied to a stop and stepped off the groomed trail, trying to catch our breath.

"We couldn't pass up a full moonrise on Hatcher Pass," said Don.

I chuckled, thinking it was a joke about my name.

Don's face was in shadow, so I could not see his expression, only that he straightened his posture. "You haven't heard the story?" he asked.

I glanced at Penny.

"Oh! I didn't think of it," she said.

Don chuckled. "Well, this whole recreation area is named after a miner named Hatcher, a long time ago," he said. "Maybe you're related."

I motioned toward the moon, now cresting a low point in the Talkeetna Mountains. It resembled a glowing beach ball nestled between sand dunes. "Is that Hatcher Pass?"

"Nope." "No." Donna and Don answered at the same time. "It's the other way," Donna continued, pointing west. "I mush my dogs up there sometimes. You just have to watch out for snow machines," she said, using the Alaskan term for snowmobiles.

Penny reminded me dinner was waiting. That morning, she had combined brown rice, carrots, celery, potatoes, rutabaga, and salmon in a Crock-Pot. She had also harvested greens that grew under grow-lights in the basement of the Lower House. Nearly all of the ingredients were local.

On the drive back to the branch, we commiserated about the latest war. Neither of us understood how Iraq was involved in 9/11, and we hoped the Bush regime did not think Americans were so dull as to confuse Iraq and Afghanistan and the alien-sounding names of Osama and Saddam. Each man's name contained a hissing sibilant that Christians might associate with the name Satan.

"God bless 'Merica," Penny drawled, and we laughed.

In the days following September 11, 2001, Bush had declared before Congress, "Either you are with us, or you are with the terrorists," carefully framing his war in terms of ultimate good versus ultimate evil. The website RaptureReady. com hit a record number of visits after the speech. Millions of Christians already longed for Biblical Armageddon and the End Times and had bought millions of copies of the books from Tim LaHaye's *Left Behind* series. It was an easy sell. Evangelicals craved to finally prove to the world—and, perhaps, reassure themselves—that they were right. The administration's words and actions helped fortify their identity.

Author and political commentator Gore Vidal responded to Bush's worldview with disbelief: "We've had bad presidents in the past," he said, "but we've never had a goddamned fool." The French, too, were not so easily gulled, and abstained from joining the US-led coalition. In retaliation, some Americans rebranded French fries as "freedom fries" and boycotted "Tar-zhay," that is, Target stores, because of rumors that the French owned it.

We had no Target store in Palmer, but this jingoistic mentality proved both highly adaptive and contagious. "God Bless the USA," the anthem sung by country music star Lee Greenwood (whom I had seen in concert in 1985) could often be heard blaring from automobiles with their windows rolled down, trolling Palmer's streets. One such vehicle was a black diesel pickup truck with dually wheels. Festooned with little American flags duct-taped to the hood, the truck had a flagpole mounted in the bed. An American flag that doubled the truck's length flapped in its wake, disconcerting motorists who drove behind it. A pair of chrome-plated "bull-balls" hung from the rear bumper.

Most vehicles around town displayed patriotic bumper stickers, which included THIS IRAQI OIL BURNS JUST FINE; NUKE 'EM 'TIL THEY GLOW, THEN SHOOT THEM IN THE DARK; I SUPPORT WAR FOR OIL; KILL 'EM ALL AND LET GOD SORT 'EM OUT and HEROES: HONOR THEIR SACRIFICE. All were in support of our military exploits, which were an expression of our power. The words reminded me of my flight training: power creates lift, which overcomes drag and gravity—but not forever. Gravity ultimately wins.

The owners of a very few cars responded with bumper stickers I had never seen before. White lettering spelled the word COEXIST on a blue background, but closer examination revealed that each letter was a stylized emblem of a world religion or social movement. The sticker's message was simple: we are much more alike than we are different, so relax. People whose cars displayed this sticker impressed me with their audacity, and I agreed with them, but I did not get one for my Ford Escort. I did not want to attract attention.

The owner of a white Chevy Blazer took the "patriotic" attitude to a new level. He had cut off the C and the O from a COEXIST bumper sticker, letters that represented Islam and the Peace Symbol. In this rendition, the Christian Cross now anchored the last letter of the word EXIST. I noticed it as I filled my Ford Escort with regular-grade gasoline at a Shell station in Palmer. I suspected the Blazer's owner was oblivious to the meaning of the other letters, which represent Paganism/Wicca, Daoism, Judaism, and gay rights. The Blazer had two other memorable details: only one headlight worked, and another sticker covered the gas cap with the word love. A toddler sat in a woman's lap in the passenger seat gumming Cheerios from a Ziploc bag. Meanwhile, the driver walked out of the station with a bottle of Mountain Dew. He wore a drawn, apprehensive expression, and when he glanced at me, I dropped my gaze to the fuel nozzle in my car.

Cozy lights beckoned from inside the Lower House. The back door squeaked in two places as Penny and I were welcomed by the aroma of a home-cooked meal. We hung our coats and kicked snow off our boots.

"I'm starving!"

"I hope you like it," she said.

We went into the kitchen. Her cat was on the counter.

"Lucky!" she shouted. She went over and picked him up. "You can't be up here, buster." But she held him and petted him and smiled at me. "You like cats?"

"I love cats." I petted him, too.

The Crock-Pot perked and bubbled. Steam hissed. She put Lucky down and went to the sink to wash lettuce and break it into pieces into a salad bowl. She added slices of jicama, lemongrass, and green apples. For dessert, she arranged a plate of Siljans Finn Crisp whole rye crackers and St. Dalfour Blueberry Spread. She then poured two glasses of Pinot Noir, her favorite.

"To something special," she said.

I did not like wine. It was too bitter, but I tried not to show it when I sipped. I put down my glass and picked up Lucky. Penny and I petted him together, until he began to purr. Holding me in a light embrace around Lucky, she came closer, and we kissed.

Footsteps approached.

"Penny, I took last year's meal schedule and added a—" Kurt walked into the kitchen. He lived in a room downstairs in the Lower House.

Penny took Lucky from me and moved away.

Kurt stopped in the doorway between the kitchen and the living room. He held a pencil and rubbed it against the air in front of him, as if erasing a mistake, and then pushed his glasses up the bridge of his nose.

"Sorry," he said, and marched back to his room.

Penny called after him. "Kurt! Have you had dinner?"

"No! Thank you."

His reaction confused me.

"I'll explain later," said Penny.

Her bedroom was in the attic. When we went there to eat, she told me that she and Kurt had dated—once. She considered him a friend, nothing more. But he still had a crush on her, and for his sake, she told me, we should avoid public shows of affection. I was still high on our kiss and open to any suggestion.

She also explained he had served in the military. The job of handyman and gear-room assistant at the branch suited him.

I ate most of the salmon in my bowl, but the stew contained more of it than I was used to, and I separated some into a little mound of flesh on my plate. I did not want to waste it, but so much seemed unnecessary.

Penny pointed. "Is it okay?" We sat cross-legged on a rug on the wooden floor in her bedroom. "I thought you liked fish."

"I do."

It seemed a bit much, but then I remembered how bears, dolphins, whales, seals, eagles, and Alaska Natives, too, all ate tons of salmon, and nonetheless plenty appeared to survive to swim upstream and spawn each fall. (Commercial fishers took 157 million salmon in 2003.) After that, they died anyway. Along the coasts, Natives roasted, smoked, fried, boiled, and dried salmon meat. They also combined salmon roe with bearberries to make a sort of jam spread. They buried the heads of salmon in leaf-lined pits for weeks and considered the result a delicacy similar to cheese. Fermented salmon were placed on a person's neck and nose to treat fever. A single Native family might eat or otherwise use thousands of salmon each year for themselves and their dogs, although snow machines had largely replaced dog teams. In the Alaskan interior, caribou were the main source of food. Natives there put caribou meat in stews and roasts and harvested greens from caribou stomachs and fat from behind the eyeballs. They turned skins into winter garments.

These Native ways of life had changed dramatically, however, since the turn of the twentieth century. Nearly all Natives now hunted with rifles and propelled their johnboats with Evinrude outboard motors. Commercial and processed foods now made up most foods they consumed, especially among young people, who acquired only 7 percent of their calories from traditional sources. Doritos were more common than whale blubber. Of the eighty thousand Natives who lived in Alaska, very few of them were true hunter-gatherers, such as the Hadza in Africa.

As I imagined a Native might do, I scooped up the glob of meat from my plate. "I love fish. I just like to get the full effect." I spooned it into my mouth like Little Mikey eating Life cereal in the television commercials I'd grown up watching, except it was squishy and viscous instead of crunchy and sweet.

"Good! I'll take you fishing in the Matanuska River," she said, and sipped her wine.

I chewed and nodded.

Lucky lay sprawled on the bed. He no doubt smelled our salmon and hoped for a bite. But we held the power, and his eyes expressed both envy and caution.

CHAPTER 22

Sacrificial Virgins

"SEE THAT GRAVEL bar?" shouted Ben from behind me. He pointed over my right shoulder and out the starboard window of the plane. "Put her down right there."

I saw nothing but trees cut by a narrow swath of boulders.

Ben chuckled over the headset. "How about I take her in this time?"

I sat in the front seat of Ben's tandem Champ. His plane reminded me of Bongo's Piper Cub on Mount Kenya, except Ben's was thirty years old, while Bongo's was closer to sixty. The Champ also had balloon tires called "bush wheels" that allowed it to land on rougher surfaces, such as gravel bars in the middle of streams hundreds of miles from the nearest airstrip.

In routine fashion, Ben banked the plane around to face the Matanuska Glacier, added carb heat to prevent ice from building up in the carburetor, pulled the power back to idle, and let the plane sink toward a forest of Engelmann spruce. He made it look easy.

It was early May, a time of year called Breakup in Alaska, when the ice that has encased rivers since October finally cracks and heaves, allowing the flow to return. Lakes thaw, too. Alaska contains some three million lakes that add up to over twenty acres in area. Many of these had now turned shades of emerald and lime, turquoise and aquamarine.

Ben held the plane's velocity just above stall speed over the treetops until the stream reemerged beneath us and continued in a more or less straight path for a thousand feet. The plane settled into ground effect three feet above the gravel bar, stained red and black from iron ore, and at thirty miles per hour we floated two hundred feet before the wheels touched down. The plane bounced and shimmied, but the tail-wheel did not alight until the plane came to a complete stop.

"And that's how we do it," he said.

Ben was not a flight instructor, but he had spent nearly as much time in the air as he had on the ground. He was a good kid, a smart kid, and like Harley he always wore a ball cap, although the logo on his advertised Talkeetna Air Taxi instead of the US Navy. If it was cold outside, meaning at least -10°F, discretion might oblige Ben to pull the hood of his gray hoody up over his ball cap, but the cap was mandatory. It added to his down-home, country-boy demeanor, which reminded me of myself at his age. In the fall, he planned to begin classes in engineering at the University of Anchorage, which did not resemble me at any age.

Until his semester started, Ben offered to teach me how to fly tail-draggers—planes with a main wheel under each wing and a small wheel or tailskid under the rearmost point of the fuselage. I had only flown planes with tricycle gear—planes with a nose-wheel under the engine and a main wheel under each wing. If I wanted to fly in Alaska, I needed to know both.

I smiled and unbuckled my seatbelt. "Smartass."

"I know. I've been coming up here with my dad since I was a kid."

We got out and looked around but saw no wildlife. The air was chilly, so after ten minutes we restarted the plane and took off. On the flight back to Palmer, we noticed a web of ATV and 4WD tracks. I spotted a homestead nearby and circled the plane to get a closer look. Ben pointed out stacks of old tires that formed a wall around the compound. Inside sat several old trucks, a bulldozer, spools of tarpaper, fuel cans, fifty-five-gallon steel drums, and racks of antlers and hides nailed to a cabin that was little more than a shack. I saw no one outside, but at least five huskies ran and jumped and barked, which meant the cabin must be inhabited. Neither of us wanted to upset anyone with a loaded weapon down there, so I turned the plane toward Palmer.

On the way back, Ben told me that even though Alaska is huge, many parts of it are not the virgin wilderness people imagine. Miners, hermits, and hunters have staked claims across the backcountry, collecting decades of "equipment" in order to live out their version of the pioneer life. In addition to homesteads, commercial mining operations have carved out so-called sacrifice areas. During the Cold War, the term described environments permanently damaged by nuclear testing that were thus considered uninhabitable.

We have sacrificed most virgin wilderness on the planet. But it is perhaps more accurate to say we have *consumed* it.

Jack London's *The Call of the Wild* and Farley Mowat's *Never Cry Wolf* have long stirred the American imagination. They formed my first impressions of Alaska as a boy. Popular songs like Johnny Horton's "North to Alaska" foreshadowed a surge in visits to national parks and enrollment in wilderness schools like Outward Bound and NOLS. After the last hippy communes disbanded, the television series *Northern Exposure* captured the Alaskan version of America's nostalgia for what President George H. W. Bush called "a kinder, gentler nation." At the pinnacle of our military, industrial, and economic success, mainstream (i.e., white) American culture yearned for the intrepid individualism of John Wayne as well as the folksy idealism of Norman Rockwell. Perhaps our success had been too complete. Maybe we had subdued the feminine in nature so well there was nothing left for the natural world to dominate—unless one went to Alaska.

However, the Alaska imagined by most people is a fable. The reality is vast but not inexhaustible, wild but not untamable. To think that it is infinite is a well-trammeled path to turning Alaska into another Gatlinburg, Tennessee, or Niagara Falls, New York—fully zoned with tram rides, balloon tours, miniature golf, and freeways lined with casinos and fast-food restaurants. In fewer than two hundred years, we have reduced Mother Nature to a mere shadow of its former self in the "Lower 48," or "Outside," or "America," as Alaskans say. Alaska might take a little longer, but we seem determined to sacrifice this virgin land, too.

Throughout April and May, I flew three or four times per week with Jacquie, though the key for my favorite plane continued to disappear. When it did, we used another plane, a Cessna 172, number 188 Victor Echo. I did not know this was Harley's favorite plane for student instruction.

Late in May, I stood on a wing strut checking the fuel level in the tanks when the steel door to the office flew open. Harley stormed out with a pursed expression, stabbing his finger at me.

"Get the hell away from my ship!" he shouted. "You, sir, are no goddamn pilot, and that bird is way out of your league!"

I climbed down. I did not understand why he shouted, and I knew the plane belonged to the company.

"Now, Harley," said Jacquie, opening her hands and walking to meet him halfway. "Calm down."

"*Calm down? Did he tell you the little stunt he pulled in Anchorage?*"

I could not hear what they said next, only that she spoke to him in low yet deliberate tones, which seemed to tame him. I appreciated Jacquie's protection, but knew I should defend myself, so I walked over.

As I got closer, he pointed at me and bristled. "Sonny, if you so much as hit a goddamn bug, you will wash that whole goddamn ship with your toothbrush! Do you hear me?"

Jacquie patted him on the shoulder and calmed him down again. He adjusted his US Navy cap and marched back into the office, but not before glaring at me in a way that meant he would watch me and scrutinize my work and expose any error, legitimate or otherwise. From that day on, we avoided each other.

With Jacquie's guidance, I practiced holding procedures, approaches, stalls, and GPS navigation. Despite a 10 percent employee discount, I spent far more than I earned, and my money from Africa was nearly gone. Fortunately, I received a letter from the Lower 48. The letter contained a check for five thousand dollars, an inheritance from my grandmother—my father's mother—who had died months earlier. It was my share of an inheritance split seven ways that my grandfather had saved by working as a pipefitter-welder for forty years. I felt grateful yet guilty. Flight lessons would consume it in a matter of weeks.

At the branch, hundreds of students were due to arrive, and Penny was busy allocating rations. The last time we had dined together was the night we skied Hatcher Pass, so we made a plan. She had heard of an upcoming town hall–type meeting and suggested we could go together. Afterward, we could go out for dinner.

A company from North Dakota called Evergreen Resources had organized the meeting. The company's business was coalbed methane extraction via a revolutionary technology called hydraulic fracturing, or "fracking." Sarah Palin, chair of the Alaska Oil and Gas Conservation Commission, had given Evergreen permission to explore for gas. Notably, Ms. Palin also supported the proposed $400 million "Bridge to Nowhere."

Most Alaskans did not own the so-called mineral rights to their land—the mineral interest estate beneath private property. If such rights were exercised by the mining company, it could declare eminent domain and erect a twenty-four-hour drilling operation to exploit whatever product it sought. Drilling methods and materials could potentially contaminate groundwater or divert it from well-taps altogether. Most homes and farms in the Matanuska-Susitna Valley obtained their water from private wells.

In addition to mineral rights, state and federal governments owned nearly all surface rights in Alaska—89 percent, an area roughly twice the size of Kenya. Most land was therefore susceptible to hydrocarbon profiteers and massive construction projects, such as the Trans-Alaska Pipeline System, which stretches over eight hundred miles from Prudhoe Bay to Valdez.

"This is unbelievable," said Penny. She wore her reading glasses and poked her index finger at the evening's program. No fewer than five hundred people, mostly men, had crammed into the auditorium at Palmer High School, "Home of the Moose," and were now seated in folding chairs waiting for the presenter to begin.

"Un-be-*lievable*," she repeated.

I leaned closer so I could speak to her and not be overheard. "At least propane's clean. I use it. You use it to cook. You said you prefer it to electric."

"I know," she said, rubbing her forehead. "I'm part of the problem."

I meant to discuss the issue, not shut her down, so I back-pedaled. "What I mean is, we may as well use what we have, right? Use what's available in gas wells we have, but wean ourselves off of it, and use more solar."

"I wish we could. But there's not enough sunlight in Alaska, not consistently."

"Well, then, geothermal. Alaska sits on a huge tectonic plate boundary."

She did not respond. I was about to bring up the wind project that Don had mentioned installing at the branch, when her face flushed and her forehead wrinkled.

"There's just so much greed. So much ignorance," she said.

"Sweetness?"

"We deplete our resources and poison the air and the water, which poisons our food and our bodies. And when things get toxic, people run away to some new, cleaner place, where everything is supposed to be fresh and unspoiled." She chuckled and shook her head. "But we are out of clean places.

"And it is *way more* than just the Exxon Valdez! Every-body knows about that one and the one they had in Prudhoe Bay. But for every big spill like that there are hundreds of smaller ones that go unreported or are covered up." She was on a roll. People in the row in front of us turned to listen. "Petrochemicals, too! Thousands of toxins dumped into riv-ers in the Lower 48 circulate to the poles, where they accu-mulate, so this *pure virgin wilderness* everyone thinks is so healthy actually has one of the highest cancer rates in the country and in the world!"

The room had quieted. The speaker for the evening stood at the front of the room. His features were East Asian, though he wore blue jeans, an open-collared shirt, and a polar fleece vest. He smiled as he listened to Penny with apparent interest.

"Of course, none of that matters to these bozos in Washington!" she said, still seated but waving a hand at the speaker. People chuckled. Some nodded. "And now—" Her voice quavered, but she set her jaw and glared at the speaker. He blinked twice.

"*Now* they want to bring it right up here to our homes and poison us firsthand and call it 'a sacrifice for the greater good.' Of course, in ten years they'll call us from their hermetically sealed cubicles thousands of miles away and apologize, 'Oh, sorry about your cancer, impossible to say how that happened!'"

Penny was passionate about healthy foods and a clean environment, I knew. But this evening, something deeper animated her. Hydraulic fracturing insulted her very notion of Mother Nature and the source of all healing and health, especially in a land so rugged yet so fragile. I shared her beliefs, though her tirade had an edge to it that suggested a more personal connection. What inner wound had this issue provoked, I wondered? Had she come to Alaska to heal by fighting for this cause as a proxy for her own inner fracturing?

She stopped shouting, but her cheeks were flushed. For a moment, her breathing was the only sound in the room. Then, the audience exploded into applause and shouts of approval. Energy reverberated off the blue-and-white cinderblock walls and evolved into a standing ovation. I clapped, too. I was so proud.

Penny blinked at me, grateful yet embarrassed. Perhaps she felt flattered by the response in a way she had not often experienced, especially from men.

She grabbed my hand and led me out of the auditorium. Groups of people followed and started to leave. They had heard all they needed to hear. Penny had convinced them to fight this "fracking" initiative.

We walked to the parking lot. People shouted compliments and hooted approval. I opened the passenger door of my Ford Escort for her, but before she got in, she pulled me close and kissed me and rubbed her hands through my hair. More people hooted.

"Can we have dinner at your cabin tonight?" she asked.

I was surprised. "Sure."

"You cook."

"Okay."

"Right now."

CHAPTER 23

Strong Enough

I STRUCK A match and touched it to a newspaper in the wood-stove. In a moment, the birch caught fire and crackled and glowed orange across the plywood floor. Candles burned on each windowsill, and Ben Harper sang "Diamonds on the Inside" from my Philips radio-cassette player with surround sound. The final touch was a bottle of Pinot Noir. I had purchased it at Oaken Keg Spirits Shops in Palmer anticipating such an evening as this, and with difficulty I now opened it and poured it into two juice glasses embossed with images of oranges.

I raised my glass. "Happy birthday."

"Oh, not until next month," said Penny. "Don't rush it."

"I know. How about, here's to a brighter, cleaner Alaska?"

We toasted and talked about the environment and fracking as I prepared a homemade pizza. I had a Red Baron Pepperoni Pizza in the freezer and could have tossed it in the oven, but I sought to impress.

"We burn so much oil and gas and coal—fossil fuels," she said between sips of Pinot. "What did we think was going to happen? Especially up here in Alaska, we can see it. The glaciers are melting, the seacoast is eroding, and the permafrost—the *permafrost*—is thawing! If that decomposes, then the carbon dioxide and methane in the atmosphere will double and warm the climate that much faster."

"It's a positive feedback loop."

"*Exactly!*" she shouted, louder than she intended.

I pulled a bag of flour down from a cupboard and arranged some bowls in which to prepare the dough. I paused to sip my wine, careful not to purse my lips. "Yeah, I've seen it firsthand on Mount Kenya and Kilimanjaro, glaciers retreating. It's incredible so many people refuse to believe it."

"Especially big business—and Christians."

"Christians?"

"You know, they deny we're part of the world and part of nature."

"Because Satan was cast down to Earth and corrupted it."

"Yes!" she said, pointing her juice glass at me. "Yes. And because Mother Earth is associated with women, and women are at the bottom the ladder."

"Hierarchy."

She held her hand flat, palm down, and raised it above her head. "God, angels, people," she said, bringing her hand down an inch with each term, "then animals, then Earth. And for people, women are lower on the totem pole than men, just above animals."

Her comments reminded me of the book by Ifi Amadiume in the O'Neals' library in Tanzania. I agreed with the author, but it was nice to hear Penny say it using real-world examples that involved everyone and everything. Unlike Rachel, Penny shared many of my principles and would require much less persuasion should I wish to convince her of my argument. Politically, socially, and environmentally, we were on the same page.

I hunted for my measuring cup, unsure which drawer or cupboard I might have stashed it in.

"I like your cabin," said Penny, warming her hands over the woodstove. "It's cozy, for a man-cave."

"A what?" I had never heard the term before.

"A man-cave," she said, and pointed to the maps on the walls and an Old West–style lamp on the table. "It's a room that a man decorates however he wants so he can have his man-friends over to watch football games or war movies. It's where men can be men," she said, sipping her wine, "or little boys."

I found the measuring cup in a corner drawer and went back to the bag of flour, still musing over the term "man-cave." In his book *The Hero with a Thousand Faces*, the mythologist Joseph Campbell explained how caves represent the archetypal womb and the sacred feminine. Both men and women contain feminine and masculine psychological traits. In the current American ethos, the word *feminine* is synonymous with altruism, compassion, relationship, emotion, gentleness, passivity, softness, weakness, and submission. Conversely, *masculine* is equated with virility, courage, individualism, dynamism, hardness, and assertiveness. Under this notation, masculine traits are responsible for analysis, order, hierarchy, and abstract thought, but can involve egocentrism, violence, and domination.

Penny described man-caves as manly places in the traditional sense. If they were an expression of men's psyche, I wondered, how could they be feminine, too? Unless, as she implied, they comforted and protected men who were immersed in psychological regression, feigning boyhood in perpetuity?

"You think I've decorated my cabin like a cave?"

"No, silly," she said. "It's just a bachelor pad, where you can relax and do as you please, like a college dorm room or something." She tapped an airplane mobile I had bought in Kenya. It was fashioned from discarded flip-flops and was the kind of thing a parent might suspend over a baby's crib. It hung by nylon fishing line from the ceiling. "Though you do keep it very neat."

"I like it." I poured two cups of wheat flour into a large pot, then added salt and a teaspoon of yeast. I turned the red-handled tap on a five-gallon jug next to the sink and added water to the mixture.

"Still no water?" she asked.

I shook my head and mixed the ingredients in the bowl using my hand. The song on the radio changed to "Kiss Me" by Sixpence None the Richer.

"You know, I saw this cabin last year when Greg was building it," she said. "I thought about moving in here, but I have such a good deal at the branch. The rent's cheap, and everything I need is right there. Although, it can be tough sometimes, living so close . . . to people." She sipped her Pinot.

When I finished punching the dough, I set the bowl on a metal cooling rack on top of the woodstove and covered it with a towel. "Do you think it's too hot?"

She shrugged. "Guess we'll find out."

I tasted my wine and tried not to grimace. I knew nothing about wine, except this was too sour for my taste.

She pointed at my neck with her wine glass. "You still haven't told me about your tattoo."

I had gotten it on my neck so it would be more visible— to me and everyone else—though there were days I tried to hide it and forget about it. Maybe it was the wine, but I tonight was different. Tonight, I wanted to bring Penny into this part of my life, so I unbuttoned the first two buttons on my flannel shirt and pulled the collar to the side to expose it. "I got it in Mexico during Carnival a few years ago. I was between NOLS courses in Baja, and we danced till dawn on the beach."

"Sounds like fun," she said, and stroked it lightly. "Is it an eagle?"

"It's supposed to be a phoenix."

"It looks more like an eagle."

"Yeah." I released my collar and returned to the cupboard. To make pizza sauce, I pulled down a can of tomato paste, a bag of brown sugar, and a bottle of balsamic vinegar.

"Does it mean anything?" she asked.

"A lot changed for me in Africa and after." I was still reluctant to tell her about the crash. "So, it means rebirth or resurrection."

I mixed the ingredients for the sauce in a smaller pot and set it aside. As for toppings, I had not bought pepperoni or sausages in a long time, so I was out, and given the evening's trajectory I decided against chopping onions and garlic. I did, however, open a can of olives.

"What happened? How did it change you?"

I did not know where to begin. The experience had been powerful, enlightening, and agonizing, but it was still too close and recent. I could not yet see all of it. I was still in the midst of it.

"I grew up religious, and now I'm not. You?"

She shook her head, swallowing a sip of wine before answering. "No. Not really."

Her answer pleased me, but I had gathered as much from our ski date.

"Do you have other tattoos?"

I patted my chest. "I have a columbine that represents my love for the mountains." I hoped to show her this tattoo later that evening. "That's all, so far."

Her eyes smiled. She sipped her wine again and set the glass on the table. I continued to slice olives as she moved in close behind me.

"Can I give you a hand?" she asked, and slid her hands around my waist and stomach.

In the background, the music changed to "Strong Enough" by Sheryl Crow:

> I have a face I cannot show,
> I make the rules up as I go.
> Just try and love me if you can,
> Are you strong enough to be my man?

I had a pretty high opinion of myself as physically strong, intelligent, and not bad looking, though I was adept at pretending to be humble. I found this attracted women even more. I was sure Penny must feel lucky to have me.

In truth, my self-confidence had never been secure. In this way, I again served as a microcosm of American culture, which harbored similar fears. Just as my country built a military stronger than any other (the United States alone accounts for approximately half of the world's annual spending on the armed forces), I exercised until I hurt myself, flew planes until I crashed, and climbed dangerous mountains to the brink of death—all in a vain attempt to convince myself I was good enough and strong enough, and that I controlled my world.

I set the pot of pizza sauce on the kitchen counter and turned to Penny. She draped her arms over my shoulders and I held her hips and we swayed, the toes of our shoes touching as we shuffled over the cold, plywood floor. She ran her fingers through the hair on the back of my head. Her body felt electric and hot to the touch. The heat focused into white-hot sparks in her eyes that exposed my soul and left a swirling sensation in my stomach like butterflies or small birds.

She brought her cheek next to mine, almost touching but not quite, and whispered, "I love you." But she said it quickly and clipped the last word short as if she pushed it out before she lost nerve. This was my chance.

"I love you, too."

Firelight flickered in the wine on her lips. She tasted tart yet salty, like a tear, and I held her and we caressed each other.

In a moment, she turned her face from mine. I opened my eyes, and she stared at the floor between our feet. She started to speak but stopped and shook her head. A tear fell from her cheek onto my sleeve.

"Penny? What's wrong?"

"I have to tell you something," she said, her head turned down as she wiped her cheek with her hand. "I . . ."

"It's okay."

She cleared her throat. "A long time ago, I was . . . raped." The last word came out strained and pinched. She buried her face in my shirt and held me but made no sound. I kissed the top of her head and stroked her hair. I was sad for her and angry with a faceless man from her past. I did not know what to say, so I stayed quiet and held her, ready to do or not do whatever she asked, whatever she needed.

She sighed and turned her face toward mine. Her eyes were puffy and watery, and I was sure they were red. But the candlelight revealed only a weak smile as she moved the hair off my forehead. Without a word, she went to the woodstove and took the pot of dough off and sat it on the counter. Then she took my hand and led me upstairs to my bedroom.

She had revealed to me her deepest secrets, but I did not have the courage to return the favor. I could not tell her about the talisman or the crash. I could not tell her about those I had hurt—in the crash, at the Nairobi police station when I demanded vengeance, when I argued with Vijay and Bob, and likely many more, directly and indirectly, human and otherwise. I was not strong enough.

After the crash, the paramedic in the ambulance had not known the extent of my two companions' injuries. One of them had acquired only superficial wounds, but the other had suffered a broken back and was airlifted to a hospital in Salt Lake City. He spent six months in bed as the fractures healed and the metal rods implanted along his spine grew secure. I had visited him while my head was still shaved and the stitches still fresh. My face was bruised and swollen, my right arm in a cast. The distal end of my right radius bone was not found at the crash site, so a rod was implanted.

I was unable to tell Penny any of this or understand the mystery behind my shiny necklace. I was oblivious. I did, however, know that concealment has consequences, and mine were fast approaching.

CHAPTER 24

Rape and Pillage

"YOU HAVE AN unusual situation," said the loan officer. She sat behind a polished wooden desk on the second floor of the Matanuska Valley Federal Credit Union in the town of Wasilla. "Unlike yourself, Penelope—"

"Penny," said Penny.

The loan office flashed a smile. "Most of our clients are unable to deposit $30,000 on a home."

Penny was not wealthy. She managed the kitchen and field rations for the branch—a rewarding, if demanding, profession, but not a lucrative one. She was, however, shrewd with money and was now ready to spend it.

To me, such a quantity seemed a fortune. And while I respected Penny's ability to amass it, guilt shadowed my respect, knowing I couldn't contribute anything. To cover the cost of a flight instructor, airplane rental, and fuel, I had cashed out my Vanguard IRA and spent all the funds inherited from my grandmother. My checking account was nearly empty and would barely cover the Instrument Rating Exam I was scheduled to take in a week. Penny offered to help pay for flight training but sounded hesitant, as if she felt obligated to offer, which only compounded my sense of shame, and I declined. If not for the meals she prepared for us each week, I would by now have registered with social services to collect food stamps.

The loan officer shifted in her chair. She wore a brown acrylic cardigan that no longer fit her, and she tugged it across her bosom in a protective manner. She appeared close to us in age, though her demeanor was jaded and stern, as if she had spent her entire adult life in an office, this office, wrangling with loan applications under fluorescent lights.

"Yet most of our applicants have steady, gainful employment," she said. "So, I'm afraid that both your incomes combined do not meet our minimum requirements for lending, even at the thirty-year rate."

Penny scooted forward in her chair and rested her fingertips on the edge of the loan officer's desk. "I understand," she said. "I just want to make it clear that Family Services in Palmer told me they need nutritionists to help plan diets for their low-income families. They said they're interested in hiring me next year when I graduate." Penny smiled and nodded in a hopeful manner. She was normally quiet, so I knew this venture must be important to her. Our future was important to her.

The loan officer's expression did not change, and she turned to me as if to ask, *And what about you?* She glanced at the scar on my forehead, the tattoo on my neck, and my necklace, and I imagined she had settled on an answer.

I cleared my throat. "Well, I will finish my flight training in a month, maybe two."

She did not flinch, except to pick her teeth with her tongue behind closed lips.

"And I know tons of people, so it won't be long, probably, before I'm out there . . . gainfully employed. Did I mention I work at the airport?" But I lied. Only in Africa would an air charter service consider a rookie like me, who had flown only half as many hours and was nearly twice as old as most newly hired pilots.

Yet Alaska was my new Neverland. Ever since that magical night at my cabin, Penny had proposed we build a home and a life together. Now the trees looked greener, the sky bluer, and the mountains brighter. She understood my work as a bush pilot might take me elsewhere, maybe away from Palmer, away from Alaska, but, she assured me, "People are more important than places." Like America's alliance with Britain, or Canada, or even Greece, she would stick with me through any hardship.

Before meeting with the loan officer, I had phoned my parents and told each of them about Penny and our decisions. They sounded happy but cautious. When I had asked my father for a loan, he told me, "We don't got no money," and asked what happened to the inheritance from my grandmother. I could almost hear him shake his head when I told him I had spent it on flight school, and he warned, "You better get growed up, or you're gonna wake up at sixty-five without havin' two nickels to rub together."

His rebuke had hung in the air like the smoke from a cheroot cigar. It only darkened when he changed the subject and asked, "Hey, has you went huntin' up there yet?"

My mother had few resources, so I had called her mostly for advice. She sympathized and suggested I pray about it and use more "elbow grease" if I needed to save money.

I smiled at the loan officer across the desk and tried to look sweet. She pursed her lips and addressed Penny. "When you find work with social services, please call me and make another appointment. I'd be happy to talk about your options then."

We shook hands with the loan officer and walked out of the Credit Union and climbed into the 4Runner.

Before starting the engine, Penny turned to me. "Well, she was a little rude."

"Yeah, but I do need to find a job, a real job."

"What about flying?"

I stared out my window without answering her. I wanted to fly professionally, but it was increasingly difficult to deny how unlikely, how far-fetched it was, especially in light of building a home and a life with Penny.

She reached over to smooth my hair, running a finger over the scar on my forehead.

"What happened here?"

I held her hand and told her about the plane crash and the attack in Uhuru Park but not the talisman: not yet. She kissed me and said she respected me for continuing to fly after the crash, but she respected me more for my willingness to try something new for our future together.

"What kind of work will you look for?"

"I don't know. I don't really have a trade."

She smiled and pointed at me. "I think I have an idea."

That afternoon, I composed a résumé. The only staff computer at the branch was in Kurt's room, so Penny guarded the door as I typed. I did not notice when she left for a moment.

The sound of heavy boots approached from the kitchen. Kurt stopped in the doorway to his room. "What are you doing?" he asked, bristling.

"Penny's helping me write something."

His faced flushed. He folded his arms across his chest and shifted from one foot to the other and back again, trying to decide which course of action to take, diplomatic or combative.

I returned my focus to the computer screen. "I won't be long."

"She's not what you think she is."

I gave no response and heard the creaky back door open and close. Penny was coming.

"You know, she was raped and had an abortion," he said. "Did you know that?"

"Kurt!" shouted Penny. He spun around. She stood in the living room, so I could not see her, only Kurt. Neither of them spoke, so I tried to interpret his reactions to her gestures.

With clenched teeth, he pushed the glasses up the bridge of his nose and marched out of the room and out of the house.

Penny exhaled and entered the room. Her face was tense, and she seemed somehow older. She did not look directly at me but came over and sat in my lap. She held me and pushed her face into my shoulder.

I stayed quiet, though I wanted to know more about her past—to know everything. Mostly, I wanted to know how Kurt, whom she had dated only once, could know so much about her, while I, the man with whom she planned to build a home, knew less. What else had she withheld from me?

That afternoon, Penny contacted her friends at Alaska Pacific University and Matanuska-Susitna College. I applied to both schools, and within one week I had secured an adjunct position to teach geography at each. They scheduled me to start in September.

In the meantime, Penny and I enjoyed cerulean skies and twenty hours of sunshine every day. We often drove to Lazy Mountain or Hatcher Pass to pick blueberries, eating them all amidst fields of blue lupine and yellow poppies while grizzly bears grazed nearby. Our hopes were as high as the days were long, and they inspired me to write a song on my guitar for her. By June, she asked me to move in with her at the branch.

After she told Don and Donna, they became noticeably cooler toward me. I mentioned it to Penny the day we moved my things out of my cabin.

"Well, you know," she said, playful yet exasperated, "they're big Christians, so . . ." We loaded my camping and climbing gear into her 4Runner.

"No kidding!" I was surprised, since Don and Donna hadn't approached me with a religious tract or an invitation to church.

"Oh, yeah, Bible-thumpers. But don't get me wrong, they're great people, and I love them to death. It's just that religions, and especially Christianity, have so much baggage."

"Yeah?"

"Oh, my God, like sexism and racism and *so many* stupid wars. Just look at our Christian president!"

I could not have agreed more. Although religious aid organizations have built schools, orphanages, and clinics for the world's poorest people, they have left behind Native cultures ruined by an imperialism that privileged its own worldview and demonized theirs, stripped them of their natural resources, and left them dependent on charity. Powerless, they have become prey for dictators and, in too many cases, supported by the nations from which those aid organizations came.

It was becoming clear to me that, in spite of its platitudes of stewardship and the brotherhood of man, religion had been one of the most powerful weapons deployed all too often by men to rape and pillage Earth and subjugate, exploit, or even destroy most of its inhabitants. In my opinion, God symbolized the human ego and the Devil its shadow archetype projected onto the "Other"—any member of any "out-group," whether human or animal. God and ego were two sides of the same coin, and the most prevalent peddlers of this dual identity were Christianity and Islam.

As for Christianity, much of its scriptural foundation is either historically inaccurate or intentionally misleading. In the 1980s and 1990s, biblical scholars at the international Jesus Seminar concluded that 82 percent of the statements and events described in the gospels concerning Jesus of Nazareth were later adaptations and forgeries. Their judgment only confirmed for me Mark Twain's opinion on the matter: "Faith is believin' what you know ain't so."

Penny was not religious. She did, however, appreciate neopaganism's reverence for nature and atheism's humanistic logic. I told her I valued both views and considered pantheism a hybrid.

"Explain," she said.

"Pantheism describes the whole universe and everything in it as being divine. It's all one."

"Isn't that like saying God?" she asked, as I put a cardboard box in the back of her 4Runner. The box was heavy with books and reminded me of the climbing injury to my sacrum, so I was careful when I pushed the box forward.

"*God* is another word loaded with baggage. I prefer to say *divine*, because it feels more holistic. But it's still a word. Maybe it's more accurate just to say it's like the vibration or the hum behind everything."

"You mean like ho-hum?" She was playing with me.

"Like an undercurrent. You can't really hear it when you think about it, only when it's perfectly quiet, and you're not thinking about it, because it's not really a sound."

"So, it's your imagination," she said, more pointedly.

"Think of it this way. Ninety-nine percent of an atom is the space between the nucleus and the orbiting electrons, which means that most of everything is nothing. But it's still there, it's still important. The atom couldn't exist without the space. The universe is the same way. Ninety-six percent of the universe is dark energy and dark matter. We can't see it, but we know it's there because we can measure its effects, and it makes up most of everything. We couldn't exist without it."

"That still doesn't make it divine or spiritual," she said. "Science will eventually figure it out."

"Maybe. Or maybe science can only see a tiny part of it. The rest is consciousness." I waved my hand in the air.

My simplistic, hipster philosophy amused her, and she smirked and folded her arms across her chest. "I think I was wrong about you."

"What do you mean?"

"I think you need to eat more meat—lean meat."

When I gave Greg the keys to the cabin, he invited Penny and me over for a big cookout he had planned that weekend. It was late June, the weekend after solstice, but he said he wanted to celebrate summer before it was gone. At least twenty of his friends showed up, and he manned the grill, flipping burgers and sliced leeks and adding dollops of sauces and layers of cheese and lemon pepper. It smelled heavenly.

Greg's guests retreated inside his home to take shelter from the wind, but I stood outside next to the grill, sipping from a bottle of Alaskan White Ale. A radio blared, and Greg squinted into the smoke of the grease that dripped onto the coals. I asked if he needed a hand with anything.

"No—well, here. Take this inside," he said, and handed me a plate piled high with hotdogs and hamburgers. "Oh! And Penny told me you two are veggies. So, these two on the end are veggie burgers, and be sure to take some green onions, too."

"You mean, the leeks?"

"Oh, hell, whatever it is—the green things."

I carried the plate to the house. Someone saw that my hands were full and opened the door for me. I walked into the sunken living room and put the plate on a long table set with chips and baked beans and various condiments. People formed a line. A gray and black husky smelled the meat and barked. Greg's wife, Susan, pointed her finger and scolded the dog, then smiled and ruffled the hair on his head.

Penny gave me a peck on the lips. "Did you get a veggie burger?" she asked.

I pointed to the table, but a woman with a blonde braid had discovered them. She stabbed one with her fork and put it on the plate of a boy who stood next to her. She shuffled the other burger onto her own plate. I was secretly grateful.

Penny shrugged. "Maybe he has more on the grill."

"It's okay. I don't mind."

"You sure? You should check."

I did not want to draw attention to myself over something as silly as meat avoidance, so I kissed Penny's cheek, filled my plate with macaroni, beans, and a hamburger bun, and went back out to the grill. The song on the radio was a new release by Gillian Welch called "Look at Miss Ohio" from the album *Soul Journey*. Wistful and melancholy, the chorus resonated with me:

> I know all about it, so you don't have to shout it
> I'm gonna straighten it out somehow
> Yeah, I wanna do right but not right now.

Greg popped a pill into his mouth and washed it down with a swig of Arkose beer. The pill came from an amber-colored prescription bottle.

I pointed at the bottle. "What's up?"

"Oh, it's these damn migraines."

"I take ibuprofen for mine."

"Yeah." He did not elaborate and flipped the last four burgers on the grill. "Did you get your veggie burger?"

I told him what happened. He chuckled and said those were the only two he had.

"It's okay. I'll have one of those."

He scooped a hamburger off the grill, delivered it to the bun on my plate, and told me to be more aggressive next time. I added a dollop of sauce—Greg's recipe of relish, vinegar, ketchup, salt, and pepper. The meaty, juicy ground beef tasted better than I remembered, and I complimented him on it.

The wind kicked up again, and we watched the trees. The dark-green leaves of the balsam poplars tossed and shook, and a small bird darted out. It could have landed on solid ground to get its bearing, but it chose instead to fly up to a small branch and endure the heaves and swirls of random forces. The bird resembled a wheatear. I pointed to it and turned to Greg, but his face had a dour cast, as though he saw something I did not, something ominous.

I felt a nervous chill, so I said the first thing that came to mind. "I love these long days."

He snapped out of his fog and appraised the burgers, sizzling. "Like they say, you only get two seasons in Alaska—winter and July."

We chuckled and drank our beer. But the joke was forced, as was my laughter. Both were ways of avoiding deeper issues.

"It goes fast—faster than you think," he said, and pointed his bottle at the bird. "It won't be long now."

CHAPTER 25

Captain America

HIGH SUMMER HAD arrived in Alaska. Students and instructors swarmed the branch, and Penny struggled to feed everyone as well as supply rations for outgoing courses. She and I shared her room and her bed, but we saw each other only late in the evenings and early in the mornings. Everyone was exhausted. By late July, however, most groups had left for the field, and Penny could take a short break. She needed to unwind, so she enrolled in a weeklong art class in the town of Homer, which was almost three hundred miles away. I rented a plane and flew her over.

"Jewel grew up here. Did you know that?" she asked.

I filled a Styrofoam cup with coffee at the Homer air terminal. "Who?"

"The singer, Jewel."

Jewel was a female singer-songwriter popular in the late '90s and early 2000s. I had heard some of her songs, such as "Foolish Games" and "You Were Meant for Me," on the radio, and I liked them, but I was hardly a devoted fan.

"She's from Homer?"

"Well, outside of town, I think," said Penny. "The house she grew up in didn't have plumbing, so they used an outhouse."

"I can relate to that."

Homer is situated at the western tip of the Kenai Peninsula on the Gulf of Alaska. Like Alaska itself, Homer is replete with logos extolling its magnificence, such as halibut fishing capital of the world, where the land ends and the sea begins, and the end of the road, where it anchors the southernmost point on the Alaskan Highway System.

After sharing a coffee in the air terminal, we kissed good-bye, and I flew back to Palmer.

The following week, I packed my Ford Escort with camping gear and some of Penny's belongings, too, and drove back to Homer. Excited to explore the area, we rented a tandem sea kayak so we could tour Kachemak Bay. For three days and two nights, we watched salmon wriggle up streams, puffins roost along the shore, and even a pod of killer whales crest across the bay. Loon yodels crooned us to sleep at night and awakened us in the morning.

On the second day, we went ashore on a deserted, pebbly beach. Our map showed a route called Grace Mountain Trail that wound through forests of hemlock and Sitka spruce to a low summit. We anchored the kayak and hiked up. At one thousand feet above sea level, we passed through the tree line, where the forest gave way to thickets of wild salmonberries, cranberries, and watermelon berries, and we picked them and ate them as we climbed higher. Penny spied a family of martens at play on a swathe of spongy sphagnum moss, and we laughed as the martens raced and tumbled.

We made it to the top in less than an hour. From the summit, we saw Cook Inlet, the entire Kenai Peninsula, and the eastern edge of the eight-hundred-mile-long Alaska Peninsula. Lush valleys descended to the sea from snowcapped peaks, and the salty marine air blended with the resinous alpine breezes. Runoff from the Grewingk Glacier turned the water zinc-gray and merged with the turquoise of the Cook

Inlet and the open Pacific beyond. The view was Olympian. We sat on the alpine tundra and took it all in.

A clicking-whistling sound caught our attention.

"Do you hear that?" asked Penny.

"Birds?"

"There. See them?"

We squinted into the low sun. Two birds perched on a rocky outcrop quilted with forget-me-nots and saxifrage. One bird was gray with black wings and a yellow throat. The other was tan. A black coloration that resembled a mask extended across the face of both birds.

"I think those are wheatears," she said, "a male and a female."

I squinted and remembered. "Yes."

"You know birds?"

"No. Not really." They cackled and whistled at each other and paid no attention to us. "But I remember seeing that kind in Africa."

"Each summer, they migrate up here, farther than any other bird, something like twenty thousand miles round trip."

"Do you know why?"

"All I know is they breed up here, and then they fly back to Africa for the winter." She shook her head. "I think they're nuts."

The two birds hopped around. It was almost eleven o'clock, and the setting sun framed them behind the rock and illuminated Penny's face with orange light. A breeze blew a lock of black hair across her face. She tucked it behind an ear.

"Oh, I don't know about that," I said.

She chuckled. "You are so corny."

I leaned over and nibbled her ear. "It rhymes with *corny*."

"Hey, that reminds me. Did you hear about that football player?"

The abrupt change of subject stung me, but I tried not to show it. "Who?"

"You know, the one who joined the Army."

"You mean, Pat Tillman?"

"That's him. I heard he's part of the Iraqi invasion, and the media are following him right into combat."

"Like Captain America or something."

She chuckled at my vapid humor, restoring a notch of my confidence.

"No, but get this," she said. "They're calling it Operation Iraqi Freedom."

"Well, that sounds happy, and we Americans will buy it—literally." I shook my head. "Iraq is the poorest, weakest nation in that region, no weapons of mass destruction—beyond what Reagan gave them, anyway—and no one's really sure what we're doing there, but nobody's asking that question."

"Oil," said Penny emphatically.

"Of course. And every good president needs his war, you know. Maybe Bush wants to finish his dad's war, too. I remember after the Gulf War hearing Bush senior say America had finally kicked its Vietnam Syndrome, something like that. Like we had absolved ourselves of failure and—"

"And all those nutty hippy movements that fought for women's rights, civil liberties, and environmental protection."

We sat in silence, lamenting the state of the world. Slowly, the birds and the scenery melted our qualms and made us smile again.

I leaned close to Penny and nodded toward the courting wheatears. "I think they have the right idea."

She reached over and held my hand. "There's something I need to tell you. Something I should have already told you."

I sat up.

Her forehead tightened, but she continued to watch the wheatears. "I've been careful, but I want you to know there's no problem." She sighed and petted my hand. "I might have herpes."

My eyes opened wider than I intended. "You mean . . ."

She nodded. "That kind. But it was such a long time ago, and it hasn't reoccurred, and the doctor said that if I watch my diet and take care of myself, I'd be fine. And I am fine. But we should still be careful, and . . ." She motioned to her daypack. "I didn't bring—"

"I have one." I was relieved we had always used condoms. I now hoped that showing strength in the face of adversity, like a Captain America, would prove my love.

"You think it's—"

"It's brand new."

She hesitated, and I was ready to shrug it off and start our descent, when she stood and took off her clothes. I took mine off, too. There, on the tundra next to the wheatears and the saxifrage and forget-me-nots, we affirmed our love under an endless Alaskan sky.

And then the sun went down.

CHAPTER 26

Trophies

"LET'S CALL IT twelve hundred even," said the man seated behind the desk.

Clouds covered the sky, and the fluorescent lights inside the building were turned off, which made it dim. The place smelled of oil and half-rotted meat, though the cool temperatures dampened the odors.

As my eyes adjusted, I saw shelves of tools, aerosol paint cans, and an old airplane fuselage. On one wall, an American flag hung next to a tier of trophy heads: two moose, a grizzly bear, a black bear, a caribou, and two wolves. A Mossberg rifle poster was tacked to the wall under one of the moose heads. The poster showed a man on horseback dressed in camouflage with a rifle slung over his shoulder, while a packhorse trailed behind with an impressive rack of elk antlers strapped atop panniers. Spectacular mountain scenery filled the poster's background and reminded me of the movie *Jeremiah Johnson*, starring Robert Redford. Capitalizing on more recent events, the tagline on the poster read, BEHIND EVERY REVOLUTION IS A PATRIOT, the name of Mossberg's newly Christened weapon.

My dad would love this place, I thought.

The wolf heads and the poster brought to mind Senate Bill 155, recently signed into action by Governor Frank

Murkowski. The bill allowed hunters to shoot wolves from helicopters, which would make more caribou and moose available for hunters. I wondered if state officials realized this would weaken the ungulate gene pool. I also wondered if they saw the irony in calling aerial wolf hunting "predator control."

At the national level, verbiage in the USA PATRIOT Act, signed into law on November 26, 2001, made it a felony to "protest the actions of a . . . corporation" engaged in the exploitation of animals or natural resources. In the broadest interpretation of this clause, a person could be accused of being unpatriotic or even considered a terrorist if they questioned interests associated with hunting, mining, or animal or crop agriculture.

It impressed me how the meaning of the words *predator* and *patriot* had nearly merged in the American vernacular. *Patriot* comes from the Latin root *pater* for father, and *patria* for fatherland. *Patria* is also the root of the Latin *patriarchalis*, or patriarchal. This term is often invoked to describe male-dominated social systems, such as exists in the United States and most nations today, as well as in many religions, in particular Islam and Christianity.

The man behind the desk growled to clear his throat. Penny nudged me.

"Sorry. How much?"

"Twelve hundred dollars." He said it slower this time before spitting chew-juice into a repurposed Coke can. His Carhartt coat was stained and frayed at the wrists, and his overalls struggled to manage his girth. Temperatures hovered in the forties, and the roller-doors on his hangar-garage stood wide open, though the man's thick black beard no doubt insulated his face. He struck me as the quintessential Alaskan outdoorsman. However, his primary trade was automotive maintenance. In previous years, he had installed engine block heaters in NOLS vehicles and in Penny's 4Runner, and with winter approaching, she urged me to get a heater as well as studded tires installed on my Ford Escort.

I pulled the checkbook out of my puffy blue down coat and leaned onto his desk to write the check. My hand shook with nerves as I wrote, and I did not know why. To distract him, I pointed my pen at the heads on the wall. "I see you hunt." It sounded dumb after I said it.

"All my life," he said. "Moose, mostly." A black Labrador Retriever laid his head on the man's thigh. The man stroked the dog's head.

I signed my name on the check and handed it to him. He took it and swiveled in his chair toward the heads.

"Now that one there," he said, as he sniffed and pointed to a moose with antlers six feet across, "the head's about all I saved of that son of a bitch." Dusty spider webs spanned the antlers.

"What happened?" asked Penny. She bent down to pet the dog, which had come around to investigate us.

"Oh, me and some buddies was up at Resurrection Creek." He turned back to us, squinting into the fading gray light. "Up in the Chugach."

Penny nodded, but I did not know the place. The dog nosed my crotch, and I pushed him aside, but he kept at it. Grizzly Man paid no attention.

"Anyways, we was up there huntin' moose, and I got this big son of a bitch, fifteen hundred pounds, right next to the cabin we was stayin' in. Huge bastard! But I didn't need it all, so we decided to divvy him up and take him out the next day on four-wheelers. Until then, we hung him in a tree. Well, that night, goddamned bear comes in, big son of a bitch, and tears him down and starts eatin' on him and maulin' the shit out of him. So, I shot the bastard."

Grizzly Man straightened in his creaky chair like he had just won an award and pointed to the bear's head. "That's him there," he said, and cackled. The head was mounted over a large *Sports Illustrated* swimsuit calendar that had not yet been turned from August to September. It portrayed an African American woman on a beach wearing a chef's hat and a red bikini. She used a stainless-steel fork to turn a steak in the flames of a grill. The title at the top of the calendar read DARK MEAT.

"Well, you do what you gotta do," said Penny.

"Yeah, them's my trophies," he said, and pushed my keys across the desk, staring into my eyes, but motioning toward Penny. "I guess she's your trophy, bud."

I blinked and glanced up at the bear and Miss August. Penny laughed again, but it was hollow and sounded as if she had practiced that laugh for so long and in so many situations, since before she could remember, that it came off without thinking, automatically, so that even she had convinced herself it was genuine.

I had occasionally heard the term *trophy wife*, usually used with reference to a younger, attractive woman married to an older, wealthy white man. Like a hunter who mounts an animal's head on a wall, the older man gets to show off the younger woman's body and the prestige that displaying her garners him. In return, she acquires a portion of his wealth. The transaction struck me as similar to that portrayed in the photos of military men and their wives the recruiter had shown me all those years ago.

I took my keys off the desk.

"We really appreciate it," said Penny.

Grizzly Man smiled. For a second, he resembled a teddy bear more than an outdoorsman. "Well, you know you're always welcome around here, Sugar. Just come on back any old time."

Penny and I walked out of the hangar-garage to our respective cars. The dog barked and capered behind us.

"Samson!" shouted the man. "Get back here!"

I continued to work at the airport on weekends, but I had not flown since our trip to Homer. I missed flying, yet I was too busy to notice its absence. On Mondays, Wednesdays, and Fridays, I grabbed a bagel and drove to Anchorage to teach at Alaska Pacific University. After grading homework, I went to Peak Fitness, worked out, and then taught classes from seven to nine o'clock at Matanuska-Susitna College. I was exhausted when I got back to the branch at ten and squeezed into bed between Penny and Lucky. She had barely touched me since Kachemak Bay.

In late September, we went for a walk, and I asked her what was wrong. Had I said something? Had I upset her?

"It's not you," she said.

"Then what? Let me help."

She grew quiet and gazed across the carrot fields.

This was the edge of the Kellogg Estate, and carrots had been harvested the previous week for the Alaska State Fair. The fair was held every fall in Palmer, and Penny and I had gone to see the fifteen-pound carrots and hundred-pound cabbages, jewelry made from bones and antlers, and all the quilts and carvings. The fairgrounds had been cold and smelled like manure. People already wore coats and fur-lined boots.

The fields of the Kellogg Estate now seemed bare and lifeless under gray skies. We walked without talking. Penny was never chatty, but she had become positively mute, and I wracked my brain. The season at the branch was over. Could it be her job? Her studies? Kurt? Someone else? I reminded her that she could tell me anything, because I loved her and she loved me, and we wanted to build a home together.

"Oh! I meant to tell you," she said. "It's so sad."

A mixture of relief and fear rippled through me.

"It's Greg. They found out he has a brain tumor."

I covered my mouth. "No."

"You probably know, he's had these terrible headaches for months, so they ran some tests and found out it's cancer. Goddamned toxins are everywhere. You can't get away from them." Her eyes filled with tears, but none ran down her cheeks.

I had seen an article posted at the Palmer Public Library stating that Alaska scored higher than the national average for nearly every type of cancer. This prevalence was likely due to an array of toxins that circulated to the poles via wind and water, as well as local fossil-fuel residues and petrochemical fertilizers. A footnote in the article pointed out that Alaska tended to attract people with individualistic, heedless attitudes, which might also play a part.

"Anyway," she said, "Greg and Susan are flying to Seattle to start treatments there."

"I'm sorry. I didn't know." I was stunned. I reeled between this news and our earlier non-conversation. We reached the end of the field and came out on Farm Loop Road, which led back to the branch.

"There's something else I need to tell you," she said. "I've decided to take a little trip."

"Okay?"

"I'm going to see my mom in New Jersey and then my brother in London. I'll be with him and his wife for Thanksgiving."

"When do you leave?"

"Monday."

"This Monday?"

"I know," she said. "I should have told you sooner. But I talked to some friends who need a pet sitter. They're travelling to the Lower 48, and I think it might be best if you stayed at their house while I'm gone."

"Because of Kurt?"

"Yeah—Kurt, and Don and Donna. You know, I work there, so my rent's next to nothing. But you don't, so when I'm gone . . ."

The cool, moist blacktop dampened the sound of our shoes, but a cacophony of emotions raged inside me. I felt deceived, cornered, like a trophy kill. I wanted to remind her I had rented my own cabin until she invited me to move in with her and suggested we buy a home together, at which point I discovered I needed a more stable income. But I said none of that and instead asked about my prearranged future.

"So, who are these friends?"

"They asked me to house-sit for them. I've done it before, but I told them you need a place to stay."

"Where is it?"

"Chickaloon."

CHAPTER 27

The Principle of Drag

JEANNIE AND DENISE were a lesbian couple who lived several miles up a dirt road near the town of Chickaloon, Alaska, population 217. Although they were skeptical of me, a man, their manner was gentle and gracious, and Penny persuaded them to entrust me with the care of their home for two months while they were away.

Denise had a Ph.D. in environmental engineering and was scheduled to give a lecture tour in the Lower 48, promoting sustainable living and home design. Jeannie would accompany her. Their home modeled their worldview: a pump automatically irrigated an indoor vegetable garden using household gray water; window space was compact but strategically placed to capture passive solar heat and light; high R-value cellulose (from newspaper) insulated the ceiling and walls; and the bathroom was equipped with a composting toilet. They had no satellite dish or cable TV, and their television played only VHS recordings. Their house did, however, draw electricity from the grid, so they had purchased a diesel generator in case the power failed.

I moved in on October 1. My primary jobs were to monitor the automated home systems and take care of Cheeks the cat and Sally the dog, a little German shepherd mix. Chickaloon was a forty-minute drive east of Palmer, which made my morning commute to Anchorage that much longer. On school days, I got up at five in the morning to walk the dog on a dirt road in the woods, feed her, feed the cat, feed myself, and hit the road by six. The class I taught started at eight.

By now, the birch, willow, and alder trees along the way had lost their leaves and stood naked and cold, and spruces appeared sickly with tops that drooped like dead flowers. Brown leaves twirled in the wind, going nowhere. The sky hung gray and bleak, while the ever-expanding night stiffened into needles of cold that pierced my thermal underwear and seeped into my bones.

I did not understand how Penny's love for me could evaporate in a few weeks. If only I had a clue, something I could hang onto, I would be okay. But there was no reference point, no up or down, left or right. My talisman—or what it represented—was all I had left. I began to wonder if the Nairobi thief's declaration was true: "This is nothing."

After evening classes, I would drive back to Chickaloon, walk Sally again, check on Cheeks, microwave something to eat, and crawl into bed. On Tuesdays and Thursdays, I graded homework and made lesson plans. When I worked at the kitchen table, Sally curled around my feet and Cheeks lay in my lap, and I petted her until she purred and in a way seemed more human—or at least more humane—than most humans. When I played my guitar and sang the song I wrote for Penny, I cried; Cheeks and Sally cuddled close, as if they knew. They were my only company, my only friends.

I continued to work at Mustang on weekends. Late in October, the airport hosted a barbeque fly-in, celebrating the centenary of the Wright Brothers' first flight in Kitty Hawk, North Carolina. (That flight actually occurred on December 17, 1903, but Jacquie decided it was more sensible to hold an

outdoor party in October.) I manned the grill, roasting hotdogs and hamburgers. But I had not flown in months. I was
not certain I wanted to continue flying, or if I just wanted
to land somewhere and confront all the shadows I had been
struggling to outdistance. I was so tired. Something inside me
was about to crash.

Harley did not attend the barbeque, and no one mentioned
him until I met Ben a few days later at the Valley Coffee Shop
in Palmer. He told me Harley had suffered a heart attack.

"I thought you knew. We all thought you knew," he said,
and ran his finger around the rim of his coffee cup.

"Is he—"

"Dead?" said Ben, and he chuckled. "Old Harley's too
grumpy to go that easy. He's at home with his wife now, but
we probably shouldn't call him or bother him. He needs his
rest."

"Of course." I sipped my coffee, guilty that I might have
caused his blood pressure to spike.

Ben was in the middle of his first semester at the University
of Alaska and said his engineering classes were intense and
left him little time to fly. When he asked about my commercial license and Penny, I told him everything. He was the first.

"I'm sorry," he said. "I know how much she means to you."

I stared out the window. It had snowed all day, and plows
with flashing yellow lights heaped dirty snow along the streets.

"What will you do?" he asked.

"I can't stay here—unless she changes her mind. And she
won't."

"Do you think you'll fly again?"

"I don't know. I've almost got my CPL, but I don't care
anymore."

Nothing had ever hit me so hard: not the plane crash, the
beating, Rachel and Steve's betrayal, the fall on the Grand

Teton, my divorce, my parents' divorce—not even a trag-
edy that struck close in the Peace Corps, when I lost a dear
friend. At that time, a fresh outlook helped me make sense of
everything. But since then, I had increased my velocity, which
also increased an effect in aviation known as parasitic drag.
It drained me, emptied me, and I lost altitude.

The next day was Halloween. After classes, I returned
"home" at ten in the evening and took care of Cheeks and
Sally and put a beef burrito in the microwave oven. I had
intentionally purchased a meat product at Carr's grocery
store that was manufactured from parts of an animal—
likely many. Now its saturated fats, cholesterol, acids, and
carcinogens would damage my own body. In this way, I
could exert some tiny degree of control over my life. I hoped
the burrito had been filled with parts of a bull, hung on a
rack, and skinned alive to die slowly, as often happens—a
big, angry, muscular bull—so I might ingest its anger and
strength. Or better yet, a cow, a female that had been raped
with a semen gun to produce veal, then executed, dismem-
bered, and consumed.

I set the timer and started the microwave. Sally and Cheeks
watched me from across the room. People would incur fines
and jail terms for committing such acts on dogs and cats as
happens every day to millions of cows, pigs, chickens, sheep,
and even fish. Although in those latter cases, we turn our
heads and say it's necessary, even scripturally condoned.

The beef burrito was turning on the plate in the microwave when the phone rang. Caller ID showed a New York
number. Thinking it might be Jeannie or Denise, I cleared my
throat and picked up the receiver.

"Bill! Hey, it's Penny!"

I heard music and voices in the background.

"Can you hear me?" she shouted.

"Yeah! How—how are you?"

"Great! I'm great! Mom's great, too. She's fine. Anyway, I'm at a pub here in New York with friends, and the *streets are packed!*"

My interests collided. She sounded happy, and I was glad yet jealous and hurt at the same time.

"Bill?"

"Yes! That's . . ." I heard a pause and lots of people and noise in the background. I wracked my brain for conversation.

"Anyway," she said, "I just had the *best* pastrami sandwich ever! You would have loved it, except it was meat. But hey, when in Rome!"

"Pastrami?"

"Yeah, it's like lunch meat, some kind of bird, turkey, I think."

"Hey, that reminds me, I saw a bird today over on—"

"What? Kurt? You saw Kurt?"

"No, a *bird!*"

"Oh! A bird. Well."

"Yeah, like one of those wheatears we saw in Homer. Remember?" I hoped to force her to recall our last intimate episode.

Instead, she laughed. "No, no, no. They're long gone. They left months ago."

Blood drained from my face, and for an instant I wished I could have flown away with the wheatears to Africa, but the shame and the thought of Rachel squelched my fantasy. The weight of the moment dragged me down along the kitchen cabinet, until I sat on the floor.

"Anyway, you should see me! I have this costume!" She slurred her words.

"Costume?"

"Yeah! I'm wearing these pointy ears and black lingerie and a black tail! So, I'm like a *sex kitten*! Is that nuts?" Pause. "Did you hear me? I said I'm a—"

"Yes! I . . . I heard you."

She laughed. "And this guy, he has this mask like Nixon or Reagan or something! And he was trying to eat me! Ha! Is that nuts?" Pause. "Bill?"

"Yeah! That's. . . . So, when do you leave for London?"

"Oh, God. Shut up! My brother—whoops! Hey, you freak!" she shouted.

"You okay?"

She laughed again. "Yeah! No, it's just the Reagan guy. He grabbed my tail!"

I said nothing.

"Hey, I better go!" she shouted. "Say hi to Lucky for me. I'll see you in about a month!"

"Is there a number I can—"

"Bye!" She hung up.

The bell dinged on the microwave. The little packet of flesh was warm again and ready to be consumed.

CHAPTER 28

Blood Sport

FOR THIRTY MINUTES, three times each week, Headline News updated me on world affairs while I rode the StairMaster at Peak Fitness. In November 2003, CNN announced that inspectors had failed to find any weapons of mass destruction (WMDs) in Iraq, although administration officials maintained that the Iraqi regime intended to develop them. Meanwhile, coalition forces bombed Baghdad, and so far, 480 US troops and about 14,000 Iraqis—including 5,000 civilians—had been killed. Americans demanded vengeance, and it mattered little whether the fatalities were terrorists or civilians, Afghanis or Iraqis. In fact, all dark-skinned people—even US citizens—could be labeled "the enemy," and anyone from South Asia or North Africa was deemed a "sand nigger" or "towel head."

Some news reports—not the headlines—reminded us that the Reagan administration had supplied the Afghan Mujahideen with weapons to fight the Soviets back in 1983. By 1994, the Mujahideen had evolved into the Taliban. Meanwhile, the CIA funded and trained another Islamist organization called Al-Qaeda and its leader, Osama bin Laden. Now, the newly minted "War on Terrorism" sounded like a plausible enough reason to lock the globe into a cycle of fear, hatred, and violence that could shift attention from the cause of the disease to its symptoms.

Somali warlords began referring to Americans as "war masters," and Afghani civilians dubbed our military "The American Taliban." We had become that which we opposed. But no matter: corporations such as Halliburton and Lockheed Martin (and restaurant chains like Burger King and Dairy Queen located on military bases) posted wartime profits of close to $12 billion per year. Killing faceless terrorists was a military-industrial blood sport that ensured a steady flow of prosperity, and more faceless terrorists.

In 2004 alone, the US military spent $400 billion, nearly half the world's total military budget. By 2015, that figure would grow to nearly $600 billion. According to the Global Energy Network Institute, an annual expenditure of $237.5 billion over ten years could provide global health care; eliminate starvation and malnutrition; provide clean drinking water and shelter for everyone; stop deforestation and anthropogenic climate change, ozone depletion, and acid rain; remove landmines; decommission nuclear weapons; resolve the debts of developing nations; produce clean energy; solve overpopulation; eliminate illiteracy; and essentially eradicate the motivations for terrorism. If only we preferred it.

But how could we prefer it if we did not know about it? As trillions of dollars bled out onto the deserts of Iraq and Afghanistan, twenty-one US states cut funding for higher education to help reduce the national debt. (Alaska and South Dakota awarded zero dollars for undergraduate student aid in 2001–2002. This occurred in the wake of a 1999 Department of Defense audit that revealed $2.3 *trillion* in Pentagon spending that could not be accounted for.)

After thirty minutes on the StairMaster, I climbed down and toweled the sweat off my face and neck. As I stretched,

CNN summarized the day's top stories: the US economy had rebounded, the Catholic Church agreed to pay $85 million to victims of sexual abuse committed by priests in Boston, and Arnold Schwarzenegger had been elected governor of California. The take-home message was clear: violence builds empires powered by capitalism, monotheism, and chauvinism. We called it patriotism.

It was seven o'clock on a Saturday evening, and Mustang Air had closed for the day. No one was around. I counted the till, shut down the computer, and locked the doors. But before I left, I made a phone call. I had been rehearsing it all day. I even scribbled down some notes, so I would not forget. I did not know why I needed to do it, only that it was important to me. But I was nervous, and I chewed on the inside of my mouth as I dialed the number.

Grizzly Man answered. "Your block heater okay?" he asked. I pictured him sitting in his garage-hangar with his dog, his mounted heads, and his gut.

"I haven't used it yet. But the studded tires work well in the snow."

He laughed lightly and waited. I chewed harder on a patch of skin at the corner of my mouth, inside my cheek. It started to bleed.

"Did you need something?" he asked.

My heart pounded. I tasted the blood from the corner of my mouth. "No. I just wanted to call and say I thought it was too bad about your moose hunt up in the Chugach." I struggled with the words.

"You mean that moose we lost."

"Well, that, too. But I mean it's too bad about that bear that came into your camp."

"Yeah, like I say, the bastard ruined the meat before we got out there with our guns, me with my .338 Weatherby, and I just lined him right up on his—"

"*Come on!*" He had given me the prompt I needed. "You know as well as I do, you cannot hang anything dead outside in bear country. That's just stupid. But you weren't being stupid, because you were intentionally baiting bears so you'd have a chance to kill one and claim defense of property, or whatever you call it."

He cackled on the other end. "Shit-fire, boy. What do you think you're gonna do with that kind of meat out there anyway? Bury it? Hang it in a tree?"

"No! Because people really don't need to hunt anymore. Especially in the United States, where we eat enough food to make us sick."

He whooped. "Hell, you go and tell that to the Natives!"

"The Natives . . . they do what they do. But times have changed, and maybe they'll have to change, too."

He laughed long and slow, as if giving himself time to consider whether to argue a point or simply tell me off. "Son, you can just pull up your big-girl panties now, cause I'm gonna say this real slow so you understand it: *People. Eat. Meat.* It's always been that way, and that's a goddamned fact. You cannot have life without death."

"Unless it's *cruel* death, which cheapens life, because it's unnecessary."

"Let me tell *you* what's *necessary*. If a bear or a wolf or a goddamned environmentalist gets in my way, I will run the barrel of my gun right up his ass and ask questions later!"

"Hunting is just blood sport that makes people feel manly and strong, because they're afraid they're not."

"And you, sir, *are an asshole!*"

"Would you shoot your dog and eat him?"

"I'll tell you who I will shoot! 'Cause if you ever set foot—"

I hung up. My heart raced, and I felt hot but elated, too, like good had triumphed over evil, even though I had not changed his mind and probably provoked him to kill even more. Still, I had come clean with someone who represented control, domination, killing, consumption, and supremacy.

High on adrenaline, I left Mustang Air and decided to treat myself. I had recently overheard two guys at the gym talking about the food at RW's Hamburger House—roast beef, BLTs, cheeseburgers, and more. They called it "meat porn."

A banner in front of the restaurant read, WELCOME HUNTERS! I went in anyway. I was tired of burritos and Hamburger Helper (because hamburger needs help) and thought I deserved a real burger for standing up for myself. I still shook from the excitement of the phone call.

The restaurant's decor was homey and simple and themed with race cars. I sat at a table next to a log-sided wall and ordered a vanilla shake, a cheeseburger cooked medium rare, and French fries. I emphasized "French" when making my order.

A white Chevy Blazer pulled up and parked outside. One of its headlights was out. A man wearing no coat or hat got out and came into the restaurant. His face was haggard, and he seemed edgy. He looked familiar, but I could not place him, and as he sat down he stumbled as though drunk and looked around to see if anyone noticed.

Then he saw me. He glanced at me again and took notice of my fleece pullover, the blue Patagonia down coat on the back of my chair, and maybe my necklace, too. He covered his face with his hands and rubbed his forehead. I tried to ignore him.

A waitress brought my food. It revived the aromas of Sunday lunches after church when I was a boy, which made me feel comfortable and safe again—until I remembered the cookout at Greg's, and his cancer diagnosis.

A sprig of parsley rested at the edge of my plate. As a boy, I learned such greenery was called a garnish. It was considered a decoration, and people should not eat it. I would later learn that plant foods in our culture are often the source of disparaging language. A person who cares for the environment might be tagged a "granola head," and a mentally unbalanced person is considered "nutty," a "fruitcake," or "fruity," which is also an antiquated, pejorative term for a gay person. And if a person suffers an illness or injury that renders them comatose, they are said to have become a "vegetable" or to have entered a "vegetative state." All are disdained and subconsciously associated with the feminine.

As I brought the burger to my mouth and prepared to sink my teeth into its juicy, bloody goodness, the man across the room shouted at me.

"Hey, you!"

My jaws hovered around the burger.

"You're an *environmentalist*, aincha?" He gave special attention to the word *environmentalist*, branding it with a gall and venom that implied he had suffered at the hands of a green organization, perhaps over land appropriations, hunting fines, restrictions on oil jobs. Who could say?

Patrons at the other tables turned to look.

"You're one of *them*!" he shouted, and dropped his hands to the table. "Bet you're a goddamned *feminazi*, too!" *Feminazi* is another pejorative term, a combination of the words *feminist* and *Nazi* used to denote a militant, radical feminist. Talk-show host Rush Limbaugh popularized the use of this word in the early 1990s.

I backed away from the burger and smiled and shook my head at the man, indicating I was none of those things. I just wanted to eat my dinner. So, with preoccupation, I opened my mouth and bit into the burger, sensing the heat, congealed fats, and perhaps the blood. But I did not taste it.

A waitress shouted at the man from the kitchen. "Cut it out, Bill!"

The shout startled me. He and I shared the same first name, and for an instant I felt as if all my bluffs and self-deceptions had been exposed.

I could see what was about to happen, so I chewed quickly and swallowed. Setting the hamburger on my plate, I opened my hands in a friendly gesture, my last attempt to defuse the man's anger.

"You're one of them *fuckers*, aincha?" he said.

He stood up, tipping his table over. The top of the ketchup bottle popped off and a glop of red splattered onto the floor. People shouted. Some cringed, others charged. I jumped to my feet. The waitress and two others rushed in from my left. I saw they would intercept him before he got to me, but I grabbed the small, metal saltshaker off my table and closed my fist around it, just in case. The assault in Uhuru Park had taught me to be ready for anything. Still, I did not want to hurt this fellow.

He moved and raised his fist, but he was clumsy and drunk. The waitress, the cooks, and a patron tackled him. He struggled as they held him down.

"*Goddamn environmentalist!*" he shouted.

The waitress, middle-aged and heavy-set, laid across one of his arms. She yelled back to the kitchen. "Patty, call the police!"

"Bill," said a brawny cook to the man, "just calm down now. It's not worth it."

"He's drunk," said the waitress. "I smell it."

"*Goddamn it!*" shouted the man. He was unable to move and getting tired.

"I know," said the big cook, agreeing with him in a tone of resignation while holding down an arm.

"But, I'm *not*." I shook my head, trying to convince the cook and everyone that I wasn't drunk and had a right to be there.

The waitress leveled her gaze at me. "You better go."

It dawned on me the drunken man was right. I was a feminist. And on the basis of social justice, environmental ethics, and animal welfare, I could no longer harm animals. I glanced at the cheeseburger on my plate. An hour earlier, I had felt vindicated, even lofty; I now realized I had been a coward for far longer.

I never ate red meat again.

CHAPTER 29

The Hard Truth

LATE NOVEMBER, AND the snow was deep. Temperatures seldom climbed into the teens, and the land lay defeated under gray skies and dusk at midday. I plugged in the block heater on my Ford Escort every night.

Denise and Jeannie returned, and so did Penny. I was homeless, so she invited me to move back in with her until I could find other accommodations.

"But this is strictly as friends," she said. We had finished dinner—homemade sushi rolls of rice, cucumbers, carrots, and avocado—and we sat in the middle of a rug in her room. A snowstorm had hit, but we were warm, and it felt cozy. Penny played Ben Harper's album *Diamonds on the Inside*. The music was wistful and slow, and I liked it, until Harper sang the chorus to "Amen Omen":

> Amen omen, will I see your face again?
> Amen omen, can I find the place within
> To live my life without you?

"If you want, you can put your things in here or in the cabin next door," she said. "But the propane's out over there, so you shouldn't leave anything that might freeze."

"Right."

We sat and listened to Ben Harper and the people moving around downstairs. Kurt's behavior had improved, and he even started to greet me again at the Lower House, though in a glib manner. News traveled fast among the half-dozen people still at the branch, the headliner being that Penny and I had "crashed and burned." I suspected Kurt was behind the gossip, though it could have been Donna. She had always treated me with polite caution, but grew aloof after Penny and I began living in sin.

"And I guess," said Penny, glancing at her bed, "you could sleep in my bed, if you want. The floor is so cold."

My mind did somersaults trying to resolve the contradiction. "But, where would you sleep?"

"You know, it might be healthy for us to sleep in the same bed for a while. It might help us heal."

"By sleeping together?"

"Just as friends." Lucky curled into her lap, and she leaned down to kiss him on the head.

I still nursed a naïve hope, a masochistic impulse that believed we might yet have a chance. So, I moved in, and late that evening we switched off the light and turned away from each other under a fluffy, cotton comforter. For a long time, perhaps an hour, I listened to her breathe and felt the heat radiate from her body. Occasionally, she brushed against me when she moved, and the thought of her lying so close yet untouchable made me tense and fidgety. I hardly slept at all that night or the next. I was exhausted, and I looked it.

In the middle of the third night, she rolled over and spooned me. Although sleep deprived, I became immediately alert. She slipped her right arm across my chest, and I moved my right arm back to rest on her hip as nonchalantly as I could manage, and we lay there, motionless and warm. I convinced myself this might be my last chance to show her my love and my faith in our future.

Her arm stayed wrapped around me in a loose embrace as I turned to face her, and she slid her hand across my back and tickled me under my arm. I giggled and tickled her between her ribs, and she started to laugh, but in a whisper. We tickled each other until we began to laugh.

"Shh!" she whispered. "He'll wake up!"

Kurt's room was directly below hers. But I continued to tickle her despite her attempts to discourage me, and now I was on top of her, and she stopped laughing and instead grabbed at my hands and kicked me.

"Stop it!" she whispered.

Sleep-deprived, I craved her love and respect, so I could regain control over my life. Maybe she wanted me to fight for her, I thought, and like a warrior I should struggle to win her back using whatever force necessary.

I grabbed her hands and pushed them to the bed, but she was strong and freed an arm and grabbed at my talisman and yanked hard until the necklace broke.

"Get off!" she yelled, and boxed my right ear, the one that had been severed and stitched. The blow stung and filled my head with a high-pitched ring.

I jumped back and sat at the edge of the bed. As the haze in my mind cleared, I saw that I had crossed a line and reached a turning point.

Someone raced up the stairs from the kitchen and stopped outside the door. A light shone underneath.

"Penny?" It was Kurt.

"It's okay, Kurt," she said.

"Are you okay?"

"It's nothing. I'm fine."

"You sure?"

"Go back to bed."

The stairs creaked as he plodded down, and the light under the door blinked off.

The ringing in my ear subsided. I stood but did not turn around. "I'm sorry. I didn't—"

"Forget about it," she said, and I heard her sigh.

I took a blanket down from the closet, and as I went to curl up on the rug, I stepped on the talisman and flinched and hopped. It pierced the skin on my right foot, the one I had broken in my flight from an elephant. Penny said nothing. Neither did I.

A map covered the entire wall. For a state the size of Alaska, only a large-area, small-scale aeronautical chart could depict its vastness with the degree of detail required. I had gotten a coffee at Vagabond, and now I studied the wall map for Native villages, rivers, glaciers, and a hundred other things in the dim light that filtered through Venetian blinds on the opposite wall.

The fluorescent ceiling lights blinked on.

"You might want to see where you're going," said Ben, as he walked into the classroom at Mustang Air. Like always, he wore his ball cap, down jacket, and flannel shirt.

"Where you headed?" he asked.

"Not sure. How's school?"

"Final exams are in two weeks." He sat down on one of the long tables in the room, the kind with white plastic tops and folding metal legs.

"You ready?"

"I'll be ready. I'd rather fly," he said, and motioned toward the map. "Where are you thinking?"

I shrugged and pretended to scan the map. "I just need to clear my head."

"Penny?"

I nodded.

"Did you guys talk?"

"It doesn't matter."

"That sucks. But maybe it's something from her past that has nothing to do with you."

He was more perceptive than he knew, but I said nothing and focused on the Brooks Range in the far north of the map.

"So, what's next?" he asked. "Have you thought about where you'll go?"

"I don't know. I might finish my CPL, go back to Africa, do something important." The pain of Alaska was fresh and made me forget the pain of Africa. I was almost happy again, until I remembered the wheatears in Homer—the breeding pair.

"You sound like Tillman."

"Who?"

"The football player, the one who joined the Army."

The comparison irritated me. "What do you mean?"

"He thinks he's some kind of hero, part of some grand cause. But all he's really trying to do is prove he's a bigger man. That's why he joined the Army, to be a badass. Because he's afraid he's not."

"So, you think I want to be a badass?"

"All I'm saying is, I think you're holding onto something that keeps you between places. You never stop long enough to catch up with yourself. And sometimes it makes you do desperate things."

"Like Penny."

"Penny, Alaska, maybe Africa."

I was uncomfortable, so I laughed. Ben did not laugh, which made me more uncomfortable, and I hovered near the map, studying it, feeling self-conscious.

"I don't know about Africa," he said, finally, "but if you want to fly someplace remote in Alaska . . ." He walked over, and instead of the Brooks Range or the Bering Sea, he pointed to a spot almost due south on the southern tip of Kodiak Island. "There's an old World War II airstrip here called Miller Field. My dad flew us out there one time when I was a kid. There's nothing there, just a weather station and a dirt strip, so you could take the 172. I remember seeing walruses and huge bears, Kodiak bears."

"Except it'll be buried in snow this time of year, right?"

"Normally, but this winter's been dry. Anyway, I think that's the one for you."

"Why?"

"Something about an island; it's what you need." His expression grew concerned. "Just remember, there's a lot of open water out there, so top off your tanks and take a life vest, and I'll show you how to put cardboard over your oil cooler to keep it warm. Check NOTAMs, too, and watch for headwinds. Anything more than five knots, I wouldn't go. That's the hard truth. It'll make too much drag, slow you down, and you only have so much fuel. And one more thing—don't tell anybody. They might not like it."

CHAPTER 30

The Fifth Principle

I PULLED INTO Mustang at seven in the morning. It was mid-December, a time of year when the sun does not rise until 10:30 and barely clears the mountaintops before falling into darkness by 1:30 in the afternoon.

No one else was around, so I sat in my Ford Escort and let the motor run and the heater blow, while I listened to National Public Radio. The war coverage explained that UN Weapons Inspectors had failed to find any weapons of mass destruction. However, US Joint Special Operations Command (JSOC) had captured Saddam Hussein, who was on trial for aiding terrorists. The Iraqi Interim Government said it would execute him when it found him guilty.

I was aware of a psychological concept called projection, where a person despises another for something they fear and loathe within themselves. Perhaps, I thought, many in the United States feared trends in feminism, organic whole foods, apostasy, and homosexuality, and so projected those traits onto other nations, such as Iraq—whether its leaders had anything to do with 9/11 or not. As for me, I was ashamed that as a young man I had projected a loathing for the feminine within myself onto others in the form of passive sexism and active animal cruelty and violence. More recently, I had used Amy, Rachel, and Penny to avoid growing up, just as the United States has manipulated nearly every sovereign nation on Earth to maintain its vision of American Exceptionalism—because we are special and play by our own rules.

I turned off the radio and the engine, and for the first time in weeks I saw the Northern Lights, silent curtains of blues, reds, and greens, mingling and slithering across the heavens. They had been there when I walked Sally the dog in Chickaloon, and when I drove to Anchorage to teach, and then back again in the evenings. But I had never stopped to look.

I grabbed my duffle and went inside. I had packed food, water, and basic supplies—iodine tablets, a first aid kit, extra clothes, a sleeping bag, and a BIC lighter. I wore a Merino wool sweater with a thick cableweave. Penny had bought it for me while visiting her brother in England. She gave it to me for my birthday.

But I needed more, so I borrowed a blue life vest from a gear locker, sectional charts for Anchorage and Kodiak, and a plotter and flight computer. The weather report said the day would be sunny, with temperatures in the twenties and a dew point of 17°F. Winds were calm. Kodiak Airport sold gas, but it was 450 miles away, so I planned to stop in Homer on the way over to refuel.

"You goin' for a swim?"

I recognized the voice before I turned to see Harley in his CPO parka and US Navy ball cap, but his face had changed. It was drawn and sallow. I could tell he had lost weight, and he moved slower, too.

He motioned to the life preserver. "Or you just gonna wear it around town?" He was still crusty, but softer. Our altercation on the tarmac seemed like years ago.

"I heard about what happened—your condition. But I'm glad you're feeling better."

"Yeah, hell, they got me so full of pills I piss purple," he said, and grunted as he sat down on a stool on the other side of the office counter.

I was at a loss for words and made small talk. "So, are you flying today?"

He shook his head. "Can't. Doc said he's gotta run some tests before he gives me the all-clear."

I nodded.

"You still ain't answered my question," he said. "Where you headed?"

I shuffled my charts together. "Local. Maybe Cordova, along the coast." It was plausible, given the life vest.

He grunted, and his gaze drifted down to his hands, which rested on the countertop with the palms facing up. Then his eyes closed, and I could not tell if he was deep in thought or if he had fallen asleep. I was relieved to see his chest rise and fall when he breathed.

"Oh, hell," he said finally, and looked up from his hands. "I guess it's been a rough year for you, too."

I kept my personal life quiet, but it was a small town, and Ben must have talked. Not that I cared anymore.

"And just so you know," he continued, "I don't agree with what they say about Alaska—that it either loves you or it spits you out. But I do think it'll teach you something. And I'm not talking about tourists, God no, but the people who live up here, and that includes *cheechakos* like you."

Was this a white flag? Was he apologizing? Either way, it was hard for me to look him in the eyes.

"And hell, I don't know you," he said. "Other than you're a decent pilot, you're learning, but I'd trust you to fly me just about anywhere—except Anchorage."

I smiled and nodded, grateful for the levity. I suspected that since his heart attack, Harley had decided petty differences were unimportant, a lesson I hoped to learn, and one I hoped our country might learn, too, before circumstances demanded it.

"All I'll say is this, then I'll get out of your hair," he said. "It just seems to me you got something inside of you that needs out. We all see it. Hell, you're wound tighter than an eight-day clock, and you gotta let that pressure out." He spoke with authority and leaned over the counter and pointed at me. "'Cause if you don't, and I mean soon, you're gonna do some goddamn dumb shit that's gonna get you killed! And you are damn lucky it ain't happened yet." He shook his claw-finger at the scars on my head.

I might have felt like a boy being scolded. Yet I was no longer a boy, which turned his words into something more like guidance or counsel, strong counsel. I was coming down and growing up. I no longer feared crashing, because I was learning to let go. But I still lacked something.

"Let what out?"

"Whatever the hell it is that wants out of you!" he said, and glanced at my talisman as though he knew its story. His warning reminded me of Stanford, who urged me to "let it go." I had thought Stanford wanted me to return the talisman I stole more than three years earlier—before Alaska, Penny, Rachel, Omari Bob, the assault, and the crash. But I was wrong. He never meant the piece of B-17 bomber, and he never meant for me to return it to the mountaintop. Or if he did, the act would only symbolize a deeper truth—to let go of Neverland (grow up) and reveal the consciousness that had opened in me during the Peace Corps.

"Well, you best be goin'," said Harley. "And don't forget your parky. It's cold as hell out there."

He put out his hand. The gesture surprised me, but I met him halfway. He did not release his grip at once, but reached across with his other hand, holding the key to 868 India Uniform.

"I hope you understand," he said.

When I took the key, something inside of me switched off as something else switched on. I enjoyed flying. It had its moments, but it was not my passion, and, as Kabiru had expressed, it was often boring. Harley had seen it in me from day one.

I nodded but said nothing. I pulled on my warm hat, zipped my down coat, took my duffle and life vest, and walked around the counter to the steel door. Cold air rushed in when I walked out. A waning crescent moon sailed high overhead, and sheets of red translucent light folded across the sky, transmogrifying into streamers of indigo and green. The light show reflected in the Plexiglas windows of the airplanes parked on the apron.

The moon's glow and Northern Lights cast my shadow onto the icy black tarmac. The eclipsed area was dark and bent and resembled Omari Bob, or Harley, or perhaps my father, and I reached high as if to thank them, forgive them, and beg their forgiveness. We shared so much in common, far more than our trifling, mostly imagined, differences. Down deep, we all wanted the same things. We wanted friendship and dignity. We wanted clean water, clean air, healthy bodies, a healthy environment, and real food. We wanted world peace.

I reached higher, as high as I could, until my shadow assumed the form of a bird, perhaps a wheatear, coming down to land. And while those birds and I had each flown over the same landscapes, using the same principles of flight, our paths now diverged.

Gravity, the first principle, gives weight and value to life. It can bring great misfortune, which can yield great learning. It is the foundation principle and makes all of the others possible.

The second principle is lift. High and ebullient, it opens our vantage to the world and our place in it. However, at great altitudes, the details and reality of life below become obscure. We are tempted to stay aloft too long, because we are afraid of the truth on the ground, which might require us to change. Many of us have deceived ourselves into clinging to this principle at all cost.

Power is the third principle. In a social sense, it is the ability to control the thoughts and actions of others. But psychologically, the desire for power issues from a perceived lack of control over one's own life. The ego adjusts for this insecurity by dominating the lives of others, whether by concession or by force. For a time, excessive power allows us to overcome the realities of gravity, maintaining lift and the pleasures of loftiness.

However, the principle of drag curbs power. Drag is the shadow that accompanies the ego's endless appetite. To overcome drag, we fixate on gaining more and more power, which ultimately drains us of humanity and empties us of love.

These principles are not inherently right or wrong, up or down. They are merely unconscious. However, in our deepest collective soul there exists a fifth principle, which is consciousness. Consciousness is our true identity. It is the eternal present moment in which everything happens. Beyond all dualities, it alone enables us to fly with the intent to become more grounded.

The sign in Africa had read *chaguo ni lako*, and at last I had made my choice. But I was only able to make it after my psyche had grown up to become conscious—conscious that my true nature is shared with all people, all creatures, and Earth itself.

The tide is turning. Like never before, humanity is on the cusp of forging a new vision of reality that holds compassion, altruism, and humility in highest esteem. *Chaguo ni letu* (The choice is ours).

A New Level of Consciousness

I NEVER FLEW to Kodiak. After talking to Harley that morning and walking out onto the tarmac, I realized my flight was no longer necessary. Instead, I packed my Ford Escort LX wagon and migrated south to complete the journey that had started for me almost ten years earlier in Africa.

My first stop was Tucson, Arizona, where I took classes at the university, marched in pro-peace demonstrations, and volunteered at a soup kitchen. In March 2004, I received an email from Penny. She thought I should know that Greg had died from brain cancer. The news shocked me and reminded me of the poisons in our environment and in our processed foods.

I wrote back to her with condolences, and a week later I received a package containing homemade bread baked with the blueberries we had picked the previous summer on Hatcher Pass. Also in the package, she had enclosed wasabi, soy sauce, seaweed, and a bamboo sushi wrap. It was a peace offering and included a short note that said that she and Lucky had moved into a rental cabin outside Palmer, and they were happy. In closing the note, she wrote, "You're still searching for who you are. I hope you find it." She was right about my search. On a subliminal level, I had known who I was for several years. However, I refused to acknowledge that person until Penny deserted me, which emptied my ego of its power and forced me to crash into the hard reality of awareness. For this, I am forever grateful to her.

In May, I packed my car and drove back to Lander. On the way, I learned that Army Ranger Pat Tillman had died. The Army initially reported that enemy combatants in Afghanistan had killed Tillman, but new information revealed he died from so-called friendly fire, a detail the Bush administration had concealed. The entire story—from why Tillman joined the Army to what he believed he fought and died for—was too sad to bear.

Not that it was his fault, or any soldier's fault. Like anyone, the men and women in the military only do what they think is right and honorable. The enemies we have created ensure that we will continue to need their services—with one caveat: *true* peace requires *true* courage. This means forging a third way that is not passive *or* aggressive, fight *or* flight, but that engages the principle of consciousness. This alone has the capacity to replace militaries with the infrastructures of reconciliation and benevolence. As German philosopher Friedrich Nietzsche wrote, "And perhaps the great day will come when a people, distinguished by wars and victories . . . will exclaim of its own free will, 'We break the sword,' and will smash its entire military establishment . . . *Rendering oneself unarmed when one had been the best-armed . . .* that is the means to real peace" (his emphasis).

A shift is underway. In days to come, perhaps we will confer more praise on everyday heroes, such as teachers, aid workers, migrant farm workers—and all those whose labor inspires, rather than sabotages, the evolution of human consciousness.

In the summer of 2004, I led NOLS wilderness courses in Wyoming, and a deep sense of contentment and abundance began to fill me. But an unresolved issue remained. So, on a warm morning in June, I drove to Hunt Field—the municipal airport near Lander—and rented a Cessna 172.

I flew north over the Wind River Indian Reservation and climbed to thirteen thousand feet. At only two hundred feet over the summit of Bomber Mountain, I flew in the same direction a B-17 had flown that fateful night in 1943. The wreckage came into view—a radio shack, cockpit, wheels, pieces of fuselage. I circled to make another pass and reached into my pocket for that scrap of metal, a sliver of aluminum painted green on one side. A hole now pierced it where a shoestring had passed. It symbolized my transition from youth to adulthood, androcentrism to egalitarianism, Peter Pan to a gentle man.

I flew even lower on the second pass, and cold, thin air rushed into the cockpit when I opened the window. I held the token in front of my face, and after everything that had happened, I still hesitated to let go. Quickly, I kissed it and tossed it into space.

I returned to Lander and never flew again.

On September 11, 2004, I met the students I would guide for the next two weeks in the Wind River Mountains. Throughout the course, a certain student carried pack-weight for an injured cohort and added insights to our evening class discussions. She told me she had studied philosophy, political science, and women's studies in college, and as a feminist she argued for equal rights and environmental protection. Her name was Kim, and though I was attracted to her, I did not approach her during the course.

After the course, she contacted me. Over the next three months, we learned we had each survived crises that showed us how true life is possible only after one accepts and reifies one's new self. Or, as spiritual teacher Eckhart Tolle points out, "True transformational change cannot come into your life until your consciousness changes." In December—one year after I left Alaska—Kim and I met for the holidays. Without effort, we fell in love on solid ground and pledged our lives to one another.

Before leaving Wyoming, I drove to the sweat lodge on the Wind River Indian Reservation one last time. I hoped to see Stanford again and, perhaps, receive his blessing.

He recognized me as soon as his nephews carried him into the sweat lodge. He smiled and winked but said nothing. After the sweat, he did not socialize much with anyone. He looked weak and tense, as though he struggled with pain. At the midnight feast in his home, he rode by me in his electric wheelchair while his nephew Cody carried a bowl of chili and a can of Diet Cherry Coke for him. Stanford overcame his chronic pain long enough to stop and turn his wheelchair toward me. He said nothing, but the smile in his eyes told me he understood: I had let go of all the pieces of my old world-view. I was now free to forge a new one.

In 2006, Kim and I moved to a remote location in the Rocky Mountains of Colorado. At first, our food choices were pesca-tarian (we sometimes ate fish). Since 2012, however, our diets have been comprised of vegan (plant-based), whole foods, and the occasional vegetarian (dairy) option when we travel. Kim and I call our food habits "veganarian." With this and all our choices, we hope to cause as little harm as possible.

We recognize that humans have dominated and, in most cases, traumatized animals for millennia. According to data gathered by Will Tuttle in *The World Peace Diet*, ten billion land animals are slaughtered each year in the world—three hundred every second in the United States alone. In 2017, fifty-two US senators voted to allow hunters to shoot wolves and grizzly bears from airplanes in Alaska. This injunction included the slaughter of wolf pups and bear cubs, as well as aerial shooting and trapping in National Wildlife "Refuges." This is but a tiny example. The physical and psychological suffering caused by humans on sentient beings is inconceivable.

Such attitudes also affect the broader environment. An article in the September 2014 issue of *National Geographic* states: "Simply put, a diet that revolves around meat and dairy, a way of eating that's on the rise throughout the developing world, will take a greater toll on the world's resources than one that revolves around unrefined grains, nuts, fruits, and vegetables." Savannas and grasslands are denuded by massive cattle feedlots, compounding the effects of desertification and groundwater depletion across the Sahel of North Africa, the Great Plains of North America, and the Loess Plateau of China.

According to David Robinson Simon, author of *Meatonomics*, "It takes dozens of times more water and five times more land to produce animal protein than equal amounts of plant protein. Unfortunately, even 'green' alternatives . . . can't overcome the basic math: the resources just don't exist to keep feeding the world animal foods at the level it wants." Tropical rainforests absorb greenhouse gases, but two acres of these forests are cut down *each minute*, in part to create cattle ranches or the crops with which to feed them. These ranches then produce staggering amounts of methane, a potent greenhouse gas.

America's love affair with guns, hunting, and armed conflict is a cognate manifestation of this toxic worldview. We have long been told, as James Brown sang, that "it's a man's world," and the phallocentric worldview expressed in bombs, knives, and guns is obvious. However, Carol Jenkins, founding president of the Women's Media Center, describes the United States as "a nation of teenage boys." Indeed, ours is a world run by the shadow form of the immature warrior archetype, its nostalgia for boyhood at once exemplified and camouflaged by terms such as "good old boys," "old boys club," and "one of the boys."

Indoctrination begins early. Walk into any toy store and witness its affinity to a military arsenal populated with muscular action figures like Thor and Captain America. Precursors of these toys were manufactured in the wake of 1980s blockbuster movies, such as *Conan the Barbarian* and *Rambo*. Many classic board games, including Battleship, Risk, and Stratego (where all the pieces are men), also imply violence.

In 1983, psychologist Dan Kiley coined the term *Peter Pan Syndrome* to describe men who never mature from adolescence, a condition triggered by masculine insecurity. Peter Pan can represent the trickster-fool archetype. He can also epitomize the transformative power of nature, initiating it in others while resisting it in himself, floating in limbo and paradox. On the national and global levels, this condition has manifested itself by America's being involved in over forty armed conflicts since the end of World War II. And in the 241 years since 1776, the United States has been engaged in military action for all but seventeen of them. Einstein recognized our propensity for madness when he commented on the development of the first atomic bomb: "We shall require a substantially new manner of thinking if mankind is to survive."

Contrary to Einstein's admonition, violence has taken increasingly perverse forms in recent decades. Following the massacre at Columbine High School in 1999, Wal-Mart reported a 40 percent increase in sales of ammunition. Gun sales increased by 70 percent. Sales spiked again after 9/11, following both of Obama's elections, and again after mass shootings in Tucson, Arizona, in 2011, in Aurora, Colorado, in 2012, and in Las Vegas, Nevada, in 2017. (In this last case, sales increased most dramatically in so-called "bump stocks," which convert semi-automatic weapons into fully automatic weapons. The Las Vegas gunman used them to spray a crowd with bullets, killing 58 and injuring more than 500. Consequently, bump stocks may soon be outlawed.) Fear makes money.

True freedom is the absence of fear. The United States wears its "freedom" on its sleeve, disguising fear with aggression. We are afraid because we know deep down that our social and economic policies of exclusion are ultimately void of humanity and untenable. On the world stage, we fear to lose our domination of wealth and power, mostly in the form of weapons and economic cachet. In short, we are afraid of reality.

Peter Pan did not want to grow up and preferred the status quo in Neverland—a place of fear, full of pirates and Indians. He did not know the difference between real and make-believe, which is the difference between childhood and adulthood. Thus, we Americans create opponents because we are too afraid to make the hardest choices of inclusion and relationship, which are feminine qualities. Trapped in ordeals of our own creation, we seek release by confronting our limits in Apocalypse, biblical or otherwise. Or, as author Isaac Asimov put it, "Violence is the last refuge of the incompetent."

Women's minds and bodies are, likewise, controlled, dominated, and socially consumed, sometimes violently. In 2017, the gender pay-gap in America was steady at 79 percent; that is, women made seventy-nine cents for every dollar earned by men in the same job. As for politics, only

19 percent of members of Congress in the United States were women, making it seventy-third among nations, tied with Panama. In 2014, a study from the University of Illinois at Urbana–Champaign found that hurricanes given female names were taken less seriously than were those with male names, with the result that storms named after women caused more fatalities.

To be fair, the rights of women and minorities have advanced further in the United States and other Western nations than in Southwest Asia and North Africa, where women hold only 7 percent of seats in governing bodies. According to the World Economic Forum, nine out of ten countries with the worst gender parity are Muslim-majority nations. Proscriptions on women in those countries range from bans on voting, driving, and holding public office to exclusion from school (85 percent illiteracy rate for women in Afghanistan), forced marriages, child marriages, female genital mutilation (FGM), floggings, canings, cutting off ears and noses, scarring and death by acid, and "honor killings." (At least five thousand women are executed each year for, say, having premarital sex or looking at another man.) On this point, it may be telling that the most popular syndicated television programming in the early 2000s in Saudi Arabia was *Desperate Housewives*, and in Afghanistan, *Baywatch*.

Worldwide, some six thousand girls suffer FGM each day, a barbaric means of controlling women and female sexuality. And in the United States (and other "developed" countries), brochures advertise women and girls as young as four and five years old—and younger—available to the discriminating tourist. Such businesses are part of a global sex trafficking industry.

This massive burden of proof might lead some to blame men, or at least white men, or certain corporations, industries, nations, and religious institutions controlled by white men. But such an exercise would devolve into yet another opportunity for the ego to identify opponents and assert superiority. The real culprit is within each of us: the failing hyper-masculine ego, which lashes out in the form of armed conflicts, terrorist attacks, and mass shootings, as well as increased violence against women, the billions of animals penned, raped, and slaughtered each year, and a planet pushed to the edge of endurance.

In *The Macho Paradox*, author Jackson Katz advises us to cultivate "a vision of manhood that does not depend on putting down others in order to lift itself up." The solution for ending warfare, developing clean energy, conserving the environment, and eradicating poverty, disease, sexism, ethnocentrism, and animal cruelty is to nourish a masculinity that venerates *all* life, celebrates our rich diversity, and reinforces an unyielding equality. This is the mature warrior archetype, wise enough to make violence unnecessary.

I do not suggest that America and the world transform in the ways in which I have. But it is worth pointing out the obvious: humanity is exhausted with violence. We crave a shift toward the intrinsic human faculties of compassion, relationship, and equality. Perhaps the most day-to-day practice with which to drive this revolution comes with the foods we eat. As David Robinson Simon advises in *Meatonomics*, "Make a choice to buy less meat, fish, eggs, and dairy—or better yet, give them up completely."

This vision of hope implies we change not only what we consume physically, but socially and economically as well. So, the true battle is always one within. To recall Laozi in the *Daodejing*: "Those who defeat others are strong. Those who defeat themselves are mighty."

In October 2004, the Nobel Peace Prize was awarded to Dr. Wangari Maathai, the Kenyan woman whom Vijay had pointed out in the crowd in Nairobi. The Prize honored her as an environmentalist and women's rights activist in the face of constant and oftentimes dangerous opposition. From her acceptance speech delivered in Oslo on December 10: "In the course of history, there comes a time when humanity is called to shift to a new level of consciousness to reach a higher moral ground. A time when we have to shed our fear and give hope to each other. That time is now."

Stanford's advice may have been less eloquent, but it was no less true. To paraphrase him, the only way forward is to let go of our thin yet burnished past and embrace a bold new adventure in consciousness—the fifth principle of flight.

I wish I could have thanked Stanford and Wangari in person. Both died in 2011. Like all great teachers, they encouraged us to choose courage over fear, compassion over violence, and love instead of hate, especially when it means getting hurt.

As we leave the old empires—the old paradigms—behind, let us chart a course for Maathai's "new level of consciousness." Together, we stand at the threshold of a new frontier.

Acknowledgments

First and foremost, I thank my parents for raising me in a rural area near the bluffs and sloughs of the Mississippi, where my imagination could run free. When I was not exploring river islands, my mother kept me busy in the garden and with 4-H projects, while my father enlisted my help in bailing hay and tending the animals we kept. Our family was never hungry, and my sister and I received the vexing luxuries of four years of dental braces and twelve years of piano lessons. Our parents gave us all they had and did the best they could, and for that I am grateful. More than anything, I thank them for the work ethic they instilled in us and the sincerity with which they loved us. I would later draw upon these raw materials when asking hard questions of life and doing my part to help foster a more sane and peaceful world—the kind of world that is possible if we put our heads and hearts together.

Many of the good citizens of Lander, Wyoming, are also like family to me. Back in 1997, the people at NOLS (National Outdoor Leadership School) put me to work, first in the office and then in the mountains. They provided a space in which I could grow as a wilderness leader, as a teacher, and as a principled human being. I especially thank those with whom I lived and worked in Wyoming, Idaho, Arizona, Utah, Alaska, Kenya, Tanzania, and Mexico.

I also extend a special thanks to the late Stanford Addison and members of the Northern Arapaho and Eastern Shoshone tribes of the Wind River Indian Reservation. One hundred years before we met, people of my ethnic affiliation committed unspeakable atrocities against theirs, yet they welcomed me into their homes and showed me nothing but generosity and kindness. I am indebted.

I also wish to offer a special thanks to the following supporters who helped fund the publication of this book and its message: Dee Brake; James Livaccari of Under the Rainbow Tree, LLC; and James R. Schneider of Vertical Performance, Inc. These individuals (and their businesses) work to transform their communities and world, one person at a time. I am honored to call them my friends.

Finally, I give my deepest gratitude and all my love to my wife, Kim Smoyer. Her advice and encouragement kept me writing when doubt descended and failure loomed. This book would not have materialized without her support. A mutual friend once confided in me: "Kim is smart, pretty, and kind—a rare combination." I couldn't agree more.

Bibliography

Adams, Carol J. *The Sexual Politics of Meat: A Feminist-Vegetarian Critical Theory*. New York: Continuum International Publishing Group, 1990.

Ali, Ayaan Hirsi. *Infidel*. New York: Free Press, 2007.

Amadiume, Ifi. *Reinventing Africa: Matriarchy, Religion & Culture*. London: Zed Books, 1997.

Barrie, J. M., and Maria Tatar. *The Annotated Peter Pan: The Centennial Edition*. New York: W. W. Norton & Company, 2011.

Bekoff, Marc. "The Psychology and Thrill of Trophy Hunting: Is It Criminal?" *Psychology Today*, Oct. 18, 2015.

Campbell, Joseph. *The Hero with a Thousand Faces*. New York: The World Publishing Company, 1949.

"Cards' Tillman Leaves NFL to Serve in Army." *Washington Post*, May 24, 2002. https://www.washingtonpost.com/archive/sports/2002/05/24/cards-tillman-leaves-nfl-to-serve-in-army/1e4d3de5-24ad-450a-9c67-f74cc33e51c8/?utm_term=.51e50f3a87a1.

Crow, Sheryl. "Strong Enough." *Tuesday Night Music Club*. Sheryl Crow. Bill Bottrell, November 1994.

D'Adamo, Peter J., and Catherine Whitney. *Eat Right 4 Your Type*. London: Penguin, 1996.

Davis, Kara, and Wendy Lee. *Defiant Daughters: 21 Women on Art, Activism, Animals, and the Sexual Politics of Meat*. New York: Lantern, 2014.

De Sieyes, Jacques. "Aces of the Air." *National Geographic* 33:1, Jan. 1918: 5–9.

Denver, John. "American Child." *Autograph*. John Denver, Joe Henry. Warner/Chappell Music, Inc., Milton Okun, February 1980. Cassette.

———. "You Say That the Battle Is Over." *Autograph*. John Denver, David Mallett. Warner/Chappell Music, Inc., Milton Okun, February 1980. Cassette.

Dinesen, Isak. *Out of Africa*. New York: Random House, Inc., 1937.

Exupèry, Antoine de Saint. (Translated from the French by Lewis Galantièr.) *Wind, Sand and Stars*. New York: Reynal & Hitchcock, 1939.

Edelman, Benjamin. "Red Light States: Who Buys Online Adult Entertainment?" *Journal of Economic Perspectives*, 23:1 (2009): 209–220.

Eisler, Riane. *The Chalice & the Blade: Our History, Our Future*. New York: HarperCollins Publishers, Inc., 1987.

Elphick, Jonathan, *Atlas of Bird Migration: Tracing the Great Journeys of the World's Birds*. Buffalo, NY: Firefly, 2007.

Gibbons, Ann. "The Evolution of Diet." *National Geographic*, Sep. 2014: 40.

Gimbutas, Marija. *The Language of the Goddess*. New York: Thames & Hudson, Inc., 1989.

Green, Tamara, and Tony Gibbons. *The Quagga: The Extinct Species Collection*. Milwaukee, WI: Gareth Stevens Publishing. 1996.

Gross, Mathew Barrett, and Mel Gilles. *The Last Myth: What the Rising of Apocalyptic Thinking Tells Us About America*. New York: Prometheus Books, 2012.

Harkey, Ira. *Pioneer Bush Pilot: The Story of Noel Wien*. Seattle: University of Washington Press, 1974.

Harper, Ben. "Amen Omen." *Diamonds on the Inside*. Innocent Criminals. Ben Harper, March 2003.

Hartung, William, and Stephen Miles. "Who Will Profit from the Wars in Iraq and Syria?" *The Huffington Post*, Oct. 1, 2014.

Herold, Marc W. "Dossier on Civilian Victims of United States' Aerial Bombing." University of New Hampshire, Whittemore School of Business and Economics, 2004. http://pubpages.unh.edu/~mwherold/dossier.

Huxley, Elspeth. *The Flame Trees of Thika: Memories of an African Childhood*. London: Chatto & Windus, Ltd., 1959.

iCasualties.org. "Afghanistan Coalition Casualty Count." Coalition Deaths by Year, http://icasualties.org/OEF/ByYear.aspx.

———. "Iraq Coalition Casualty Count." Iraq Coalition Casualties: Fatalities by Year, http://icasualties.org/Iraq/ByYear.aspx.

Jones, Lisa. *Broken: A Love Story*. New York: Scribner, 2010.

Katz, Jackson. *The Macho Paradox: Why Some Men Hurt Women and How All Men Can Help*. Naperville, IL: Sourcebooks, Inc., 2006.

Klaper M.D., Michael, *Vegan Nutrition: Pure and Simple*, 4th ed. Summertown, TN.: Book Publishing Company, 1999.

Kaufmann, Walter. *The Portable Nietzsche*. New York, Viking Penguin, Inc., 1954.

Lindbergh, Charles. "Is Civilization Progress?" *Reader's Digest*, Jul. 1964: 64–74.

Markham, Beryl. *West with the Night*. New York: North Point Press, 1942.

McPhee, John. *Coming Into the Country*. New York: The Noonday Press, 1976.

Miedzian, Myriam. *Boys Will Be Boys: Breaking the Link Between Masculinity and Violence*. New York: Lantern, 2002.

Miers, Earl Schenck. *Billy Yank and Johnny Reb: How They Fought and Made Up*. New York: Rand McNally and Company, 1966.

Nash, Roderick. *Wilderness and the American Mind*. New Haven, CT: Yale University Press, 1967.

Private Pilot Manual, 2nd ed. Englewood, CO: Jeppesen Sanderson, 1988.

Ray, Sugar. "Fly." *Floored*. Sugar Ray. David Kahne, June 1997. Cassette.

Sharp, Daryl. *Jung Lexicon: A Primer of Terms & Concepts*. Toronto: Inner City Books, 1991.

Simon, David Robinson. *Meatonomics: How the Rigged Economics of Meat and Dairy Make You Consume Too Much—and How to Eat Better, Live Longer, and Spend Smarter*. Newburyport, MA: Conari Press, 2013.

Stone, Merlin. *When God Was a Woman*. London: Harvest/Harcourt Brace, 1976.

Tennyson, Alfred. "In Memoriam A.H.H." *The Literature Network*. n.d. http://www.online-literature.com/tennyson/718/.

Thom, Trevor. *Air Pilot's Manual: Flying Training v. 1–4*. Ramsbury, UK: Airlife Publishing, Ltd., 1988–1989.

Tuttle, Will. *The World Peace Diet: Eating for Spiritual Health and Social Harmony*. New York: Lantern, 2005.

Tzu, Lao. *Tao Te Ching*. Trans. D. C. Lau, New York: Penguin, 1963.

Vogler, Christopher, *The Writer's Journey: Mythic Structure for Writers*, 3rd ed. Chelsea, MI: Sheridan, 2005.

Welch, Gillian. "Look at Miss Ohio." *Soul Journey*. Gillian Welch. David Rawlings, June 2003.

"What the World Wants Project." *Global Energy Network Institute*, Jun. 30, 2016. http://www.geni.org/globalenergy/issues/global/qualityoflife/what-the-world-wants-project.shtml.

Wilson, E. O. *The Future of Life*. New York: Vintage, 2002.

Wood, Bruce, and David Petersen. "A Beginner's Guide to Deer Hunting." *Mother Earth News* 120 (Nov/Dec 1989): 98.

Yeoman, Ann. *Now or Neverland: Peter Pan and the Myth of Eternal Youth: A Psychological Perspective on a Cultural Icon*. Toronto: Inner City, 1998.

Zondervan New International Version Bible. Grand Rapids, MI: Zondervan Corporation, 1984.

About the Author

BILL HATCHER teaches geography and anthropology in southern Colorado, where he lives with his wife, Kim, and their cat, Mitts. He is also the author of *The Marble Room: How I Lost God and Found Myself in Africa*. He can be reached through his website at www.billhatcherbooks.com.

About the Publisher

LANTERN BOOKS was founded in 1999 on the principle of living with a greater depth and commitment to the preservation of the natural world. In addition to publishing books on animal advocacy, vegetarianism, religion, and environmentalism, Lantern is dedicated to printing books in the U.S. on recycled paper and saving resources in day-to-day operations. Lantern is honored to be a recipient of the highest standard in environmentally responsible publishing from the Green Press Initiative.

lanternbooks.com